THE ENGLISH CONSTITUTION

The English Constitution addresses two burning contemporary and complementary questions: one regarding the so-called English 'question', the changing identities of England and English-ness, and a second regarding the changing shape of the Anglo-British constitution. It is suggested that there are both internal and external pressures that are driving the reformation of our constitutional order. There are internal pressures of decay, even corruption, and popular apathy, and there are external pressures brought to bear by the geopolitical challenges of the new world order and the new Europe. The 'project' of constitutional reform inaugurated by the present government is supposed to reflect these pressures. This book challenges this assumption, arguing that a far more radical re-constitution is required, involving deeper institutional reforms (the most pressing being the abrogation of monarchy, and the established Church), geopolitical reforms to recast the devolutionary settlement and redefine English regionalism, and perhaps most importantly, conceptual reform, reform that will embrace the need to rebalance the constitution and to promote greater accountability and democracy.

It is intended that the book will provide a stimulating text for both academics and students, advancing a series of original ideas on a subject of considerable contemporary interest. Along the way it discusses most of the major topics, institutions and debates which are ordinarily addressed in public law courses, and equivalents in non-law disciplines.

The English Constitution
Myths and Realities

IAN WARD
University of Newcastle-upon-Tyne

HART PUBLISHING
OXFORD AND PORTLAND, OREGON
2004

Hart Publishing
Oxford and Portland, Oregon

Published in North America (US and Canada) by
Hart Publishing c/o
International Specialized Book Services
5804 NE Hassalo Street
Portland, Oregon
97213-3644
USA

Distributed in the Netherlands, Belgium and Luxembourg by
Intersentia, Churchillaan 108
B2900 Schoten
Antwerpen
Belgium

Hart Publishing is a specialist legal publisher based in Oxford, England.
To order further copies of this book or to request a list of other publications please write to:

Hart Publishing, Salter's Boatyard, Folly Bridge,
Abingdon Road, Oxford OX1 4LB
Telephone: +44 (0)1865 245533 or Fax: +44 (0)1865 794882
e-mail: mail@hartpub.co.uk
WEBSITE: http//www.hartpub.co.uk

British Library Cataloguing in Publication Data
Data Available
ISBN 1-84113-431-7 (paperback)

Typeset by Hope Services (Abingdon) Ltd
Printed and bound in Great Britain on acid-free paper by
TJ International Ltd, Padstow, Cornwall

For Freya

Preface

We are cursed, it seems, to live in interesting times. It is certainly the fate of anyone who embarks upon writing a book on the Anglo-British constitution. For a constitution that takes so much pride in its sheer conservatism, things appear to be changing mighty fast. According to one prominent contemporary commentator, we presently 'live in times of exciting and profound constitutional debate'.[1] According to another, now 'is a time for asking new constitutional questions and for debating new constitutional possibilities'.[2] The legal academy is buzzing. As we shall see in due course, so are English courtrooms; or at least some of them. According to one leading member of the judiciary, the Anglo-British constitution is presently 'at an intermediate stage between parliamentary supremacy and constitutional supremacy'.[3] The implication is clear. Finally, it seems, we are going to get a proper constitution.

There is an immediate context for these observations; that described by the much-vaunted 'modernization' proposals with which the 'new' Labour government came to power in 1997. As I write this Preface, new proposals have been presented for the reform of the House of Lords, along with the abolition of the office of Lord Chancellor, and all manner of vague promises regarding wider judicial reform. We have already witnessed the inauguration of a Human Rights Act, as well as devolution. Beyond the immediate borders of the increasingly fragmentary 'united' Kingdom, the 'new' Europe is presently debating a suitably 'new' constitution. Meanwhile, the darker underbelly of governmental practice is, once again, being laid bare by another judicial inquiry. This time it is the Hutton Inquiry, and the supposition that members of the present government are not only indirectly responsible for the suicide of a civil service scientist, but are also guilty of lying both

[1] See N MacCormick, *Questioning Sovereignty: Law, State and Practical Reason*, (Oxford, Oxford UP, 1999), 78.

[2] B Hadfield, 'Towards an English Constitution' [2002] 55 *Current Legal Problems*, 189.

[3] Lord Justice Laws in *Prolife Alliance v BBC* [2002] EWCA Civ 297 para 34.

to Parliament and the British public in the matter of going to war in Iraq. Interesting times indeed.

And interesting times should be polemical times too. And this is an unashamedly polemical book. It does not claim to provide a comprehensive account of 'our' constitution. No book can do that, no matter how strongly it might make that claim. Indeed, I am not entirely sure what either the 'our' or the 'constitution' might mean in such a statement. But, if it eschews the pretence of comprehensiveness, this book certainly hopes to be challenging, even antagonistic. Political and legal debate is supposed to be antagonistic; or at least it is in a genuinely democratic and liberated community. And there is much towards which we should feel antagonistic; an arcane system of monarchical government, an absurdly inappropriate established Church, a largely corrupt and ineffective legislative body, a putatively despotic model of government, and a judiciary that appears to be institutionally unrepresentative, as well as reluctant, at least on the whole, to acknowledge its irreducibly political responsibilities.

We should then welcome the opportunity that constitutional reform offers. It gives us the chance to re-think, perhaps re-imagine what 'our' constitution could be and should be. Back in 1790, the radical Tom Paine famously recommended that the English should, like the French, offer up their constitution as a 'burnt-offering to reason'. Perhaps, two centuries on, the opportunity has finally arisen. The five chapters that make up this book investigate the state of 'our' constitution, its myths and its realities. And they do so with a particular aspiration, to project the possibility of re-imagining a distinctively English constitution; one that is rooted in a specifically English tradition of radical republican public philosophy.

The first chapter will examine the image of the Anglo-British constitution as it was cast by the great Victorian jurists, most famously and most particularly Walter Bagehot and Albert Venn Dicey. The political constitution described by the former, and the legal constitution described by the latter, have long held a complementary, and deeply reactionary, sway over the corridors of Westminster and Whitehall, as well as countless law school lecture halls. Bagehot and Dicey are long dead. But their grip on our constitutional imagination is barely weakened. We must prise it away. The jurisprudence that sought to legitimate the Anglo-British constitution must be laid to rest, just as must the Anglo-British state itself. The time for a decent burial is long past. The second chapter addresses the particular mythologies that attach to

Parliament and government. It is here that the smell is foulest. Ours is a thoroughly rotten system of government, corrupt to its very core. It is only when we have appreciated just how rotten it is, that we can properly imagine its reform. The respective Houses of Parliament, as we shall see, are corrupt and supine, woefully inadequate in the matter, not just of calling government to account, but in securing the interests of those it claims to represent. Parliament, the body that is supposed to be 'sovereign' in 'our' constitution, has, sadly, long since lost the use of its vital organs. This particular body may still be twitching. But only just. Government, meanwhile, has assumed the position of virtually limitless political power. The idea that we live in an 'elective dictatorship' is no longer controversial. This should trouble us.

The third chapter flirts with a possible saviour, the judiciary. For centuries the role of the judiciary in 'our' constitution has been clothed in its own myriad mythologies, not least those of the 'separation of powers' and 'judicial independence'. As we shall see the tortuous process by which the law of judicial review has developed is a testimony to the residual strength of these particular mythologies. More recently, it has been suggested that a contemporary 'renaissance' in judicial review, along with a more 'antagonistic' judiciary, signals the rise of a new and more assertive judiciary, one that has recognised the limitations which pervade Parliament and which is more ready to curtail governmental excesses. It is an assertion that gains added credence in the context, not just of European integration, but also the arrival of a new Human Rights Act. Perhaps the judiciary can breathe new life into the body of 'our' constitution. Perhaps.

The fourth chapter will take a rather closer look at the experience of European integration, along with the complementary geopolitical challenges of devolution and the 'new' world order. The cancer of internal decay which presently afflicts the increasingly diseased body of the Anglo-British constitution is joined by the seemingly irresistible pressures which attach to the much-heralded 'end' of the nation-state. Constitutional reform, it seems, is going to happen, whether or not we like the idea. No one seriously believes the kingdom is 'united'. Not that many care any more. But we, particularly we in England, need to think rather urgently about what is going to replace it.

Finally, in chapter five, we will take a closer look at the past in order to make some kind of sense of the future. We will investigate the present, essentially Whiggish, even reactionary, process of constitutional reform. Rather than drifting from one apparently unplanned venture to another, it will be suggested that the time has now come for 'root and branch' constitutional reform; for casting aside all the fripperies of the Anglo-British constitution, its monarchy, its Church, its House of 'lords', whether it be selected by genes or governments; as well as all its more modern failings, its over-mighty parties, its specious system of parliamentary 'representation', above all its thoroughly rotten and corrupted system of government. And in its place we will explore the alternative notion of an English constitution, and an English constitutional philosophy. We shall excavate one of the great traditions in English political and constitutional thought, that of the 'Good Old Cause', and we will explore the extent to which it chimes with the related ideas of a 'commonwealth' and a 'common law' constitution. It is here, in the past, that a better, more liberal, more equal, more tolerant, and more progressive constitutional future may lie.

The author wishes to acknowledge the support of the Art and Humanities Research Board in enabling the completion of this book.

Contents

1

The Old Boundaries

ACCORDING TO THE nineteenth-century French commentator, Alexis de Tocqueville, 'in England the constitution can change constantly, or rather it does not exist at all'.[1] What Tocqueville meant, of course, is that the English constitution 'does not exist' because it is 'unwritten'. Any study of the English constitution tends to be premised on a consideration of this peculiarity. The classical justification tends to follow the line that such a constitution is inherently more fluid, an expression of 'pragmatic empiricism'.[2] The idea that we have no written constitution is only partly true. The English constitution is, of course, written. It is simply not collected in one formal document that looks like a constitution. Instead it is collected in various statutes and cases, and most particularly perhaps various defining treatises.

The organic nature of the English constitution has been nowhere better expressed than at the outset of the one of the most influential of these treatises:

> Our law very often reminds one of those outskirts of cities where you cannot for a long time tell how the streets come to wind about in so capricious and serpent-like a manner. At last it strikes you that they grew up, house by house, on the devious tracks of the old green lanes; and if you follow on to existing fields, you may often find the change half complete. Just so the lines of our constitution were framed in old eras of sparse population, few wants, and simple habits; and we adhere in seeming to their shape, though civilisation has come with its dangers, complications and enjoyments. These anomalies, in a hundred instances, mark the old boundaries of a constitutional struggle. The casual line was traced according to the strength of deceased combatants; succeeding generations fought elsewhere; and the hesitating line of a half-drawn battle was left to stand for a perpetual limit.[3]

[1] A de Tocqueville, *Democracy in America*, (London, Fontana, 1994)), 101.

[2] C McCrudden, 'Northern Ireland and the British Constitution', in J Jowell & D Oliver (eds) *The Changing Constitution* (Oxford, Oxford UP, 1994), 326.

[3] W Bagehot, *The English Constitution*, (Cambridge, Cambridge UP, 2001), 182–83.

The treatise from which this quotation is taken is Walter Bagehot's *The English Constitution*. It, along with Albert Venn Dicey's *Introduction to the Study of the Law of the Constitution*, is the primary subject of this first chapter. Both treatises were written during the second part of the nineteenth century; an age in which the state of the Anglo-British constitution was a defining concern.[4]

Bagehot's *English Constitution*, originally a series of essays written for the *Fortnightly Review*, takes the form of an institution-based study of the relation between the constitution and government. Ultimately, it is a study of the politics of the Anglo-British constitution. In contrast, Dicey's *Law*, written for an exclusively academic audience presented a rather more theoretical account of the 'principles' of the constitution. They describe, then, two sides of a coin; presenting alternative and complementary mythologies of the Anglo-British constitution. And they have, in their different ways, defined the landscape of modern Anglo-British constitutionalism.

But before we take a closer look at these two defining commentaries on our constitution, we must first divine the context within which they were written. For both Bagehot and Dicey shared an ulterior motive for venturing their particular constitutional visions; the need to somehow sanctify the Anglo-British state.

I POLLITRICKS AND PRINCIPLES

The Greatest Revolution Ever Known

The first context is set by the 'Great and Glorious' revolution of 1689. No historical event in English history was more entrenched in the mind of the Victorian constitutional historian. The classic description could be found in Macaulay's *History of England*, by its author's admission a 'romance' of English history. Thousands of Victorian Englishmen and women were to be enraptured by Macaulay's romance, and more particularly his account of 1689. Everything, it seemed, had flowed from the seismic events of this particular year. In Macaulay's words, it presaged, a 'history of physical, of moral, and of intellectual improve-

[4] M Loughlin, *Sword and Scales: An Examination of the Relationship between Law and Politics*, (Oxford, Hart, 2000), 139. For the same sentiment regarding the impact of nineteenth century constitutional texts, see D Castiglione, 'The Political Theory of the Constitution', (1996) 44 *Political Studies*, 417.

ment'.[5] As AJP Taylor observed, for Macaulay and his generation, the settlement of 1689 was 'a unique display of political genius'; and a uniquely English display.[6] The great Whig historian, Herbert Butterfield, reached the same conclusion; for the likes of Macaulay the events of 1689 had become 'part of the inescapable inheritance of the Englishman'.[7] So obsessed was Macaulay with the 'Great and Glorious' revolution that his projected 'history of England' never got beyond it, dwelling lovingly for hundreds of thousands of words on the various events that heralded and then celebrated the coronation of William III.

It was the manner of this coronation that so fascinated Macaulay, as it did so many Whig historians. The diminutive Dutch prince had sat obediently under a canopy of state, alongside his wife Mary, whilst he listened to Lord Halifax read out what amounted to the conditions under which he would be allowed to assume the throne; conditions which included the iconic Declaration of Right. When Halifax had finished, William had humbly replied, 'We thankfully accept what you have offered us', and everyone cheered politely. William then spoke of his determination 'to preserve your religion, laws and liberties'. Macaulay wrote 'we cannot but be struck by its peculiar character'.[8] According to the contemporary diarist Abraham de la Prynne, it was, quite simply, 'the greatest revolution that was ever known'.[9]

The Declaration and the subsequent Bill of Rights, was supplemented by an Act of Settlement in 1701, which plainly stated that it was 'for the further limitation of the Crown and better securing the rights and liberties of the subjects'. Taken together these three instruments, according to Whig historiography, sanctified the 'revolution principles' of 1689, at the apex of which was the supreme principle of the sovereignty of Parliament. The English were finally liberated from their 'state of ignominious vassalage', as Macaulay described the Stuart dynasty, and were ready for the 'wants of a modern society'. From this 'auspicious union of order and freedom', he further suggested, 'sprang the prosperity of which the annals of history had furnished no example'.[10] All was set fair:

[5] T Macaulay, *The History of England*, (London, Penguin, 1986), 52.

[6] AJP Taylor, *Essays in English History*, (Harmondsworth, Penguin, 1976), 56.

[7] H Butterfield, *The Englishman and his History*, (Glasgow, Collins, 1944), 2.

[8] Macaulay, above n 5, 287–8.

[9] In W Speck, *Reluctant Revolutionaries: Englishmen and the Revolution of 1688*, (Oxford UP, 1988), 241.

[10] Macaulay, above n 5, 290–4, 486.

> Our parliamentary institutions were in full vigour. The main principles of our government were excellent. They were not, indeed, formally and exactly set forth in a single written instrument; but they were to be found scattered over our ancient and noble statutes; and, what was of far greater moment, they have been engraven in the hearts of Englishmen during four hundred years.[11]

Macaulay was not the first to suggest that, in lieu of any more tangible alternative, the English constitution might be located in some kind of corporeal metaphor. In his *Reflections on the Revolution in France*, Edmund Burke had suggested that a love for the English constitution defined the 'English mind'. We shall revisit this thought in due course.

Perhaps most striking of all was Macaulay's assertion that the 'Great and Glorious' revolution had actually changed no part of the English constitution. The success of the 'revolution' instead evidenced the residual strength of the constitution itself, and the innate 'love of freedom' that characterised the English. In terms of constitutional law, the revolution, and even the Declaration that defined it, merely reinforced the 'vindication of ancient rights'.[12] What Macaulay was alluding to was, of course, the mythology of the 'common law constitution'; something to which we will, once again, return in due course. It defined England's past, and Macaulay confidently asserted, it defined the present and the future. For:

> In all honest and reflecting minds there is a conviction, daily strengthened by experience, that the means of effecting every improvement which the constitution requires may be found within the constitution itself.[13]

But then it had all started to go wrong. By 1726, Jonathan Swift would have his Gulliver inform the king of Brobdingnag, that the famed 'revolution principles' of 1689 had failed to prevent a 'heap' of revolutions and murders, or more recently the reduction of politics to the level of 'avarice, faction, hypocrisy, perfidiousness, cruelty, rage, madness, hatred, envy, lust, malice, and ambition'.[14] In fact, the prophets of doom were present from the very inception of the 'modern' system of Parliamentary government. In his satirical essay *Alexander Bendo*, composed in 1675, the notorious Earl of Rochester prophesied that the coming age of Parliamentary supremacy would also be the age

[11] Macaulay, above n 5, 290.
[12] *Ibid*, 292.
[13] *Ibid*, 294.
[14] J Swift, *Gulliver's Travels*, (London, Penguin, 1985), 143, 167–77.

of the political 'mountebank', an age in which the success of the aspiring politician would be entirely dependent upon his ability to ensure 'how the people are taken with specious miraculous impossibilities'.[15] Three years later, another poet, John Dryden, watched the chaos of the 1678 elections, the first to be fought along obviously party lines, with a mixture of horror and fascination and could only conclude that 'Wit and Fool are Consequents of Whig and Tory'.[16]

As the seventeenth century passed into the eighteenth, it became sadly apparent that the 'rage of party' was all-consuming. It was, to use Henry Fielding's term, the age of 'pollitricks'. In his novel *Jonathan Wild the Great*, Fielding warned that modern politicians, like the monarch whose powers they had taken, were driven by the same need to pander to the baser 'passions of men'. The 'hat' which any politician wears at any given moment is of little importance, except and insofar as it seems to fit the occasion and the head.[17] Fielding's contemporaries were wholly unimpressed with a politics that was defined by party. In his *Contests and Dissensions*, Swift noted that party politics so divides a 'nation' that every subject is left with 'but half their strength and wit, and honesty, and good nature'.[18] The acuity of Swift's analysis has echoed down the centuries. Defoe's *Tour Throughout the Whole Island of Great Britain* described a country apparently entranced by the theatre of political discord, one in which town after town was engaged in a seemingly endless series of squabbles and punch-ups over 'revolution principles' that no one could anyway define with any kind of confidence. Democracy had, quite literally, run riot.

A Great Juggle

By the middle of the nineteenth century, the Victorian mind was obsessed by the challenge of 'pollitricks'. The advent of the 'Great' Reform Bill in 1832 did little to settle the nerves. It was intended, like all subsequent reform bills, in the words of Lord Grey, to 'prevent the necessity of revolution'. And it was limited to removing 140 'nomination' boroughs and extending the franchise to all £10 householders in

15 Rochester, *The Complete Works*, (London, Penguin, 1994), 93–94.
16 'To the Reader—Absalom and Achitophel', in J Dryden, *Works*, (Oxford UP, 1987), 177.
17 H Fielding, *Jonathan Wild the Great*, (London, Penguin, 1986), 79, 102–3.
18 J Swift, *Works*, (Oxford UP, 1984), 54.

the formerly 'close' boroughs. But it was enough to set the alarm-bells ringing. The Duke of Wellington commented acerbically that the 'revolution is made, that is to say, that power is transferred from one class of society, the gentlemen of England, professing the faith of the Church of England, to another class of society, the shopkeepers', many of whom were 'atheists'. A 'new democratic influence', he warned, was pending; and it was not something to be welcomed.[19] In his *Lectures on the Relation between Law and Public Opinion*, Dicey would suggest that the 'transcendent importance of the Act lay in its effect upon public opinion', and it was for this reason that the Act could be 'regarded' as announcing a 'revolution' in English constitutional culture.[20] According to the altogether more sympathetic Whig historian, George Trevelyan, writing in the early part of the twentieth century, the 'nation' had, finally, become 'master of its own house'.[21]

At the time, however, the weight of intellectual opinion was altogether more wary, and the emergence of Chartism in the years immediately following 1832 seemed to confirm their worst fears. For the Chartists, as for many others of a radical mind in nineteenth century England, it had become all too obvious that the great 'revolution principles' had been perverted by the Whig oligarchies that dominated Parliamentary politics, and by the politicians that they spawned and then corrupted. Reform was the very least that England needed and deserved, and reform it would have. As the banner of the radical journal the *Northern Star* threatened, 'Peaceably if we may, forcibly if we must'.[22]

According to Thomas Carlyle, Chartism 'exaggerated' all the counter-mythologies of the 'Good Old Cause' and the 'Great and Glorious' revolution in 'the wonderfulest way'. There was, he suggested, a 'sullen revengeful humour of revolt abroad', the kind of humour that had resulted in one king losing his head, and another his throne. Carlyle himself was thoroughly confused by remembrances of the 'Good Old Cause' of the mid-seventeenth century, horrified by images of levellerism, thrilled by the thought that a new Cromwell

[19] See F Prochaska, *The Republic of Britain 1760–2000*, (London, Allen Lane, 2000), 58–61, and I Ward, *A State of Mind? The English Constitution and the Popular Imagination*, (Gloucester, Sutton, 2000), 173–74.

[20] A Dicey, *Lectures on the Relation Between Law and Popular Opinion in England during the Nineteenth Century*, (Basingstoke, Macmillan, 1994), 42.

[21] G Trevelyan, *British History in the Nineteenth Century and After*, (London, Pelican, 1965), 241.

[22] D Newsome, *The Victorian World Picture*, (London, Fontana, 1998), 44.

might emerge to save the 'chosen people'.[23] Bagehot came to very much the same conclusion, observing that whilst Cromwell died 'the spirit which culminated in him never sank again, never ceased to be potent'.[24] In the end, the Chartists came and went, confused, like Carlyle indeed, by the alternative ideologies, 'ancient' and socialist, that were on offer, and never entirely sure just how violent their revolution ought to be. The great Chartist rally at Kensington in 1848 ended when its leaders accepted the Chief Commission of Police's offer of a free taxi-ride if they agreed to go home quietly.

But the revolutionary moment recurred, time and again during the later part of the nineteenth century. The mood had become dangerously iconoclastic. Richard Cobden urged that it was time to sweep away the 'great juggle of the English Constitution', a 'thing of monopolies, and Church-craft, and sinecures, armorial hocus-pocus, primogeniture, and pageantry'.[25] A generation later, the republican Charles Bradlaugh would refuse to take the parliamentary Oath of Allegiance; as he did not believe in either God or the monarchy, it would, he pointed out, be nonsensical to do so. After eight years of agonised debate, the House of Commons finally agreed, and approved an Affirmation Act which admitted that heathens could indeed govern the country. It made more sense, as fellow radical Henry Labouchere informed the House, than the kind of 'meaningless' verbiage and 'mumbo-jumbo' that was found in the Oath, the kind of 'trash', he added with a relish, that is more commonly found 'among African savages'.[26]

This was the context within which Walter Bagehot wrote his *English Constitution*, and whilst he shared none of the political principles of Cobden or Bradlaugh, he did share their innate iconoclasm. He too, as his *English Constitution* would reveal, thought that much of the constitution was 'mumbo-jumbo'. The essays that made up the *English Constitution* were composed between 1865 and 1867. It was in the summer of 1867 that 200,000 of what Queen Victoria termed the 'worst sort of people' met in Hyde Park to demand further reform of the franchise.

23 T Carlyle, *Selected Writings*, (London, Penguin, 1986) 115–200, 302–7. For a commentary see, S Heffer, *Moral Desperado: A Life of Thomas Carlyle*, (London, Phoenix, 1995), 147–53, 166–68. Carlyle was not alone in invoking the spirit of Cromwell. A young Matthew Arnold also 'prayed daily' for a 'new Oliver'. See I Hamilton, *A Gift Imprisoned: The Poetic Life of Matthew Arnold*, (London, Bloomsbury, 1998), 56–59, 97.

24 Bagehot, above n 3, 177–78.

25 In Dicey, above n 20, 441.

26 In Ward, above n 19, 185.

A begrudging Disraeli piloted a second Reform bill through a doubting Parliament. It granted the franchise to urban householders, and in so doing added a mere million voters to the roll. The Act was intended to preserve 'our constitution in church and state'. It was not, Disraeli pointedly added, supposed to enhance democracy. It 'will never be the fate of this country to live' under a 'democracy', Disraeli advised the House of Commons.[27] Thomas Carlyle noted the passage of the 1867 Act and the passing of 'our poor old England'.[28]

Others, however, had rather grander aspirations. John Bright, founder of the Reform League just two years earlier, had consciously resurrected memories of the 'Good Old Cause' and announced that the 'powers of the good are gaining steadily on the powers of evil', and that they were doing so, moreover, through the vehicle of 'public opinion', without which 'Parliament had no more power than the smallest vestry'.[29] Amongst those who appeared to have enrolled in the cause of democracy was William Gladstone who, as Prime Minister in 1884, ushered through a third Reform Act which increased the electorate from 3 to 5 million, taking in household suffrage in the counties. According to Gladstone, 'every man who is not presumably incapacitated by some consideration of personal unfitness or of political danger, is morally entitled to come within the pale of the constitution'.[30] Disraeli, it seemed, had got it wrong. The age of democracy, or at least a kind of democracy, was pending.

And so perhaps was the age of republicanism. In November 1871, in a notorious speech in Newcastle, the radical MP Charles Dilke appealed for a renewal of 'republican virtues' of 'self-government', and closed with the observation 'if you can show me a fair chance that a republic here will be free from the political corruption which hangs about monarchy, I say, for my part, and believe that the middle classes in general will say, let it come'. With something of an understatement, the *Times* sniffed that Dilke's speech lacked 'delicacy'. Bradlaugh similarly denounced England's 'nominal monarchy', with all its 'princely paupers' drawing their moneys from the public purse whilst 'honest' paupers starved to death in the gutter; an observation that has lost little of its pertinence over time.[31]

[27] S Weintraub, *Disraeli: A Biography*, (London, Hamish Hamilton, 1993), 437–58.

[28] In A Briggs, *Victorian People: A Reassessment of Person and Themes 1851–67*, (London, Penguin, 1990), 22.

[29] *Ibid*, 205–6.

[30] In R Jenkins, *Gladstone*, (Basingstoke, Macmillan, 1995), 246–47.

[31] R Jenkins, *Dilke: A Victorian Tragedy*, (Basingstoke, Macmillan, 1996), 69–73.

Joseph Chamberlain's Birmingham constituents heard similar declamations. The future, they were informed, lay with the 'republican spirit', in the idea 'that in all cases merit should have a fair chance, that it should not be handicapped in the face by any accident of birth or privilege; that all men should have equal rights before the law, equal chances of serving their country'.[32] Between 1871 and 1874, eighty-four republican clubs were founded throughout England. Journals such as *Reynold's*, the *Republican* and the *Northern Tribune* churned out articles invoking the memory of past heroes of the 'Cause', Cromwell and Lilburne, Wilkes, Cobbett and the Chartists.

The context within which Bagehot published his *English Constitution* and within which Dicey began to ruminate on his 'law' of the constitution, was, then, one in which the perversions of 'pollitricks' appeared to have undermined the very foundations of the 'Great and Glorious' revolution. Bagehot would turn a cynical eye on events, and seek solace in executive power. Dicey, in contrast, would look to reinvest the central mythology of parliamentary sovereignty

Treading Upon Fairyground

The political context of mid and late Victorian England spawned a cultural complement, a broader concern with the apparent drift that had taken possession of the national mind, and soul. Victorian England was an inordinately worried place; excited by change, but just as much terrified by it too. We are not so different today. The fear sprang from the pages of letters and essays written by Victorian intellectuals such as Carlyle, Matthew Arnold and Alfred Lord Tennyson. The latter was haunted by the thought that he lived in a world in which faith had dissipated, in which there was now 'no anchor, none'.[33] Not one to underplay the danger, Tennyson warned of the impending '"doom" of democracy', of the 'common deluge drowning old political commonsense':

[32] See T Nairn, *The Enchanted Glass: Britain and its Monarchy*, (London, Picador, 1988), 326–31, D Cannadine, 'The Context, Performance and Meaning of Ritual: The British Monarchy and its Invention of Tradition, 1820–1977', in E Hobsbawn & T Ranger (eds), *The Invention of Tradition*, (Cambridge UP, 1992), 118–19, and R Williams, *The Contentious Crown: Public Discussion of the British Monarchy in the Reign of Queen Victoria*, (Aldershot, Ashgate, 1997), 42–43.

[33] 'Morte d'Arthur', l.18, in A Tennyson, *Selected Poems*, (London, Penguin, 1991), 71.

> Chaos, Cosmos! Cosmos, Chaos! Once again the sickening game;
> Freedom, free to slay herself, and dying while they shout her name.
> Step by step we gain'd a freedom known to Europe, known to all;
> Step by step we rose to greatness,—thro' the tonguesters we may fall.
> . . .
> Bring the old dark ages back without the faith, without the hope,
> Break the State, the Church, the Throne, and roll their ruins down the slope.[34]

In his poem *Dover Beach*, Matthew Arnold famously described the 'melancholy, long, withdrawing roar' of a political and theological culture that was shortly to be replaced by the 'confused alarms of struggle and flight', and, worse still, popular democracy.[35] In a letter to another anxious Victorian, Arthur Clough, Arnold confirmed that the 'constitution of the state' is a reflection of 'individual moral constitutions', an 'inward condition of the mind and spirit'; and England's spirit was ebbing away with the political tide.[36] Arnold's essay *Culture and Anarchy* mused long and wistfully on the 'England of Elizabeth', on the fond memory of Albion's former Fairy Queen and her fairy realm.[37]

Melancholy was not the sole preserve of the nostalgic poet. Dicey was given to acute melancholy.[38] In one of his final letters, looking back from the vantage point of the 1920s, Dicey confessed to a 'terrible moral and political desperation' which the 'present circumstances' of England brought 'upon' him.[39] Bagehot, too, was troubled. He feared complacency, and an England that was too 'comfortable' in its melancholy. But he also feared the opposite; an overwrought imagination. In his essay *Physics and Politics*, he railed against 'philosophers, each of whom wants some new scheme tried'.[40] Above all, as the introduction to the 1872 edition of *The English Constitution* emphasised, he feared the 'pervading spirit' of 'great change' that was sweeping across the English and their political culture.[41] As Asa Briggs has commented,

[34] 'Locksley Hall Sixty Years After', ll.127–30, 37–38, and also 250, in Tennyson, *ibid*, 337–38, 342

[35] 'Dover Beach', ll.25, 36 in M Arnold, *Works*, (Oxford UP, 1992), 136.

[36] In E Alexander, *Matthew Arnold and John Stuart Mill*, (New York, NY, Columbia UP, 1965), 4–6, 245–46.

[37] In M Arnold, *Culture and Anarchy and Other Writings*, (Cambridge UP, 1993), 64.

[38] R Cosgrove, *The Rule of Law: Albert Venn Dicey, Victorian Jurist*, (Chapel Hill, NC, Univ. of North Carolina Press, 1980), xiv–xv.

[39] *Ibid*, 284.

[40] N St John Stevas, *Walter Bagehot*, (London, Eyre & Spottiswoode, 1959), 47.

[41] Bagehot, above n 3, 194. For his comments on complacency, in an early essay on Bishop Burnet, see D Newsome, above n 22, 4.

Bagehot was convinced that he was living in what was fast taking the appearance of a 'world of nightmare'.[42]

A generation earlier, the erstwhile radical turned arch-conservative, Samuel Taylor Coleridge, composed his essay *On the Constitution of the Church and State* in a desperate bid to affirm his own personal apostasy, reminding his compatriots that the 'harmonious development' of citizen and state was entirely dependent upon a shared constitutional morality. It was the great lesson of English 'history'.[43] A similar conclusion would be implied in Dicey's discourses on religion and the state of the established Church in the later chapters of his *Lectures on the Relation between Law and Public Opinion*, composed in 1898.[44]

Coleridge's anxieties, like those of Arnold and Tennyson indeed, spoke to a particular concern regarding the fate of the 'chosen people', the people who, to use Patrick Collinson's resonant phrase, ever since the sixteenth century had thought to live their lives 'in the pages of the Bible', the people of the 'new Hierusalem' celebrated through the generations from Spenser to Bunyan to Blake.[45] The idea of the 'chosen people' was no less dear to the Victorian heart than it was to the Elizabethan. Wellington's observation, after Waterloo, that 'the hand of God was upon me' echoed Cromwell's at Marston Moor, 'God made them as stubble to our swords'.[46] It was the kind of sentiment, and the kind of military triumph, that reassured Thomas Arnold that the English were indeed 'one of the chosen people of history, who are appointed to do a great work for mankind'.[47] It was for these people, of course, that the Church of England was 'established'.

The idea of a 'chosen people' was, of course, tied firmly to that of monarchy. The English monarchy was supposed to represent the English people; even if, by the nineteenth century that people had been nominally recast as Anglo-British. As Gaunt famously declared in Shakespeare's *Richard II*:

[42] Briggs, above n 28, 95.

[43] S Coleridge, *On the Constitution of Church and State*, (London, Dent, 1972), 15, 33–38, 56–61.

[44] See *Lectures*, chs 10 and 12.

[45] P Collinson, *The Birthpangs of Protestant England: Religious and Cultural Change in the Sixteenth and Seventeenth Centuries*, (Basingstoke, Macmillan, 1988), 10.

[46] In J Paxman, *The English: A Portrait of a People*, (London, Michael Joseph, 1998), 93.

[47] Newsome, above n 22, 92.

> This throne of kings, this scept'red isle,
> This earth of majesty, this seat of Mars,
> This other Eden, demi-paradise,
> This fortress built by Nature for herself.[48]

A century and a half later, this monarchic idyll would be reaffirmed in Blackstone's *Commentaries*, with its paean to a monarchy that was the 'the fountain of justice, and general conservator of the peace of the kingdom'.[49] A similar sentiment could be found in Bolingbroke's idea of a 'patriot king', also presented in the middle of the eighteenth century.[50]

And one particular monarch obsessed the Victorians; Elizabeth I, the personification of the 'chosen people'. The Elizabethan poet-courtier Edmund Spencer penned his epic *Faerie Queene* with the express purpose of describing 'the most excellent and glorious person of our soveraine the Queene, and her kingdome in Faery land'; a tone that resonated down the centuries finding its most recent expression in Princess Diana's desire to the be a 'Queen of Hearts'.[51] Elizabeth had known how to perform her role. 'We princes', Elizabeth readily acknowledged, 'are set on stages in the sight and view of all the world duly observed'.[52] 'Crowned we see they are, and inthronized and anointed', as the Elizabethan jurist Richard Hooker observed.[53]

In 1792, Dorothy Wordsworth recorded a visit to Windsor where she espied the periodically insane King George III and his grotesquely bloated son, the future Prince Regent. George had made a concerted effort to reinvest the theatricality of monarchy, regularly cajoling some of the less willing members of his vast family into strolling along Windsor terrace in full public view. Dorothy was entranced. 'I fancied myself treading upon Fairy-Ground', she declared, 'and that the gay company around me was brought there by enchantment'. She could only conclude that it was 'impossible to see the King and his Family at Windsor without loving them, even if you eye them with impartiality

[48] W Shakespeare *Richard II*, 2.140–43.
[49] W Blackstone, *Commentaries on the Laws of England*, (London, Walker, 1826), 1.266.
[50] Viscount Bolingbroke, 'The Idea of a Patriot King' in *Political Writings*, (Cambridge UP, 1997)
[51] For a discussion of Spencer's expressed intent, see G Waller, *Edmund Spencer: A Literary Life*, (Basingstoke, Macmillan, 1994), 101.
[52] S Greenblatt, *Renaissance Self-Fashioning*, (Univ of Chicago Press, 1980), 167.
[53] R Hooker, *Of the Laws of Ecclesiastical Polity*, (Cambridge UP, 1989), 147.

and consider them really as man and woman'.[54] Republicans such as William Hazlitt were thoroughly frustrated by such obeisance, unable to comprehend why subjects should be so happy to 'worship' at the 'shrine of monarchy'.[55] But they were.

At the same time, however, the shadow of the Fairy Queen was cast far over successor Princesses. It certainly shrouded Victoria, from the very moment of her coronation. Needless to say, chroniclers had purred at Elizabeth's two-day coronation pageant in 1559.[56] Victoria's coronation, by contrast, was a shambles, replete with a drunken Prime Minister collapsing in the aisle, and a myopic Archbishop of Canterbury so determined to ram the coronation ring on the wrong finger that he rendered his fledgling Fairy Queen in need of medical attention.[57] And whereas Elizabeth had happily 'ravished' her subjects 'wonderfully', as one chronicler put it, with her theatrical progresses, Victoria was appalled at the idea of anyone ravishing anybody.[58] Indeed, following the death of her beloved Prince Albert in 1861, Victoria decided to retire from public view, even writing to *The Times* in an effort to explain herself, acknowledging the 'desire of her subjects to see her', but adding that there were 'other higher duties than those of mere representation'.[59]

She could not have been more wrong. As Disraeli respectfully countered, England expects its Queens to play the role of 'Queen Titania', the 'Fairy Queen' of her 'enchanted isle'.[60] *The Times* editorial responded in like terms. Representation was the Queen's greatest duty. It was, it added, 'impossible for a recluse to occupy the British throne without a gradual weakening of that authority which the Sovereign has been accustomed to exert'. Unless the Queen once again performed her 'public functions' it would 'confirm in their views those who suggest

[54] See A Byatt, *Unruly Times: Wordsworth and Coleridge in their Time*, (London, Vintage, 1997), 107, and C Hibbert, *George III: A Personal History*, (London, Viking, 1998), 300–1, 390–93.

[55] W Hazlitt, *Selected Writings*, (London, Penguin, 1992), 378–84, 430–33, and E Smith, *George IV*, (London and New Haven, Conn, Yale UP, 1999), 149–52.

[56] For commentaries, see J Neale, *Queen Elizabeth I*, (London, Pimlico, 1998), 64–67, and Ward, above n 19, 31–32.

[57] E Longford, *Victoria RI*, (London, Weidenfeld & Nicolson, 1998), 79–83.

[58] For descriptions of Elizabeth's various progresses, see E Talbert, *The Problem of Order*, (Chapel Hill, NC, Univ of North Carolina Press, 1992) 83–84, 88, and S Greenblatt, above n 52, 166–69.

[59] See Longford, above n 57, 7, 321–21, 329–30, Prochaska, above n 19, 100–3, and L Strachey, *Queen Victoria* (Harmondsworth, Penguin, 1971), 106.

[60] Longford, above n 57, 401–6, and Weintraub, above n 27, 460–61, 547.

that the Throne is only an antiquarian relic and Royalty itself a ceremony'. Without a 'proper intercourse in the world', the residual love of 'the great mass of the nation' would be lost.[61] The warning was stark. The 'pompous body of a king', as Shakespeare's Richard II famously observed, is nothing more than a 'brittle' illusion.[62]

It would be a mistake to underestimate Victoria, or her subjects' capacity for adoration. Denied a 'Fairy Queen', they settled for, and eventually came to admire, a rather schizophrenic monarch; on the one hand the mighty Empress of a mighty Empire, and on the other a shrewd and sober housekeeper. Victoria became the icon for the scrupulous, well-managed households of middle England, and in doing so recast the monarchy for the twentieth century. This was the kind of 'temperate' monarchy that Tennyson appraised in his *Ode on the Death of the Duke of Wellington*.[63] The *Morning Post* praised 'our Queen' as 'the highest type of English lady, English wife and English mother'.[64] The echoes of Gloriana were faint, but just discernible.

Victoria's *Leaves of a Journal of our Life in the Highlands*, the second edition of which was published in 1868 in an effort to somehow re-engage monarch with subjects, was received by the *Telegraph* with the gushing observation 'Thank God there are many thousand English homes like this'. Give or take a few dozen servants there probably were. The royal family at Balmoral was, apparently, an apposite symbol of 'that pure light of household love which shines by so many English hearths'.[65] In the words of Lytton Strachey, more than ever Victoria had become the 'living symbol of the victory of the middle classes', and all their 'prim solidarity'.[66]

Victoria survived, and so did the monarchy. By the time of her death in 1901, she was almost as revered as Elizabeth. The English have always admired longevity in their Fairy Queens. But it tends to be forgotten just how deep was the crisis that afflicted Fairyland in the mid-nineteenth century. And it was amidst this crisis, as well as the associated reform agitation of 1866–67, that Bagehot sat down to compose his *English Constitution*.

[61] Longford, above n 57, 347–48, Strachey, above n 59, 183–85, and M Homans, *Royal Representations: Queen Victoria and British Culture 1837–1876*, (Univ of Chicago Press, 1998), 70–71, 142–43.

[62] Shakespeare, *Richard II* 4.1.287–88

[63] 'Ode on the Death of the Duke of Wellington', l.165, in Tennyson, *Poems*, 283.

[64] Homans, *Representations*, 24–28, and Williams, *Crown*, 200

[65] Homans, above n 61, 133–34, and Williams, above n 32, 203.

[66] Strachey, above n 59, 29, 116–17.

II DIGNIFIED AND EFFICIENT

Mystery and Magic

Bagehot was fully appraised of the performative role of monarchy, just as he was of Victoria's performance, the transfer of the 'pride of sovereignty to the level of petty life' and 'nice and pretty events'.[67] His discussion of the Anglo-British monarchy in his *Constitution* was framed by the famous distinction between the 'dignified' and the 'efficient' aspects of the constitution, between those aspects that appear to give the constitution a certain legitimacy, and those that actually make government work.[68] The dignified aspects are 'those which appeal to the senses', that 'which is mystic in its claims; that which is occult in mode of action; that which is brilliant to the eye'.[69] Both Houses of Parliament had 'dignified', as well as 'efficient', aspects. But far and away the most 'dignified' institution of all was the monarchy; or at least it should be.

The opening to Bagehot's first chapter on monarchy brilliantly encapsulated the mix of journalistic irony and political perception that defined *The English Constitution*:

> The use of the Queen, in a dignified capacity, is incalculable. Without her in England, the present English government would fail and pass away. Most people when they read that the Queen walked on the slopes at Windsor—that the Prince of Wales went to the Derby—have imagined that too much thought and prominence were given to little things. But they have been in error; and it is nice to trace how the actions of a retired widow and an unemployed youth become of such importance.[70]

Bagehot fully understood the Dorothy Wordsworths of England. Men and women prefer to be 'governed by the weaknesses of their imagination', than by the exercise of their reason.[71] Thus, whilst he affirmed that monarchy is the 'most national thing in the nation', the 'standard to which the eyes of the people perpetually turn to keep them together', it is also an institution that exists to furnish 'a visible symbol of unity to those still so imperfectly educated as to need a symbol'.[72]

[67] Bagehot, above n 3, 37.
[68] *Ibid*, 5.
[69] *Ibid*, 7.
[70] *Ibid*, 34.
[71] *Ibid*, 34.
[72] *Ibid*, 41.

The English, Bagehot observed, always 'defer' to the 'theatrical show of society', to 'a certain pomp of great men' and, most especially, to 'a certain spectacle of beautiful women'. For them, the 'higher world, as it looks from without, is a stage on which the actors walk their parts much better than the spectators can'. Life in England is still a 'charmed spectacle', at the 'climax' of which can always be found the ultimate icon of the Fairy Queen, for whom the 'baser sort', so readily 'governed by the weakness of their imagination', retain an entirely 'mystic reverence'. In this sense, the popular worship of the monarchy furnishes English constitutional culture with its 'occult' thrill.[73] Most importantly, 'Its mystery is its life. We must not let in daylight upon magic'.[74]

Bagehot did, of course, breeze through the various nominal duties of the English monarch, the assenting to legislation, and the appointment of ministers and bishops and so on. He also famously noted the monarch's three 'rights'; 'the right to be consulted, the right to encourage, and the right to warn'. A 'king of great sense and sagacity', of which there are occasionally one or two, Bagehot pointedly added, 'would want no other'.[75] But all in all, the formal responsibilities did not add up to much. The vast majority of documents that had to be signed by the monarch, he concluded, 'contain no matter of policy' and could as well be signed by a 'clerk'.[76] Moreover, 'if the two Houses unanimously sent it up to her', the Queen would have to 'sign her own death-warrant'.[77] In terms of genuine power, Bagehot was keen to impress that his monarch was, to all intents and purposes, impotent.

This, according to Bagehot, was a good thing. For the vast majority of monarchs, as history reveals, are of 'inferior ability', something which means that whilst 'idle' monarchs are to be welcomed, the 'active and meddling fool' is a menace to all and sundry.[78] The problem with monarchs, Bagehot advised, is that most are too stupid or too mad to be allowed any nearer to real power, and those that are not genetically disadvantaged suffer from the fact that, with every passing day, their office distances them from reality. A 'monarch in the recesses of a palace, listening to a charmed flattery, unbiased by the miscella-

[73] Bagehot, above n 3, 60, 64–65, 82, 248, See, also Nairn, above n 32, 334

[74] Bagehot, above n 3, 50.

[75] *Ibid*, 60.

[76] *Ibid*, 49–50. For a general discussion of this nominal function, see also 52–54.

[77] *Ibid*, 48.

[78] *Ibid*, 54, 57, 66–67.

neous world, who has always been hedged in by rank, is likely to be but a poor judge of public opinion'.[79] Few defences of the principle of monarchy have been quite so refreshingly contemptuous of those who inhabit the institution itself.

In a justly famous remark, Bagehot declared that 'A republic has insinuated itself beneath the folds of a monarchy', by which he meant that English monarchs, no matter how semi-detached or mad they might be, served the purpose of acting 'as a disguise' for the 'upper ten thousand' who enjoy real power in Britain, and whose interests are almost exclusively represented in 'government'.[80] This, ultimately, is the real purpose of monarchy, its primary duty; as it keeps the masses entertained, it provides those who govern, in other words the great Whig oligarchies, with the facility, and the opportunity, to do pretty much as they wish. Bagehot ascribed this to the general mood of 'matter-of-factness' that was slowly sweeping away the dusty myths of English constitutionalism.[81] In time, he even insinuated, monarchy itself might be swept aside. It is 'not essential', and very often 'not even in a high degree useful'. Once a people has been educated in such a way that it no longer needs to be deluded, then an 'unroyal form of parliamentary government' becomes necessarily more preferable.[82]

The Ruder Sort

Seen in this way, the English constitution becomes a series of essentially Faustian bargains, between monarch and subjects, between monarch and executive, between politician and citizen. But such a scheme of bargains, of course, has its price. The gullibility of the English is integral to Bagehot's view of the constitution. But it is also deeply troubling. As Dicey was to affirm with even greater vigour in his *Lectures on Law and Opinion*, people who could be deluded by majesty could also be deluded by 'pollitricks'. The 'ruder sort of men', as Bagehot attested, are far too easily lured by 'what is called an idea', whilst the emergent fancy of 'public opinion' means nothing more or less than the 'opinion of the boneheaded man at the back of the omnibus'.[83] The thinking

[79] *Ibid*, 160.
[80] *Ibid*, 44–46.
[81] *Ibid*, 167.
[82] *Ibid*, 170.
[83] *Ibid*, 7, 30.

man, like the thinking monarch, is the real menace to a well-ordered society. It was for this reason that Bagehot so feared precipitate reform of the franchise. The 'masses are infinitely too ignorant to make much of governing themselves, and they do not know mind when they see it'.[84] It is unsurprising, then, that the 1872 edition of the *Constitution* pointedly bemoaned the 'calamity' of the 1867 Act, and the arrival of the 'ignorant multitude of the new constituencies'.[85]

Of course, such comments must also be placed within the immediate and personal context of Bagehot's own serially unsuccessful attempts to secure election to Parliament. Having finally gained selection, he stood as Liberal party candidate in Bridgwater, only to be cheated by a corrupt count; but not before admitting that he hated 'the Liberal enthusiasts', or indeed any other kind of enthusiast.[86] In his later rather whimsical essay, *The Advantages and Disadvantages of Becoming a Member of Parliament*, he identified what, at least for him, was the essential problem in aspiring to be a politician. A 'man who tries to enter Parliament must be content to utter common thoughts, and to bind himself to the formularies of common creeds, or he will not succeed in his candidature'.[87]

But whilst he reserved this withering contempt for his putative colleagues and indeed constituents, Bagehot was shrewd enough to appreciate that reform was justified, not as a matter of principle as such, but in the matter 'gross appearance'. In his earlier essay *Parliamentary Reform*, he had acknowledged that there was a need to make Parliament better reflect the 'true judgment of the nation', or at least appear to.[88] In the *English Constitution*, he affirmed that the 'single, unbending franchise of 1832 simply did 'not look right'. The 'working classes' feel that their 'interests' are 'misconceived or neglected', and that 'the thoughts of Parliament are not as their thoughts'. Thus, whilst the 'representation' as it stood was 'adequate', it just did not seem to be so.[89] Everything about the English constitution is about 'representation'.

Bagehot had already addressed the matter of electoral reform, and the collateral issue of party politics, in a famous essay on *The*

[84] Bagehot, above n 3, 186.
[85] *Ibid*, 200, 205.
[86] Briggs, above n 28, 108, and St John Stevas, above n 40, 16–17.
[87] W Bagehot, *The Advantages and Disadvantages of Becoming a Member of Parliament*, in St John Stevas, above n 40, 461.
[88] Bagehot, *Parliamentary Reform*, in St John Stevas, above n 40, 432.
[89] Bagehot, above n 3, 120–21.

Character of Sir Robert Peel written in 1856. In the eyes of many it was Peel who had first begun to dismantle the mystique of the constitution. It was Peel who had sought to introduce the English people to their government, inviting them to read his Tamworth 'manifesto' in 1834, to vote for him, and thereby to participate in the policy-making of the nation. In his novel *Coningsby*, a young Benjamin Disraeli dismissed Peel's manifesto as a blatant 'attempt to construct a party without principles', to reduce politics to a 'mere pandering to public ignorance'.[90] It was a widely shared contempt, and fully endorsed by Bagehot. Peel had made politics popular, thereby abasing the dignity of the politician to the 'repute of the commonalty'. 'No man', Bagehot observed, 'has come so near our definition of a constitutional statesman—the powers of a first-rate man and the creed of a second-rate man'.[91] Peel epitomised the new breed of politician, the dissimulating puppet of popular opinion. There was more than a hint of Swiftian paradox in Bagehot's conclusion that 'Constitutional statesmen are obliged, not only to employ arguments which they do not think conclusive, but likewise to defend opinions which they do not believe to be true'.[92]

The matter of party was, of course, revisited in *The English Constitution*. The governing 'principle of Parliament is obedience to leaders'. Government, Bagehot affirmed, is:

> essentially a government by means of party, since the very condition of its existence is that the Ministers of the Crown should be able in general to guide the decisions of Parliament, and especially of the House of Commons; and all experience proves that no popular assembly can be made to act steadily under recognized leaders except by party organisation.[93]

In short, whilst he retained a fashionable contempt for Peel, Bagehot was quite accepting of party governance. It was, in his view, the only sensible means of ensuring effective government.[94]

The same characteristic tone, a mix of the pragmatic and the ironic, pervades Bagehot's discussion of politics and Parliament in his *Constitution*. The House of Lords, so 'decorous' in its 'dullness', potentially of great value as a reflective revising chamber, but in practice stuffed with hereditary peers and thus worse than useless.

90 B Disraeli, *Coningsby*, (London, Penguin, 1989), 95, 125.
91 W Bagehot, *The Character of Sir Robert Peel*, in St John–Stevas, above n 40, 164–66.
92 *Ibid*, 177.
93 Bagehot, above n 3, 99.
94 *Ibid*, 101–3.

Interestingly, Bagehot's suggested alternative, a selected chamber of 'life' peers, is very much in vogue today.[95] And the House of Commons, its 'expressive' role so easily perverted by men like Peel; men who simply talk, pouring 'out in characteristic words the characteristic heart of the nation', and in so doing nourishing the rudest prejudices of the 'ruder' sort.[96] It would not matter so much if Parliament was not so omnipotent. But it can, for good or bad, 'legislate as it wishes'. As we shall see, for the likes of Dicey, this capacity was the great virtue of the Anglo-British Constitution. For Bagehot, however, as his account of Parliament and politics shows, there was much to contemplate in this particular constitutional arrangement.[97]

The Efficient Secret

Bagehot's *Constitution* actually opened, not with a study of monarchy, or the overarching framework of the constitution, but with a commentary on the Cabinet. The reason was simple. The Cabinet had emerged as the most powerful institution in modern government; the 'hyphen which joins, a buckle which fastens the legislative part of the state to the executive part of the state'.[98] According to Bagehot, the 'most curious point about the Cabinet is that so very little is known about it'. Famously, he defined it as 'a board of control chosen by the legislature, out of persons whom it trusts and knows, to rule the nation'.[99] The changing nature of politics has rather dated this observation. Today, the situation is reversed, with the Cabinet very obviously chosen by the Prime Minister, rather than by Parliament. But this should not detract from the prescience of Bagehot's insight. The fastening of the executive and the legislative, in the institutions of Cabinet and Prime Minister, was, Bagehot famously concluded, the 'efficient secret' of the constitution.

And it destroyed the great Lockean myth; that the English constitution was characterised by a separation, and a balancing, between notional 'powers'. If the monarchy provided the 'dignity' that the

95 Bagehot, above n 3, 89.

96 *Ibid*, 117. The Commons, according to Bagehot, has five roles; the expressive, the elective, the teaching, the informing, and the legislative. *Ibid*, 94–95.

97 *Ibid*, 80–81,103–5.

98 *Ibid*, 10.

99 *Ibid*, 10–11.

exercise of government required, the 'efficiency' was secured in the 'close union, the nearly complete fusion of the executive and legislative powers'.[100] This was the only balance that mattered to Bagehot. An 'efficient' constitution, Bagehot declared, needs a 'conclusive' power somewhere. The 'splitting of sovereignty into many parts', in contrast, 'amounts to there being no sovereign' at all. In comparison with jurisdictions such as the American, the 'excellence' of the English constitution can be found in its 'unity'; that 'in it the sovereign power is single, possible, and good'.[101]

The fetish for sovereignty was characteristic of the age. For constitutional pedants, such as Dicey, sovereignty lay in the fiction of the 'Queen in Parliament'. Bagehot, never one to stand on ceremony, confirmed that 'ultimate sovereignty in the English constitution is a newly elected House of Commons'. Sovereignty, for Bagehot, is a matter of practical politics, not constitutional nicety. The House of Commons 'can despotically and finally resolve' any matter it pleases; so it is the sovereign power in the nation.[102]

The dissonance between reality and fancy in the matter of sovereignty was only one of many anomalies that Bagehot detected in the substance of British government. The very relation between executive and legislative, the 'buckle' that fastens the constitution, is itself a 'specific peculiarity'.[103] So too is the rather odd relation between the English mind and the bureaucratic. The governance of Britain, Bagehot shrewdly observes, had a 'sort of leaning towards bureaucracy', even though the image of the bureaucrat was so widely abused in English culture.[104] The English need strong government; but they abhor those who undertake to govern.

And then there are the particular anomalies that attach to the two most senior offices in government, those of the Prime Minister and the Lord Chancellor. Bagehot does not dwell long on the office of Lord Chancellor, but what he has to say is sufficiently incisive:

> The whole office of the Lord Chancellor is a heap of anomalies. He is a judge, and it is contrary to obvious principle that any part of administration should be entrusted to a judge; it is of very grave moment that the Lord

[100] *Ibid*, 8–9.
[101] *Ibid*, 150, 154–55.
[102] *Ibid*, 154–55.
[103] *Ibid*, 122.
[104] *Ibid*, 132, 142. See also 180–81.

> Chancellor, our chief judge, sits in the cabinet, and makes party speeches in the Lords.[105]

Whilst this particular 'heap' is finally, nearly a century and a half later, on the verge of despatch, the anomalies that attach to the office of Prime Minister remain. According to Bagehot, the Prime Minister is the head of the 'efficient' part of the constitution, 'some one man' chosen by the party in government to 'head that party, and consequently to rule the nation'.[106] The office epitomises the 'efficient secret' of the constitution. Not that Bagehot was unduly troubled. As a matter of political pragmatics, nations need leaders, individuals who can 'settle the conversation of mankind'.[107]

And, finally, there are the 'greatest' of these anomalies, prerogative powers. Much of the power of the executive, as we shall see in the next chapter, is derived from the particular anomaly of prerogative power; a power that is nominally vested in the Crown, but enjoyed, in effect, by Prime Minister, Cabinet and government.[108] As Bagehot fully appreciated, 'the executive Government, because it is the most powerful' interest in the constitution, is thereby also the 'most dangerous of all sinister interests'.[109] The purpose of Parliament, accordingly, is not to check the power of the executive as such, merely to provide some kind of measure of accountability. MPs can question ministers, not in aid of actually influencing what they do, but more, as Bagehot put it, to 'amuse the public'.[110] Once again, the observation is acute; the matter of government, like that of monarchy, is a matter of representation.

Inventing the Constitution

Subsequent political and constitutional history has reinforced Bagehot's reputation. His portrayal of the 'dignified' and 'efficient' aspects of the constitution, and particularly his incisive analysis of modern government, and its despotic potential, has proved to be percipient. Approving Harold Wilson's observation, that Bagehot's *Constitution* 'will never be out of date', Peter Hennessy has recently

[105] Bagehot, above n 3, 145.
[106] *Ibid*, 9.
[107] *Ibid*, 200.
[108] *Ibid*, 49.
[109] *Ibid*, 80.
[110] *Ibid*, 125–26.

suggested that contemporary constitutional historians continue to 'live' in his 'shadow, almost his thrall'.[111] Plaudits are many. For Asa Briggs, the *English Constitution* is a 'brilliant diagnosis' of a constitution in decline, whilst for Robin Gilmour it remains a 'classic analysis of the realities of world-power' and an 'enduring' one.[112] Bagehot's most recent biographer has lauded a 'mind of extraordinary keenness and subtlety'.[113]

But perhaps the most vivid paean of praise is Sir Kenneth Wheare's:

> Bagehot found the English constitution. It took some finding: it was not by any means obvious; there was little to guide him. At the same time, in the modern sense, he invented the Constitution; he made of it a working and living structure. He had the gift of breathing life into it; he created it. It is not an exaggeration to say that before Bagehot wrote, there was no English constitution that people could recognise or apprehend as a living and working thing. And it was not a skeleton or museum piece that he assembled; he did not confine himself to the anatomy of the subject, he went far beyond anatomy and combined the physiology, the pathology and the psychology.[114]

If one event defined mid-Victorian England and its pretensions, and indeed the brilliance of Bagehot's analysis of the English constitution, it was the ceremonial opening of the Great Exhibition in 1851. Sat on a mock throne, Queen Victoria listened to the Archbishop of Canterbury bless the event as an expression of 'Divine Providence'. She then set off to look at the exhibits, a vast and often bizarre array of the 'dignified' and the 'efficient', colonial tributes aside weapons for the extermination of 'savages', steam-engines, looms and an apparently bottomless number of things made of steel plates. The *Times* applauded the 'second more glorious inauguration of the sovereign', and praised the Exhibition's 'fairy-like' qualities. The *Chronicle* took a more earthy line and celebrated a 'Great Parliament of Labour'.[115] Both were right. Victoria, and her Exhibition, had managed to sprinkle a little Fairydust over the mundanity of modern life. Nowhere was the seamless affinity between the efficient and the dignified more apparent than at Hyde

[111] P Hennessy, *Hidden Wiring: Unearthing the British Constitution*, (London, Gollancz, 1995), 42.

[112] Briggs, above n 28, 95, and D Gilmour, *The Victorian Period: The Intellectual and Cultural Context of English Literature 1830–1890*, (Harlow, Longman, 1993), 163, 166.

[113] St John Stevas, above n 40, 21.

[114] K Wheare, 'Walter Bagehot: Lecture on a Master Mind' (1974) 60 *Proceedings of the British Academy*, 25.

[115] Ward, above n 19, 178–79.

Park in the summer of 1851. The affinity founded the Anglo-British state and empire. It made sense of it all.

As David Marquand has recently confirmed, the English constitution amounts to little more than a 'palimpsest of sometimes discordant myths, understandings and expectations, reflecting the changing values of succeeding generations'.[116] The same sentiment can be found in Martin Loughlin's observation that 'If we are to examine the foundations of politics and law, we must enter the realm of myth'.[117] No one understood the implications of this truth better than Bagehot. His *English Constitution* remains the definitive account of the 'representative' nature of an ultimately imaginary constitution.[118] And it is for this reason that we should, like Bagehot, nurture our capacity for iconoclasm. Bagehot was an ironist and a cynic, which is another reason why his treatise remains so compelling. Irony and cynicism has long characterised English political commentary; and long may it. Pomposity is there to be pricked. Few things are more pompous than the Anglo-British constitution, and rarely has it been so expertly and so comprehensively pricked than in Bagehot's *English Constitution.*

There is one final irony, of which Bagehot would no doubt have approved. In the Introduction to his great treatise, *An Introduction to the Study of the Law of the Constitution*, Dicey opined that 'No author of modern times has done so much to elucidate the intricate workings of English government'.[119] It was meant to be a complement, of a kind. The use of the word 'government', as opposed to 'constitution', was, of course, careful. Dicey realised that whilst he and Bagehot were both talking about the same constitution, they were also talking about two very different things.

III THE ORACLE

Dicey's Principles

Born in 1835, Albert Venn Dicey was a relatively young man when Bagehot published his *English Constitution*. He was also, as we have

[116] D Marquand, 'Pluralism v Populism', (1999) 42 *Prospect*, 27.

[117] M.Loughlin, *Sword and Scales: An Examination of the Relationship between Law and Politics*, (Hart, 2000), 23.

[118] Homans, above n 61, 101–15.

[119] A Dicey, *An Introduction to Study of the Law of the Constitution*, (London, Macmillan, 1959), 19.

already noted, a troubled one, trapped by history, refusing to abandon a visceral loyalty for a political party, and a creed, that of the 'old' Whigs, which was in a state of terminal decline.[120] In many ways, his political affinities mirrored those of one of his greatest intellectual heroes, Edmund Burke; intellectually libertarian, sentimentally conservative.[121] And with the political ambiguities came theological torment. Dicey lived and died a confirmed member of the Church of England. In later years, he was a prominent member of the Synthetic Society, a group of prominent Victorians intellectuals who spent their evenings worrying about Arnold's 'long, withdrawing roar'.

In his later *Lectures on the Relation Between Law and Public Opinion*, Dicey would clearly align the 'development of freedom of opinion' in England with 'the breaking up of established creeds, whether religious, moral, political, or economical.[122] In doing so, he would admit the force of a new intellectual faith; the theology of reason, of the 'sophisters and economists' against whom Burke wrote with such venom in his *Reflections on the Revolution in France*. And it was these 'sophisters' who threatened to make Arnold's prophesy come true, men like Jeremy Bentham whose *Introduction to the Principles of Morals and Legislation* ridiculed all the 'splenetic and revengeful' deities who populated the conservative imagination.[123] And yet, in his essay *Modern English Law*, Dicey proclaimed himself an 'unrepentant Benthamite'. The 'history of modern English law', he affirmed, 'is the history of a gigantic revolution produced by the ideas of one man'.[124] In his later *Lectures*, he would again pay tribute to a 'genius' who had somehow devised a utilitarianism that 'fell in with the habitual conservatism of Englishmen'.[125] It was a vital, if strained, accommodation.

Whilst Bentham remained the great icon of utilitarianism, for lawyers of Dicey's generation, it was his student John Austin who really dominated the jurisprudential landscape. In his *Province of Jurisprudence Determined*, published in 1832, Austin followed his

[120] For a general, and famous, commentary on Dicey's politics, and particularly his Whig affinities, see I Jennings, 'In Praise of Dicey',(1935) 13 *Public Administration*, 123–25, and Cosgrove, above n 38, 118–20.

[121] In his later essay, *The Statesmanship of Wordsworth*, Dicey paid great tribute to the poet's Burkean sentiments. See A Dicey, *The Statesmanship of Wordsworth*, (Oxford UP, 1917), 67.

[122] Dicey, above n 20, 438–39. See also Cosgrove, above n 38, 6–7.

[123] J Bentham, *An Introduction to the Principles of Morals and Legislation*, (London, Methuen, 1982), 18–19.

[124] In Cosgrove, above n 38, 181.

[125] Dicey, above n 20, 174.

mentor in roundly rejecting the 'senseless fictions' of both theology and ideology, of 'natural justice' and the 'rights of man', of 'unalienable liberties' and 'social contracts'.[126] Law, according to Austin, was to be understood solely as a function of reason. And of 'unitary' sovereignty. The very first sentence of the *Province* declared that laws 'properly so called, are commands', and such a command is, in simple terms, merely 'a rule of positive morality set by a determinate author'.[127] It was not just a matter of principle, but of effective government; which is why, as we have seen, Bagehot approved the principle, whilst also betraying certain misgivings.

Dicey was critical of certain aspects of Austin's *Province*, not least its failure to distinguish cleanly between legal and political sovereignty.[128] In general, however, he was totally convinced, both by the Benthamite distinction between positive law and positive morality, and by Austin's particular assertion that a rational and coherent legal system must be rooted in a concept of sovereign authority. Reverence of these two related ideas defined the zealot of positive jurisprudence, and few were more zealous than Albert Venn Dicey.

As a result of this intellectual affinity, two implications were irreducible. First, a constitution is a system of positive rules, not positive morality. Accordingly, the English constitution should be understood in terms of 'all rules which directly or indirectly affect the distribution or the exercise of the sovereign power of the state'.[129] Ironically, of course, as Ivor Jennings pointed out, Dicey's *Law* is less about rules than it is about principles, most particularly the 'revolution principles' still cherished by the 'old' Whigs.[130] Or at least most of them. Famously, three broadly defined 'principles' underpinned Dicey's *Law*; 'the legislative sovereignty of Parliament', the 'universal rule' of law, and the 'conventions' of the constitution.[131] A fourth, the 'separation of powers', was conspicuously missing; for reasons we shall consider shortly. The second implication flowed from the first. The 'present day students of the constitution wish neither to criticise, nor to venerate, but to understand', and it is for this reason that a 'professor' of constitutional law has a 'duty' not to 'attack nor to defend the constitution,

[126] See J Austin, *The Province of Jurisprudence Determined*, (Cambridge University Press, 1995), 19–20, 38–57, 73, 154.

[127] *Ibid*, 10, 21, 116–24.

[128] Dicey, above n 119, 74.

[129] *Ibid*, 23.

[130] Jennings, above n 120, 128.

[131] Dicey, above n 119, 35.

but simply to explain its laws'.[132] And that, quite simply, is what Dicey tried to do; to detach the politics from the constitution, and to convince everybody that he was right to do so. There was no hint of irony in Dicey, no temptation to prick pomposity. The Vinerian Professor loved pomposity. He lived for it.

The Spirit of Legality

The first edition of Dicey's *Law* was published in 1885, amidst the general furore that accompanied Gladstone's third Reform Act. One of Dicey's predecessors as Vinerian Professor at Oxford University had been Sir William Blackstone, and just as Blackstone penned his *Commentaries* as a laudatory to English law as it then was, so too did Dicey compose his *Law* as a paean to the English constitution as it stood, and as it had been. Only it was no longer just an English constitution. It was now an Anglo-British constitution, a symbol of Empire, and expression of a 'unitary' and 'united' kingdom, at the apex of which there was a 'single unrivalled agency'. This 'agency' was 'parliamentary sovereignty', the principle which Austin had sanctified, and over which Macaulay had encouraged his readers to swoon.[133] It was this principle and the great statutes with which it was entrenched, most notably successive Acts of Settlement and Union, which, according to Dicey, founded the very idea, and the reality, of the 'united' Kingdom of Great Britain.[134]

The principle of 'parliamentary sovereignty' was, as Dicey famously declared, the 'very keystone of the law of the constitution', as well as the 'dominant characteristic of our political institutions'.[135] Dicey immediately identified two particular and related features of Parliamentary sovereignty; namely that Parliament has 'the right to make or unmake any law whatever; and, further, that no person or body is recognised by the law of England as having a right to override or set aside the legislation of Parliament'.[136] The first of these features is often termed 'continuing' parliamentary sovereignty. According to

[132] *Ibid*, 3–4.

[133] See N Walker, 'Beyond the Unitary Conception of the United Kingdom Constitution?' (2000) *Public Law*, 387–88.

[134] Dicey, above n 119, 43–50. See also Jennings, above n 120, 128–29, suggesting that Dicey 'saw the constitution of 1885 through Whig principles'.

[135] Dicey, above n 119, 70–71.

[136] *Ibid*, 40.

Dicey, it is this 'continuing' nature of sovereignty that secures the renowned 'flexibility' of the English constitution.[137] It found historical authority in Blackstone's assertion that 'what the parliament doth, no authority upon earth can undo'.[138]

Until recent times, it has also earned consistent judicial approbation, in famous cases such as *Cheney v Conn*, where it was bluntly asserted that 'What Parliament enacts is the highest form of law'.[139] A similar sentiment could be found in Lord Reid's statement in *Madzimbamuto*:

> It is often said that it would be unconstitutional for the United Kingdom Parliament to do certain things, meaning that the moral, political and other reasons against doing them are so strong that most people would regard it as highly improper if Parliament did these things. But that does not mean that it is beyond the power of Parliament to do such things. If Parliament chose to do any of them the courts would not hold the Act of Parliament invalid.[140]

It could also be found in Lord Justice Maugham's uncompromising dismissal of the thought that one Parliament might somehow bind another.

> The legislature cannot according to our constitution bind itself as to the form of subsequent legislation, and it is impossible for Parliament to enact that in a subsequent statute dealing with the same subject matter there can be no implied repeal.[141]

Dicey, of course, was wholly dismissive of the thought that one Parliament might 'make laws which cannot be touched by any subsequent Parliament'.[142]

The classical theory of 'continuing sovereignty' inheres a variety of paradoxes and collateral implications. Parliament, for example, is empowered to 'make or unmake' any law it likes, except of course, any law that might impinge upon its power to 'make or unmake' any law it likes.[143] And then there is the vexed relation between parliamentary

[137] Dicey, above n 119, 127–28.

[138] Blackstone, *Commentaries* 1.160.

[139] *Cheney v Conn* [1968] 1 All ER 779.

[140] *Madzimbamuto v Lardner-Burke* [1969] 1 AC 723.

[141] *Ellen Street Estates v Minister of Health* [1934] I KB 597.

[142] Dicey, above n 119, 64–68.

[143] An argument that might seem whimsical; except that history reveals rather too many examples of anti-democratic parties rising to power and then trying to emasculate legislative assemblies. For a famous prophesy of this see Carl Schmitt's essay *The Crisis of Parliamentary Democracy*, (Cambridge, Mass, MIT Press, 1988), composed in pre-Nazi Germany.

sovereignty and any lingering belief in a 'separation of powers'.[144] Whilst there was much that Dicey admired about the United States, the divided sovereignty that characterises such federal constitutional orders was dismissed as a 'political contrivance' and a 'waste of energy' that can only result in 'weak government'.[145] The collateral idea of constitutional review was also the subject of Dicey's particular criticism.[146]

For others, however, the idea of a 'separation of powers', and a system of constitutional review, was altogether more appealing. According to Harold Laski, writing only a generation after Dicey, 'it would be of lasting benefit to political science if the whole concept of sovereignty were surrendered'. He continued, 'That, in fact, with which we are dealing is power; and what is important in the nature of power is the end it seeks to serve and the way in which it serves that end'.[147] Bagehot would have nodded. We shall revisit this truth, and the case for a separation of constitutional powers, in due course.

Alongside parliamentary sovereignty, the 'keystone' of the constitution, Dicey placed considerable stock in the potentially countervailing principle of the rule of law. Dicey's 'rule of law' was the product of a long jurisprudential evolution. The more immediate influence was familiar; the 'revolution principles' of Whig historiography.[148] But Dicey was prepared to go further back still, even so far as the Norman conquest.[149] The opening passages of his chapters on the 'rule of law' moreover, conceded the particular origin of the principle in the traditions of civic republicanism; of the kind which had characterised the 'Good Old Cause' of the mid-seventeenth century.[150]

By the rule of law, Dicey asserted:

> We mean, in the first place, that no man is punishable or can be lawfully made to suffer in body or goods except for a distinct breach of law established in the ordinary legal manner before the ordinary courts of the land.[151]

[144] See Carol Harlow's observations in her 'Power from the People?: Representation and Constitutional Theory', in P McAuslan & J McEldowney, *Law, Legitimacy and the Constitution*, (London, Sweet & Maxwell, 1985), 65–68.

[145] Dicey, above n 119, 138–44, 155–57, 171.

[146] *Ibid*, 159–71,

[147] Quoted in Harlow, above n 144, 72.

[148] Jennings, above n 120, 130.

[149] Dicey, above n 119, 183.

[150] Dicey, above n 119, 184–85.

[151] Dicey, above n 119, 188.

Dicey pointedly contrasted this to 'every system' of 'arbitrary' government.[152] And then continued:

> We mean in the second place, when we speak of the 'rule of law' as a characteristic of our country, not only that with us no man is above the law, but (what is a different thing) that here every man, whatever be his rank or condition, is subject to the ordinary law of the realm and amenable to the jurisdiction of the ordinary tribunals.[153]

Dicey did not shy away from the potential conflict between the 'rule of law' and 'parliamentary sovereignty', admitting that the 'two principles' may 'appear to stand in opposition to each other, or to be at best only counterbalancing forces'.[154] However, he continued:

> But this appearance is delusive; the sovereignty of Parliament, as contrasted with other forms of sovereign power, favours the supremacy of the law, whilst the predominance of rigid legality throughout our institutions evokes the exercise, and thus increases the authority, or Parliamentary sovereignty.[155]

Dicey hoped that in defining the rule of law in terms of both liberty and equality, he might be able to neutralise the apparent conflict; liberty is subject to the law. This, he concluded, preserves the 'spirit of legality' which defines the English constitution.[156] It admits a 'different sense' of the principle of the rule of law; one which holds that the 'general principles of the constitution' are 'with us the result of judicial decisions determining the rights of private persons in particular cases brought before the law'. This recourse had a very obvious resonance, as Dicey admitted, with the older 'common law' idea of the 'rule of law'.[157]

Perhaps the most controversial aspect of Dicey's discussion of the rule of law was the long attached commentary on the French *droit administratif*.[158] According to Dicey, the *droit administratif* possessed two defining characteristics. First it presumed a body of law devoted to 'special rights, privileges, or prerogatives as against private citizens'.

[152] Dicey, above n 119, 188.

[153] Dicey, above n 119, 193.

[154] For a discussion of this issue, ultimately denying that there is an irreducible conflict, see T Allan, *Constitutional Justice: Liberal Theory and the Rule of Law*, (Oxford UP, 2001), 201–42.

[155] Dicey, above n 119, 406.

[156] Dicey, above n 119, 414.

[157] Dicey, above n 119, 195. The solution is broadly approved by Allan, above n 154, 214–15.

[158] Dicey, above n 119, ch12.

Second it complied with an overarching principle of the separation of powers.[159] No such characteristics, he continued, could be found in English constitutional law, and therefore there was no comparable domain of administrative law in English jurisprudence. Once again, the historical *rationale* for Dicey's thesis could be traced back to the seventeenth century. With the defeat of the Stuart 'tyranny', he confirmed, the 'powers of the Crown' must now 'be exercised in accordance with the ordinary common law principles which govern the relation of one Englishman to another'.[160]

It was only in the 1915 edition that Dicey grudgingly admitted the reality of an emergent Anglo-British administrative law. The context to this admission, as Wade noted, was Dicey's general feeling that the principle of the rule of law was itself in a state of decline, not least because militant reformists, whether they be Home Rulers, suffragettes or trades unionists, no longer displayed an uncritical obeisance to rulings of the courts.[161] Subsequent critics have long berated Dicey for his reluctance to admit the scope of administrative law. The otherwise devoted Wade admitted that he 'long threw a chilly shadow over administrative law', whilst de Smith suggested that Dicey's ability to convince generations of lawyers that England was indeed devoid of an administrative law was a considerable 'misfortune'.[162] Of course, it is rather easier to criticise Dicey with the benefit of hindsight. It is now very obvious that a distinct administrative law exists in English jurisprudence. It was not, perhaps, quite so obvious in 1885. Moreover, the suggestion that the 'common law' principle of the 'rule of law' could anyway fill the void was not only defensible in context, but was also, for reasons that we shall encounter, rather prescient.

Fanciful Dreams

The final part of the Dicey's *Law* was given over to the subject of conventions, the other bits of 'law' which could not be brought within the purview of either Parliamentary sovereignty, and statute, or the

159 Dicey, above n 119, 336–38.
160 Dicey, above n 119, 379–81, 387.
161 See Wade, 'Introduction' to Dicey above n 119, cxliv–v.
162 W Wade and C Forsyth, *Administrative Law*, 7th edn, (Oxford UP, 2000), 7, and SA de Smith, *Judicial Review of Administrative Action*, (London, Sweet & Maxwell, 1995), 5.

common law. Dicey presented two definitions of conventions; one wide and one rather more restrictive. The wider definition presented conventions as 'consisting' of 'customs, practices, maxims, or precepts which are not enforced or recognised by the courts' and which 'make up a body not of laws, but of constitutional or political ethics'. These rules can be contrasted with the 'true law of the constitution'.[163]

The narrower definition of conventions describes those 'rules for determining the mode in which the discretionary powers of the Crown (or of the Ministers as servants of the Crown) ought to be exercised'. Understood in this way, Dicey repeated, conventions 'of the constitution' are 'intended to regulate the exercise of the whole of the remaining discretionary powers of the Crown, whether these powers are exercised by the Queen herself or by the Ministry'.[164] One convention which Dicey discusses at some length is that by which Parliament is dissolved. According to Dicey this is a supreme convention, a 'right of appeal to the people' which 'thus underlies all those constitutional conventions which, in one way or another, are intended to produce harmony between the legal and the political sovereign power'.[165]

As we shall see in the next chapter, the question of enforceability is definitive, and notorious; according to Dicey 'by far the most perplexing of the speculative questions suggested by a study of constitutional law'.[166] Conventions are mere 'rules' as opposed to legal rules, rules which 'have nearly the force of law', but not quite.[167] Some conventions, such as the summoning of Parliament each year, are regularly enforced. Others, such as those of ministerial responsibility, are only intermittently observed. The reason for this inconsistency is, quite simply, that conventions are rather more political, even moral, instruments. As Dicey admitted, they 'make up the constitutional morality of the day'; a definition that was to be echoed by Frederick Maitland, who distinguished conventions as 'rules of constitutional morality'.[168] Conventions bridge the respective worlds of constitutional law and political morality.

Dicey revisited the murkier realm of constitutional morality in his second great treatise, his *Lectures on the Relation between Law and*

[163] Dicey, above n 119, 417, 469–70.
[164] Dicey, above n 119, 423, 426.
[165] Dicey, above n 119, 438.
[166] Dicey, above n 119, 39.
[167] Dicey, above n 119, 24, 441.
[168] Dicey, above n 119, 422, and also F Maitland, *The Constitutional History of England*, (Cambridge UP, 1965), 398.

Public Opinion in England during the Nineteenth Century, published in 1905, where he again conceded that the institutions of government 'everywhere depend upon beliefs or feelings' and the 'opinion of the society in which such institutions flourish'.[169] Ultimately, the various 'fictions' of the English constitutions, he concluded, resemble nothing but the 'most fanciful dreams of *Alice in Wonderland*'.[170] It was a striking admission; for no one had worked harder to erase the fanciful from the study of the law of the constitution.

Despite the apparent concession to constitutional 'fictions', the *Lectures* provided a striking political supplement to the jurisprudence of the *Law*. There is, most obviously, a grim Austinian determination in the prospectus, to provide a 'novel and interesting view of modern legislation', one that would show how 'a mass of irregular, fragmentary, ill-expressed, and, as it might seem, illogical or purposeless enactments, gains a new meaning and obtains a kind of consistency when seen to be the work of permanent currents of opinion'. The search for 'consistency', if nothing else, is itself consistent. The crucial difference, however, is that Dicey composed the *Lectures* as an exercise in history, rather than in the science of law. For this reason, the early lectures in particular, with their wistful account of the rise, and fall, of the principle of liberty, can be placed in that vast catalogue of mournful Victorian epitaphs for the lost principles of Whig liberty; a late echo, perhaps, of Arnold's 'long, withdrawing roar'.[171]

Dicey dreaded democracy, and he particularly dreaded the kind of democracy that evinced itself in terms of 'opinion'.[172] Such opinion was guided, not by principle, but by the 'stress of circumstances'.[173] The:

> democratic idea that the people, or any large number of the people, ought to have whatever they desire simply because they desire it, and ought to have it quickly, is absolutely fatal to that slow and sure kind of progress which alone has the remotest chance of producing fundamental and beneficial social changes.[174]

It is this organic 'kind of progress', Dicey confirmed, that defines the English political 'way'.[175]

[169] Dicey, above n 20, 1.
[170] Dicey, above n 20, 93.
[171] See, for example, Lectures 2 and 3.
[172] Dicey, above n 20, lxxii.
[173] Dicey, above n 20, 301.
[174] Dicey, above n 20, lxxxvii–viii.
[175] Dicey, above n 20 ,vii, lx, 301.

As a young man, Dicey had flirted with a more radical Toryism. He had, for example, shown a keen interest in the reform of legal education, even in the broader campaign for an improvement in the education of women. After 1867, however, he turned sharply against any further reform of institutions, particularly any reform that might inflame 'public opinion'.[176] Much later, in private correspondence, he wrote 'I am rather anxious to save up carefully such strength as I have, as I am doing all I can to fight the constitutional innovations proposed by the Government'.[177] By then, the particular innovation that he really feared was the prospect of Irish secession, along with a collateral anxiety regarding mooted reform to the House of Lords, the possibility of female suffrage, and the pending torrent of social reform legislation. In each case, Dicey was convinced that the prophecy advanced in his *Lectures* had come to pass: the grand edifice of the Anglo-British constitution was threatened by nothing other than a reckless pandering to 'public opinion'.[178]

Aside from a traditional distaste of parties, shared alike by high Tory and 'old' Whig, Dicey's *Lectures* betrayed their author's particular distaste for the kind of democracy advocated by the 'collectivists'. The 'Introduction' to the second edition of the *Lectures* painstakingly listed all the contemporary collectivist legislation, such as the 1908 Old Pensions Act, the 1911 National Insurance Act, and the 1913 Trade Union Act. 'Revolution', he opined, 'is not the more entitled to respect because it is carried through not by violence, but under the specious though delusive appearance of taxation imposed to meet the financial needs of the State'.[179] Where others saw social reform, Dicey saw a fundamental threat to liberty and the English 'way'. Collectivism threatened Whig libertarianism whilst it perverted Benthamite utilitarianism. It represented government 'by experts' who 'think they know what is good for the people' better than the 'people themselves'.[180]

Not that Dicey was particularly keen on the 'people' sharing in public government. But he was genuinely concerned that their capacity to govern their private lives should be constrained as little as possible. The

[176] Dicey, above n 20, lecture 7.

[177] In Cosgrove, above n 38, 111.

[178] For a discussion of this context, see Cosgrove, above n 38, 214–17 and J.McEldowney, 'Dicey in Historical Perspective—A Review Essay', in McAuslan & McEldowney, *Law*, 52–3.

[179] Dicey, above n 20, xxxiii–liii.

[180] Dicey, above n 20, lxxiii, 15–16. See also a lengthy, and mournful, reflection in chapter 9.

'traditions of the aristocratic government', he observed, had been replaced by a new and grasping 'middle-class' elite; an elite originally inspired by a spirit of conservative 'humanism', but which had now been thoroughly sequestered by 'collectivists'.[181] Even worse, the 'working classes' were being encouraged to have opinions and to voice them. The banner of liberty had been tossed away, sacrificed to the primitive democratic yearnings of the ignorant 'wage-earner'.[182] It is difficult, in this context, to disagree with David Sugarman's blunt assertion, that Dicey's *Lectures* were an expression of an unremittingly 'reactionary politics'.[183]

In private correspondence, Dicey observed that;

> The presumption is in favour of the existing state of affairs, because on the whole it may be assumed to be the permanent will of the nation. Add to this that a constitutional change once made is, or ought to be, final, and therefore ought not to be made by any body of men who do not clearly represent the final will of the nation. Till modern times this has been the practice, though not the theory, of English constitutional government, and it is, as I have pointed out, recognised as a democratic principle in every true democracy.[184]

Dicey was at pains to suggest that he did not reject the 'democratic principle'. He simply refused to accept any democratic impulse that seemed to threaten the supervening 'principles' of liberty.

The older Dicey became, the more troubled he became, the more convinced that collectivist conceptions of democracy threatened to overcome the 'principles' of 1689, as well as the union of the 'United' Kingdom. The introduction to the 1915 edition of the *Law* was dedicated to this anxiety. Much of Dicey's final years were taken up with similar concerns. He was particularly troubled by the prospect of Irish Home Rule; something that had obsessed him since Gladstone's failed initiatives of the 1880s.[185] In his 1886 pamphlet tellingly entitled *England's Case Against Home Rule*, Dicey advised that Home Rule could only mean one thing, a 'moral check' on the supremacy of Parliament.[186] Dicey was certainly not the first of his countrymen to

[181] Dicey, above n 20, 58–59.
[182] Dicey, above n 20, 310.
[183] D Sugarman, 'The Legal Boundaries of Liberty: Dicey, Liberalism and Legal Science', (1983) 46 *Modern Law Review*, 111.
[184] In Cosgrove, *Dicey*, 161.
[185] See Cosgrove, above n 38, 114–40, 228–60.
[186] A Dicey, *England's Case Against Home Rule*, (Richmond Pub, 1973), 24, 134.

have presumed that the future of England, and its Empire, depended upon ruling the Irish. And he would not be the last.

The Authorised Version

The figure of Albert Venn Dicey towers above Anglo-British constitutional law, just as that of Walter Bagehot does over the political analysis of the constitution. As Brian Simpson affirmed, Dicey's *Law* was taken to be the 'best book and the best written book' on the constitution, and it is 'around Dicey that nearly all lawyers study constitutional law'. 'The oracle', he concluded', 'spoke, and came to be accepted'.[187] Even though he fervently disagreed with much that Dicey wrote, Harold Laski readily admitted that he was the 'most considerable figure in English jurisprudence' at least since Maitland.[188] It is still Dicey, more than anyone, who haunts the lecture rooms of English law schools, as well as the pages of English constitutional law texts, his spirit kept marching by later disciples such as HWR Wade, who edited the final, and thus essentially definitive, edition of Dicey's *Law*.[189] As Carol Harlow has recently confirmed, it was Dicey's 'authorized version' of the constitution that 'undeniably inserted' itself 'into the national consciousness'.[190] And, as we have already noted, it was this same presumed orthodoxy that received repeated judicial approval in cases such as *Cheney*, *Madzimbamuto* and *Ellen Street Estates*.

In recent years, however, Dicey's reputation has declined quite dramatically. Andrew Marr suggests that the Diceyan notion of parliamentary sovereignty is consciously 'meaningless', a mere 'cloak behind which the modern state has swollen and grown without overly alarming or shocking the people'.[191] Less caustic, perhaps, but no less trenchant is Martin Loughlin's observation that whilst the Diceyan 'method' remains dominant, there is a growing awareness that the

[187] AWB Simpson, 'Common Law and Legal Theory', in AWB Simpson (ed), *Oxford Essays in Jurisprudence*, (Oxford UP, 1973), 96–97.

[188] Obituary to Dicey, quoted in Cosgrove, above n 138, 293.

[189] See M Loughlin, *Public Law and Political Theory*, (Oxford UP, 1992), 140–46, 185–87.

[190] C Harlow, 'Disposing of Dicey: from Legal Autonomy to Constitutional Discourse?' (2000) 48 *Political Studies*, 356.

[191] A Marr, *Ruling Britannia: The Failure and Future of British Democracy*, (London, Michael Joseph, 1995), 109–10.

claims of constitutional positivism were overblown.[192] Robert Stevens agrees, suggesting that the 'reign of Dicey' is 'coming, relatively peacefully, to a close'.[193] Rather like the Cheshire Cat in *Alice in Wonderland*, the Diceyan smile remains, but the juristic Cat has all but disappeared; only with the increasingly sour and melancholic Dicey, it would be rather more appropriate to envisage a grimace than a smile.

The problems with Dicey's constitution, and more particularly its 'keystone', the sovereignty of Parliament, are both empirical and theoretical. The empirical problems flow from the simple fact that the world has changed since the late nineteenth century. Indeed, it began to change during Dicey's lifetime, as the Empire began to crumble away. Section 4 of the 1931 Statute of Westminster clearly challenged Dicey's conception of absolute unitary sovereignty, providing that any later parliamentary legislation could not be 'deemed to extend' to former dominions unless 'it is expressly declared in that Act that that Dominion has requested, and consented to, the enactment thereof'.[194] In practical terms, the statute simply reflected reality. As Lord Denning suggested in *Blackburn v A-G*, 'Freedom once given cannot be taken away'.[195] In the earlier *British Coal Corporation* case, Lord Sankey famously distinguished between the theoretical niceties that might come to bear in such cases, and the blunt 'realities'.[196] And this was certainly the view reaffirmed by the Court of Appeal in *Manuel v A-G* in 1983.[197]

The 1931 Statute, then, appears to take the form of some kind of fundamental piece of legislation; one that might serve to constrain future Parliaments. It has often been suggested that the 1707 and 1800 Acts of Union are also fundamental, and binding on future Parliaments. The 1800 Act even affirmed that Anglo-Irish Union was established 'for ever'. The status of the Acts was explored in the case of *MacCormick v Lord Advocate* in 1953, where it was argued that the style 'Elizabeth II' was in contravention of the 1707 Act, insofar as there had never been an Elizabeth I of Scotland, only of England. The case failed on the grounds that the title of the monarch fell within the prerogative.[198] But

[192] Loughlin, above n 189, 22–26.

[193] R Stevens, *The English Judges: Their Role in the Changing Constitution*, (Oxford, Hart 2002), xiv.

[194] As Wade admitted in his Introduction to the *Law*. See, above n 119, lxxxiii–xcii.

[195] *Blackburn v A-G* [1971] 1 WLR 1040.

[196] *British Coal Corporation v R* [1935] SC 520.

[197] *Manuel v A-G* [1983] Ch.77.

[198] *MacCormick v Lord Advocate* 1953 SC 396.

successive Scottish courts have been divided as to whether the 1707 Act was some kind of fundamental, and binding, law. It could certainly be argued that the 1707 Act defines how subsequent Parliaments must describe their monarch. Moreover, as Neil MacCormick has suggested, there is certainly an arguable case that the 1707 Act, in effectively abolishing the independent states of England and Scotland, could be said to have 'founded' a British 'state'. Certainly Dicey recognised that the Act established an identifiably distinct British Parliament.[199]

The idea that such 'fundamental' statutes might require 'express' repeal was articulated by Lord Wilberforce, speaking in 1966:

> In strict law, there may be no difference in status, or as regards the liability to be repealed, as between one Act of Parliament and another, but I confess to some reluctance to holding that an Act of such constitutional significance as the Union with Ireland Act is subject to the doctrine of implied repeal or obsolescence—all the more so when these effects are claimed to result from later legislation which could have brought them about by specific enactment.[200]

A still more recent example of legislation that appears to constrain future Parliaments is the 1972 European Communities Act. Cases such as *Factortame* have clearly concluded that the 1972 Act sets the conditions by means of which it can be repealed; most obviously that such repeal must be explicit rather than implied. These cases have also seen British courts striking down parliamentary legislation that is deemed to be incompatible with European Union law. The challenge to Dicey's 'keystone' is stark. As Neil MacCormick has suggested, the European experience in particular appears 'to drive a wooden stake through the heart of the old constitution, the doctrine of parliamentary sovereignty'. In simple terms, he continues, we now live in a 'post-sovereignty' age, as part of a European 'commonwealth' that is constituted by a series of 'no-longer-fully-sovereign states'. And this is a good thing; for going 'beyond' the unitary conception of sovereignty, he adds, is a 'profoundly exciting possibility that can become an actuality only if people truly grasp the possibility intellectually and in their political imagination'.[201]

[199] See N MacCormick, 'Does the United Kingdom have a Constitution: Reflections on *MacCormick v Lord Advocate*, 29 1978 *Northern Ireland Legal Quarterly*, 1–20.

[200] Quoted in B Hadfield, 'The Belfast Agreement, Sovereignty and the State of the Union' (1998) *Public Law*, 606.

[201] N MacCormick, *Questioning Sovereignty: Law, State and Society in the European Commonwealth*, (Oxford UP, 1999), vi, 95, 131–33.

The 'new' Europe, as we shall see, is representative of the challenges posed by the so-called 'new world order'. Like MacCormick, Neil Walker has emphasised that we must, in our 'plural world', develop alternative 'plural' ideas of sovereign authority.[202] Dora Kostakopoulou has recently advanced a similar notion of 'floating' sovereignty; a concept that is almost infinitely malleable and, thus, very different from Dicey's stolid and uncompromising orthodoxy.[203] The Diceyan vision of the 'unitary' state is, as Michael O'Neill succinctly put it, 'out of fashion'.[204] At best, what is left is a principle of what Dawn Oliver terms 'inhibited parliamentary sovereignty'.[205] We shall revisit these suppositions in chapter four when we take a closer look at the geopolitical implications of our 'new world order'.

The theoretical doubts, which are also practical to some degree, oscillate round the thought that Dicey's idea of constitutional law as a system of rules was anyway just plain wrong. As even he conceded in his later *Lectures*, the relation between law and politics is never clear. Back in 1979, John Griffith focussed his critique of Dicey in precisely these terms. Laws, he affirmed, 'are merely statements of a power relationship and nothing more', whilst constitutions are expressions of 'authority'.[206] Carol Harlow likewise confirms that 'legal and political worlds never have been, and never can be, discrete'. Law, accordingly, 'cannot endure as a world neutrally detached from the contests of political argument but must take its proper place as a facet of political society rather than as an autonomous and external force acting upon it'. In this context, Dicey's attempt to cast constitutional sovereignty as distinct from political power is flawed, a 'classic fudge'.[207] Martin Loughlin reaches the same conclusion. By attempting to 'sever' public law from its political 'roots', the Diceyan 'myths' of constitutional 'objectivism' have 'become too tarnished' to be taken seriously.[208]

According to Trevor Allan, the proliferation of 'strange notions' that appear to underpin our constitutional culture, are the result of taking the 'questionable dogmas' of Dicey and others 'rather too literally'.

202 Walker, 'Pluralism', 317–19.

203 D Kostakopoulou, 'Floating Sovereignty: A Pathology or a Necessary Means of State Evolution?'(2002) 22 *Oxford Journal of Legal Studies*, 135–56.

204 M O'Neill, 'Great Britain: From Dicey to Devolution', (2000) 53 *Parliamentary Affairs*, 93.

205 D Oliver, *Constitutional Reform in the UK*, (Oxford UP, 2003), 354–57.

206 J Griffith, 'The Political Constitution', (1979) 42 *Modern Law Review*, 1–3, 19.

207 Harlow, above n 190, 357–59, 366.

208 Loughlin, above n 189, 230–31.

Most obviously, the pretended 'separation of legal rule from political principle' is 'ultimately incoherent'. Legal sovereignty cannot be sensibly distinguished from political sovereignty, and political sovereignty is an indelibly moral concept.[209] Sovereignty, therefore, is 'necessarily' limited by 'moral constraints'; constraints which are defined by the 'political consensus' upon which the legitimacy of the constitution is founded.[210]

Accordingly, Allan tries to accommodate a 'different' Dicey; the Dicey who championed common law conceptions of the 'rule of law' rather than the Dicey who made so much of Whig principles of 'parliamentary sovereignty'.[211] Positing an alternative 'common law' constitutionalism, Allan resurrects the kind of sentiment, and jurisprudence, that found a famous expression in *Dr Bonham's Case*, and Lord Chief Justice Coke's observation, that:

> It appears in our books, that in many cases, the common law will controul Acts of Parliament and sometimes adjudge them to be utterly void: for when an Act of Parliament is against common right and reason, or repugnant, or impossible to be performed, the common law will controul it, and adjudge such an act to be void.[212]

The recourse to this particular tradition, set firmly within its own very particular jurisprudential mythology, is prescient. It admits that constitutions are indeed 'moral' instruments; the historical product of a long, irreducible process of what Allan terms 'moral reasoning'.[213] The challenge to Dicey is plain. We shall revisit this too in due course. First, however, we need to strip away some more of the myths that shroud our constitution, the various masks of pretended legitimacy behind which governmental power lurks.

[209] Allan, *Law, Liberty and Justice: The Legal Foundations of British Constitutionalism*, (Oxford UP, 1993), 283–84, 289. For a similar critique see Allan's more recent *Constitutional Justice*, above n 154, 6 and 13–21.

[210] Allan, above n 154, 220–21.

[211] Allan, above n 209, 1–2.

[212] *Dr Bonham's Case* (1609) 8 Co Rep 118.

[213] See Allan, above n 209, 4–10, 43, and also above n 154, 204–8.

2

The Mask of Anarchy

IN 1817, SAT on the banks of Lake Geneva pondering the virtues of free love, a young Percy Bysshe Shelley read accounts of a 'massacre' at St Peter's Field outside Manchester. Sixty thousand had assembled to listen to the famous radical Henry 'Orator' Hunt. They had been drilled for months and marched to the field carrying banners proclaiming 'Votes for All' and 'Reform or Death'. Haunted by memories of the Corn law riots the previous year, the Manchester magistrates had first ordered in the yeoman, and, when they were repulsed, a waiting troop of Hussars. Fifteen minutes later, eleven lay dead, and four hundred injured. In honour of the victims of the 'Peterloo massacre' Shelley penned *The Mask of Anarchy*. The world 'anarchy' was pivotal. The magistrates claimed that their actions were intended to prevent 'anarchy'. It is an excuse that is familiar to history. As Shelley knew, the real anarchy was the action of a government that felt no compunction in seeking recourse to the 'law' in order to suppress the call for constitutional and political reform. This was the 'anarchy' which came up from behind:

> Last came Anarchy: he rode
> On a white horse, splashed with blood;
> He was pale even to the lips,
> Like Death in the Apocalypse
>
> And he wore a kingly crown;
> And in his grasp a sceptre shone;
> On his brow this mark I saw—
> I am God, and King, and Law.[1]

Shelley's poem was a paean to corruption, to the lost idylls of the 'Great and Glorious' settlement of 1689.

The constitution, as both Shelley and Bagehot noted, had become a façade, a mask for the overwhelming dominance of government; this is its 'efficient secret', the 'close union, the nearly complete fusion, of the

[1] 'Mask of Anarchy' ll.30–37 in P Shelley, *Complete Poetical Works*, (Oxford UP, 1971), 338–39.

executive and legislative powers'. Rather more recently, in 1973, the Royal Commission on the Constitution confirmed that 'government responsibilities have, within the lifetime of many people now living, widened immensely', reaching into all 'areas of public and even personal life'.[2] As Peter Hennessy has recently confirmed, any study of our constitution is 'overshadowed by the fact' that the last century has 'belonged to the executive'.[3] It is a conclusion that should trouble us. In his 1988 Radcliffe Lectures, Lord Scarman observed that 'We have achieved that total union of executive and legislative power which Blackstone foresaw would be productive of tyranny'.[4] It is common now to talk of a 'crisis of legitimacy' brought about by the seemingly irresistible march of executive power.[5] This too should trouble us.

The purpose of this chapter is to investigate the 'efficient secret' of our constitution a little further, more particularly the relationship between the legislative and the executive in modern Britain. It will take us to the very heart of modern government, and to the law which is supposed to define it, and to constrain it. It will take us to the law relating to Parliament, and its presumed sovereignty and to its assumed 'privileges'. And it will lead us to investigate what Hennessy terms the 'hidden wiring' of the constitution, to the twilight world of government, to the abuses of prerogative, to the customs of Cabinet convention, and finally to the office of our *de facto* head of state, the Prime Minister.[6]

I HOGWARTS-ON-THAMES

Puerile, Pathetic and Utterly Useless

In his *Rural Rides*, the early nineteenth century Tory Radical William Cobbett recounted touring England in search of some kind of com-

[2] Vol 1 Cmnd 5467/1973.

[3] P Hennessy, *The Hidden Wiring: Unearthing the British Constitution* (London, Gollancz, 1995), 146.

[4] Lord Scarman, *The Shape of Things to Come*, (London, Blackstone, 1989), 12, 16.

[5] For a general overview, see P McAuslan & J McEldowney 'Legitimacy and the Constitution: The Dissonance between Theory and Practice', in P McAuslan & J McEldowney (eds), *Law, Legitimacy and the Constitution*, (London Sweet & Maxwell, 1985), 1–38.

[6] P Hennessy, *The Prime Minister: The Office and its Holders since 1945*, (London, Penguin, 2001), 53–60.

monalty. What he found, famously, was division, exploitation and disengagement; the products, indeed, of the 'old corruption' against which he regularly railed in his *Weekly Register*. Cobbett discovered what Bagehot was to chronicle a generation later; a constitution that had become a mask for supervening governmental power. But where Bagehot merely smiled inwardly, and Shelley spat invective onto the page, Cobbett's conclusion was rather more sober. If the apparently irresistible drift of endemic and institutionalised corruption was not halted, then future generations would one day wake up to find their 'Great and Glorious' constitution thoroughly perverted.[7] He was right.

Tom Nairn has recently resurrected the spectre of 'old corruption', hanging around, as he neatly puts it, 'Hogwarts-on-Thames'.[8] The alignment of metaphors, and institutions, is apposite. Parliament has become a caricature, seemingly the home of overgrown schoolchildren who spend much of their days immersed in the internecine rituals of fading power; 'self-indulgent constitutional pontificating', as one member of the Scottish Assembly puts it.[9] The disempowerment is critical. As Austin Mitchell admits, being a member of the House of Commons is 'merely an opportunity to heckle the steamroller'.[10] And the heckling is not pretty. As Dicey feared, modern politics has become an exercise in primal 'shouting'.[11] Jeremy Paxman agrees, condemning a Commons that appears to exist in some kind of 'parallel universe' to reality, its 'farmyard noises which signify approval or scorn' making the 'business of democracy seem cheap'.[12] Perhaps the most pertinent mammalian metaphor was Nancy Astor's; MPs sit in the House of Commons 'like dogs on a leash'.[13]

What was once, as David Cannadine asserts, intended to be a 'theatre of state' has been relegated to little more than a 'palace of varieties'.[14] Andrew Marr is just as caustic, dismissing the 'splashy

[7] W Cobbett, *Rural Rides*, (London, Penguin, 1985).

[8] T Nairn, *Pariah: Misfortunes of the British Kingdom*, (London, Verso, 2002), 73.

[9] Duncan McNeil MSP, quoted in A Page & A Batey, 'Scotland's Other Parliament: Westminster Legislation about Devolved Matters in Scotland since Devolution', (2002) *Public Law*, 514.

[10] In A Marr, *Ruling Britannia: The Failure and Future of British Democracy*, (London, Michael Joseph, 1995), 157.

[11] Correspondence from 1912, quoted in R Cosgrove, *The Rule of Law: Albert Venn Dicey, Victorian Jurist* (Univ. of North Carolina Press, 1980), 245.

[12] J Paxman, *The Political Animal: An Anatomy*, (London, Michael Joseph, 2002), 98, 126.

[13] *Ibid*, 104.

[14] D Cannadine, *In Churchill's Shadow: Confronting the Past in Modern Britain*, (Oxford UP, 2003), 4.

surface of crisis and resignation, confrontation and scandal' which barely masks the 'huge depths of cynicism and indifference' that pervade modern Britain.[15] It is not just that Parliament fosters corruption, though, as we shall shortly see, it certainly does that. It is also the fact that Parliament seems to be so inadequate a representative body. More old Etonians sit in the House of Commons than members of ethnic minorities.[16] Such a situation is ridiculous. No wonder we fail to relate to those who are supposed to represent us. As Raymond Williams noted, as long ago as 1983, even if Parliament is representative in the sense of being an elected body, it is certainly no longer representative in the sense of typifying the electorate; if indeed it ever was.[17] And, as a result, as Tom Nairn observes, the electorate has become 'stubbornly and increasingly cynical about politics and the state'.[18]

It was not always so. The English used to be enthused about their Parliament. In his *De Republica Angolorum*, written at the end of the sixteenth century, Sir Thomas Smith advised that in Parliament 'every Englishman is intended there to be present, either in person or by procuration and attorneys, of what preheminence, state, dignity, or quality soever he be, from the Prince' down to 'the lowest person of England'. It represented, Smith continued, the Aristotelian ideal cast in the particular guise of the English commonwealth, 'the common doing of a multitude of free men collected together and united by common accord and covenants among themselves'.[19] But then the age of 'pollitricks' advanced, and by the mid-nineteenth century Bagehot could be found dismissing an institution that had become a rest home for the unremittingly 'idle'.[20]

Some of the 'idle' have done their best to defend their institution, and its place in the public imagination. Enoch Powell suggested that 'the British nation could not imagine itself except with and through its Parliament'.[21] But this is nonsense. Back in 1958, in his introduction to the tenth edition of Dicey's *Law*, Wade admitted that it was 'undeni-

[15] Marr, above n 10, 106.

[16] See T Wright, 'England, Whose England', in S Chen & T Wright (eds), *The English Question*, (London, Fabian Society, 2000), 13.

[17] R Williams, 'Democracy and Parliament', (1983) *The Socialist Society*, 10–16.

[18] Nairn, above n 8, 3.

[19] J Blythe, *Ideal Government and the Mixed Constitution in the Middle Ages*, (Princeton, UP, 1992), 273–7, and W MacCaffrey, *Elizabeth I*, (London, Edward Arnold, 1993),368.

[20] W.Bagehot, *The English Constitution*, (Cambridge UP, 2001), 83–84, 119–21.

[21] Hennessy, above n 3, 27, 141, 146.

able that Parliament has suffered in the eyes of the general public a loss of prestige over the last seventy years'.[22] Jeremy Paxman goes further still, and concludes that 'we are almost at the point where we could dispense with Parliament altogether'.[23] Even the inmates are losing hope. 'God I hate this place', the former leader of the Liberal Democrats, Paddy Ashdown, observes, 'It is puerile, pathetic and utterly useless.[24]

A century and quarter ago, Anthony Trollope's novel, *The Prime Minister* opened with the gambit 'I can conceive no vainer object of ambition than a seat in the British Parliament'.[25] Politicians, so the mid-Victorian believed, are in it more for themselves than for the common good. It was this sentiment that underpinned Bagehot's essay on Peel. Little has changed. Simon Heffer's dismissal of the modern politician is not exceptional:

> As a general rule, politics has now become a career. It is practised by politicians to the exclusion, or near-exclusion, of anything else in their lives. As a result of this regrettable fact, politicians are more often than not on the make: usually to satisfy their own egos and lust for power, fame and publicity, but sometimes seeing politics as a useful medium in which to attract women (or, as is now increasingly ashionable, men) or to make money.[26]

Jeremy Paxman is equally acerbic:

> In much of the popular mind, politicians are all the same. They're a bunch of egotistical, lying narcissists who sold their souls long ago and would auction their children tomorrow if they thought it would advance their career. They are selfish, manipulative, scheming, venal. The only feelings they care about are their own. They set out to climb the greasy pole so long ago that they had lost contact with reality by the time they were in their twenties. You cannot trust a word any politician says and if you shake hands with them, you ought to count your fingers afterwards.[27]

And so we should. In his *Autobiography*, former Prime Minister John Major confessed to regretting the necessity of spinning the electorate all kinds of 'nonsense' on a regular basis.[28]

[22] Wade, 'Introduction' to A Dicey, *An Introduction to the Law of the Constitution*, (London, Macmillan, 1959), xxii.

[23] Paxman, above n 12, 157.

[24] In Paxman, above n 12, 181.

[25] A Trollope, *The Prime Minister*, (London, Penguin, 1994), 17–18.

[26] S Heffer, *Nor Shall My Sword: The Reinvention of England*, (London, Weidenfeld & Nicolson, 1999), 78.

[27] Paxman, above n12, 13.

[28] J Major, *The Autobiography*, (London, Harper Collins, 1999), xx.

Given the veracity of Gladstone's observation, made over a century ago, that our constitution 'presumes more boldly than any other the good sense and the good faith of those who work it', this lack of trust is a serious problem.[29] Moreover, the more powerful the politician, the less inclined we are to trust them, and the more inclined to recall Gwilym Lloyd George's wonderfully scatological aside, 'Politicians are like monkeys; the higher they get up the tree, the more revolting are the parts they expose'.[30] In one sense such iconoclasm is healthy. We are right to hold senior ministers and politicians in contempt when they are discovered to have abused their office. But the corrosion of trust that follows from such discovery is not so healthy. The balance is fine.[31]

It is, of course, a problem throughout western liberal democracies; but it seems to be especially corrosive in Britain. In recent years, popular attention, and contempt, has tended to focus on two new terms in the political lexicon; 'sleaze' and 'cronyism'. We shall encounter various examples of 'sleaze', of both the financial and moral variety, shortly.[32] 'Cronyism', the preferring of political favours for friends, and party donors, is no less reprehensible, and something which appears to have entered the soul of the present government. Minister after minister is selected by the Prime Minister from within a small coterie of chums and donors, rather than from the serried ranks of his own Parliamentary party.[33] The furore surrounding the appointment of Lord Falconer as first 'Dome minister', and then Secretary of State for Constitutional Affairs, is merely the most blatant example of this essentially presidential habit; a habit we shall also return to in due course.

What is it They Really Want?

If one aspect of our politics attracts particular popular contempt, it is the machinations of party; the machinations against which the likes of

[29] Quoted in Hennessy, above n 3, 27. See also J Morison, 'The Case Against Constitutional Reform?' (1998) 25 *Journal of Law and Society*, 521.

[30] In Paxman, above n 12, 238.

[31] For an overview of the problem, see P Heywood, 'Political Corruption: Problems and Perspectives', (1997) 45 *Political Studies*, 417–35.

[32] A Doig, 'Sleaze: Picking up the Threads or "Back to Basics" Scandals?', (2001) 54 *Parliamentary Affairs*, 365–66, 374.

[33] See A Doig, S McIvor & J Moran, 'A Word Desperately Seeking Scandal?: New Labour and Tony's Cronies', (1999) 52 *Parliamentary Affairs*, 678–87.

Swift and Fielding wrote nearly two hundred years ago. Politics has been thoroughly perverted by party, and so have politicians. Writing in the1940s, George Bernard Shaw commented that 'Practically nobody in these islands understands the Party System'. As far as he could tell, parties seemed to exist in order to ensure that public opinion remained emasculated, and to ensure that legislation is cast by the 'quality' rather than 'the mob'. In England's so-called democracy, he continued, the powers of 'Everyman' extend no further than the ability to choose between alternative policy 'idols' presented by indistinguishable groups of men drawn from the same political elite.[34] Nothing has changed in the intervening sixty years. As one MP, Tony Wright, has recently confessed, the dominance of party is 'profoundly debilitating' in its effect on democratic politics.[35] It has also, as Eric Barendt rightly concludes, effected a fatal 'imbalance' in our constitution.[36]

To a considerable extent, politicians and electorate have engaged in a mutually sustaining, and mutually destructive, pact. Whilst the poorest 40% of Britain are unable to name one MP, the chattering classes remain entranced by those who perform in the theatre of 'ill-repute'.[37] Promises demanded, promises made, promises broken. Roy Jenkins attested to the modern politician's determination to convince the electorate that he or she 'had the philosopher's stone' and could therefore realise any whim or wish.[38] Daniel Defoe long ago bemoaned the loss of dignity which was bound to result from this kind of intense, and ultimately deluded, relationship. Too great an interest in government merely makes it 'familiar' and 'consequently contemptible to the People'. It is not well, he continued to 'warm' the 'Minds of the Rabble, who are more capable of Action than Speculation, and are animated by Noise and Nonsense'.[39] Jonathan Swift reached much the same conclusion in his *Contests and Dissensions*. Politicians make their careers by encouraging the 'rash, jealous and inconstant humour of the People'.[40]

[34] G Shaw, *Everybody's Political What's What*, (London, Constable, 1944), 23, 30, 46.

[35] Wright, above n 16, 14–16

[36] E Barendt, *An Introduction to Constitutional Law* (Oxford UP, 1998), 36.

[37] For a commentary on political literacy, see P Norris, 'The Twilight of Westminster? Electoral Reform and its Consequences', (2001) 49 *Political Studies*, 887–90.

[38] In Paxman, above n 12, 90.

[39] D Defoe, 'The Original Right of the People of England Examined and Asserted', in *The True-Born Englishman and Other Writings*, (London, Penguin, 1997), 97–103.

[40] J Swift, *Works*, (Oxford UP, 1984), 25–56.

Because of our engagement in this Faustian pact with our politicians, we retain an ultimate responsibility for them. Such a responsibility is the price of democracy. The Victorian critic Thomas Carlyle concluded that there was no more 'ugly an exhibition of human stupidity' than that of excitable Englishmen trying to work out who to vote for.[41] In truth, having finally secured universal suffrage, the problem appears to be less one of over-excitement, than one of crushing indifference. The 'first-past-the-post' electoral system that presently governs Westminster elections is geared to perpetuating a two-party system, with both parties reassured that soon enough their time to govern will return. In 1997, Tony Blair was swept to a majority of 179 seats, despite having polled only 44% of the votes of the 71% who could be bothered to turn out.

The very system of representative government has become an ever less credible apology for genuine democracy. Tom Nairn rightly berates the periodical 'electoral debauches' timed at the whim of sitting governments, a vast 'vaudeville' of 'Punch and Judy shows' scattered up and down the country, all good 'cheap thrills' and entertainment, but quite vacuous in terms of genuine democratic participation.[42] And so fewer and fewer of us bother to vote.[43] The turnout in the last general election in 2001 sunk to 59%, the lowest figure since the 1918 'khaki' election; which was itself a peculiarly aberrant election. In certain urban constituencies less than one in three staggered forth to the polling booth. 2001 represented the 'landslide victory of the Apathetic tendency'.[44] There can be no stronger case for electoral reform. The statistics for local and European elections make for even more sorry reading, as do turnouts for elections to the newly established assemblies in Edinburgh and Cardiff. In Wales, only 46% turned out for the first 1999 elections to the Welsh Assembly. A month later, just 28% of Welsh voters turned out for elections to the European Parliament.[45] We shall revisit the democratic question in the final chapter.

[41] T Carlyle, *Selected Writings*, (London, Penguin, 1986), 302.

[42] Nairn, above n 8, 1, 5.

[43] See Marr, above n 10, 25–27.

[44] Nairn, above n 8, 58. For a general analysis of the problem, see C Pattie & R Johnston, 'A Low Turnout Landslide: Abstention at the British General Election of 1997', (2001) 49 *Political Studies*, 286–305, M Harrop, 'An Apathetic Landslide: The British Election of 2001', (2001) 36 *Government and Opposition*, 309–11 and J Curtice, 'The Electoral System: Biased to Blair?' (2001) 54 *Parliamentary Affairs*, 803–14.

[45] L McAllister, 'The New Politics in Wales: Rhetoric or Reality?', (2000) 53 *Parliamentary Affairs*, 593–94.

Where political power used to be conveyed through the ballot box, it is now discerned through the media of public opinion; the monster Dicey so feared. In 1957, Harold Macmillan expressed himself baffled by the elusive vicissitudes of middle-class opinion. 'I am always hearing of the middle classes', he mused, 'What is it they really want?' He wrote to the Director of Conservative Central Office with the simple request 'Will you put it down on a sheet of paper and I will see if I can give it to them'.[46] As Dicey prophesied, the age of popular politics has seen the fancies of popular opinion overwhelm the aspirations of political and constitutional principle. Austin Mitchell pointedly observes that where 'once Parliament controlled the executive', today government only listens 'to a fourth estate that obsesses it'.[47] Parliament has become an institution of 'comparative impotence'.[48]

Tom Nairn is succinct. Today's Britain is the 'diseased descendent of representative oligarchy', such that by the end of the 1990s our political system had come:

> to mean nothing but inebriate parliamentary majorities based on a minority of the votes cast, generating machismo-power, think-tank mania, mediaeval staggering fits like the Poll Tax, unrestrained petty-bourgeois optimism, and Sovereignty-delusions which the rest of the world now snigger at.[49]

Privileges

One of the collateral effects of the mythology of parliamentary sovereignty is the presumption that Parliament should regulate itself. Historically, Parliament has been very precious in protecting its 'privileges'. Coke recognised their existence in his *Institutes*, whilst Article 9 of the Bill of Rights stated that 'Freedom of speech and debates or proceedings in Parliament ought not to be impeached or questioned in any Court or place out of Parliament'.[50] Of course, 'proceedings' is a vague conception, generally assumed to include the composition of the House and cognisance of its own affairs. The freedom of speech uttered in parliamentary 'proceedings' has always been particularly jealously

[46] R Hattersley, *Fifty Years On: A Prejudiced History of Britain Since the War*, (London, Little Brown, 1997), 117.

[47] In Paxman, above n 12, 285.

[48] McAuslan & McEldowney, above n 5, 24.

[49] T Nairn, *After Britain: New Labour and the Return of Scotland*, (Cambridge, Granta, 2000), 57, and also above n 8, 70.

[50] See D Oliver, 'Regulating the Conduct of MPs: The British Experience of Combating Corruption', (1997) 45 *Political Studies*, 542–44.

guarded. It was famously invoked in order to forestall any proceedings against the MP Duncan Sandys when, in 1938, he raised a matter of national security in possible breach of the Official Secrets Act.[51]

The ultimate authority for the nature of parliamentary privilege is Erskine May's *Parliamentary Practice* which affirms:

> The 'law of Parliament' includes those aspects of Parliamentary activity that depend for their effectiveness on recognition by the courts, and such law—although it may be unwritten—is changed only by way of statute. But most parliamentary procedure and usage derives from the admitted right of each House to regulate its own proceedings, a right which led a former clerk of the Commons to observe, 'What does it signify about precedents? The House can do what it likes. Who can stop it?[52]

Needless to say, 'privilege' has been long abused. Freedom from arrest in civil law suits was notorious for much of the nineteenth century. In the *Duke of Newcastle* case, for example, it was held that members of either House were exempted from arrest for bankruptcy, whilst in *Stourton* the court refused to hold a member of the House of Lords in contempt for ignoring an order relating to his estranged wife's property.[53] And members of both Houses have always been conspicuously keen to evade the liquor laws that apply to everyone else; something that was famously accepted by the Lord Chief Justice in the *Graham-Campbell* case.[54] Similarly, the House has continued to evade all manner of statutory responsibilities, including the Trade Descriptions Act regarding the sale of bogus claret, as well as a host of work and safety responsibilities, including the negligent diffusion of blue asbestos fibres, food poisoning, and the pollution of water-tanks.[55]

Just occasionally courts have intervened where it is thought that Parliament might have overreached itself. Famously, in *Stockdale v Hansard*, an attempt to assert that Parliamentary resolutions carried legal force was struck down.[56] And in *Bradlaugh v Gossett*, it was held that Parliament cannot expect to define the limits of its privileges as and when it pleases. From time to time, Lord Justice Coleridge sug-

[51] See C Munro, *Constitutional Studies*, (London, Butterworths, 1999), 221.

[52] Erskine May, *Parliamentary Practice*, quoted in D Oliver & G Drewry 'The Law and Parliament', in D Oliver & G Drewry (eds), *The Law and Parliament*, (London, Butterworths, 1998), 8.

[53] *Duke of Newcastle v Morris* (1870) LR 4 HL 661; *Stourton v Stourton* [1963] P 302.

[54] *R v Graham-Campbell ex p Herbert* [1935] 1 KB 594.

[55] See G Lock, 'Statute Law and Case Law applicable to Parliament', in Oliver and Drewry, above n 52, 56–57.

[56] *Stockdale v Hansard* (1839) 9 As & El 1.

gested, cases would be 'put' in which 'it would be the plain duty of the court at all hazards to declare a resolution illegal and no protection to those who acted under it'. If, he added, there were to be 'unseemly conflicts between the courts and the House', then that is the price paid in a society that subscribed to the principle of the rule of law.[57]

Rather more recently, in *Rost v Edwards*, it was reaffirmed that the principle of the rule of law was 'no less important' than the principle enshrined in Article 9, and implied that 'this country's citizens should have free and unrestricted access to the courts of the land and, subject to the rules of the court, be able to present their cases fully and freely'. The mythology of 1689 was countered with that of 1215 and Magna Carta: 'To no one will we deny or delay right and justice'.[58] As Lord Salmon observed in 1976, Article 9 is 'a charter for freedom of speech in the House', and 'not a charter for corruption'.[59] A further, if rather more oblique, example of changing judicial attitudes to 'privilege' can be seen in the *Pepper v Hart* case in 1993, in which the House of Lords reversed earlier authority, most famously Lord Simmonds judgment in *Magor and St Mellons*, which held that courts could not look to parliamentary debate in order to ascertain 'the intention of Parliament'.[60] There was no sense, as Lord Bridge opined in *Pepper*, in courts continuing to 'wear blinkers' when the 'points' they are 'called upon to resolve had been addressed in the House'.[61]

There is, perhaps then, a discernible change of mood. And yet, the weight of precedent reveals a judiciary generally unwilling to challenge the broad principle of Article 9.[62] Instead, it has preferred to leave matters of privilege to the Committee of Privileges, and more recently the reconstituted Committee of Privileges and Standards. This in turn has led to a rather *ad hoc* approach; the uncertainties of which were exemplified in the recent Zircon 'case'.[63] A century ago, the nineteenth-

[57] *Bradlaugh v Gossett* (1884) 12 QBD 275.

[58] *Rost v Edwards* [1990] 2 WLR 1293. For a commentary, see P Leopold, 'Proceedings in Parliament: the Grey Area', (1990) *Public Law*, 475–81.

[59] In Leopold, *ibid*, 77.

[60] *Magor and St Mellons RDC v Newport Corp* [1950] 2 All ER 191.

[61] *Pepper v Hart* [1993] AC 593. For a discussion of the case and its implications, see G Marshall, 'Hansard and the Interpretation of Statutes', in Oliver & Drewry, above n 52, 142–54.

[62] See, for example, *Edinburgh and Dalkeith Railway v Wauchope* (1842) 8 Cl & Fin 710, and *British Railways Board v Pickin* [1974] AC 765.

[63] The 'case' involved the showing of intelligence sensitive film in the precincts of Westminster, a matter that was, accordingly, nominally covered by privilege. See P Leopold, 'The Application of the Civil and Criminal Law to Members of Parliament and Parliamentary Proceedings', in Oliver and Drewry, above n 52, 73.

century jurist Sir William Anson suggested that the law of privilege resembles little more than 'local custom'.[64] Little has changed.

Standards

In 1994, the House of Commons commissioned a report from the Nolan Committee on Standards in Public Life. The immediate context was set by the Committee of Privileges' investigation into two MPs who had received money for asking questions in Parliament. It soon became apparent that there was a vigorous market for buying questions, costing roughly a thousand pounds a throw.[65] The Committee of Privileges concluded that the behaviour of the two MPs had fallen 'short of the standards the House is entitled to expect of its Members'. The observation of one MP called before the Nolan Committee was more prosaic; too many of his colleagues too readily behaved like a 'bunch of crooks'.[66]

In spring 1995, the Nolan Committee completed its report, entitled *Standards in Public Life*. Rather whimsically, it opened by describing 'The Seven Principles of Public Life', which it believed to be 'Selflessness, Integrity, Objectivity, Accountability, Openness, Honesty, and Leadership'. There were fifty-five recommendations, including the need to ban paid advocacy, and the desirability of stopping the practice of MPs contracting with firms which provided 'paid parliamentary services to multiple clients'; in other words lobbyists. There was, the Report noted, considerable 'public disquiet' at the apparent decline in 'standards of behaviour in public life', and particularly in Parliament; something which was all the more regrettable since the House of Commons 'is at the heart of our democracy', and the 'standards' of MPs, accordingly, 'are crucially important to the political well-being of the nation'. These standards, it continued, had slipped considerably short of what the public expected. The most incendiary recommendation suggested that 'internal systems for maintaining standards', meaning the voluntary Register of Interests, 'should be supported by

[64] W Anson, *Law and Custom of the Constitution* (Oxford UP, 1922), 196.

[65] D Oliver, above n 50, 1997, 545–47.

[66] Oliver, *ibid*, 548–50. For a series of articles on the Nolan Commission and the general context within which it worked, see F Ridley & A Doig (eds), 'Sleaze: Politics, Private Interests and Public Reaction', (1995) 48 *Parliamentary Affairs*, 551–749, special edition.

independent scrutiny', preferably a Parliamentary Commissioner for Standards who would operate within the ambit of the House's own rules on standards, and would not, therefore, threaten the principle of Parliamentary privilege.[67]

For a while the House did seem to be duly chastened. The Select Committee on Public Standards accepted virtually all of the report, whilst the Labour party spokesman, Jeff Rooker, admitted that 'by and large we have proved ourselves incapable of putting our own house in order'. Self-regulation, he continued, had become 'self-delusion'. Others, however, pontificated grandly about the threat to their privileges, and the need to safeguard Parliament's sovereignty. Tony Benn cited Article 9 of the Bill of Rights. Ian Duncan Smith pleaded that 'somebody from outside this place' might not appreciate the 'pressures' that MPs work under. The bogey-man of judicial competence to review Parliamentary privileges was duly invoked.[68] Eventually, however, after much grumbling, a Parliamentary Commissioner for Standards was duly set up, alongside a newly reconstituted Committee on Standards and Privileges and a revitalized Members' Register of Interests.

The sleaze did not, however, go away. The Hamilton affair in 1995 was particularly grubby and demeaning, revealing as it did, not just the venal stupidity of the MP in question, but also the willingness of Conservative party whips to 'dissemble' before the Committee on Members' Interests in order to try to get the matter hushed up.[69] Next to emerge was the uncovering of mass bribery of MPs in the al-Fayed 'Cash for Questions' investigation. This, in turn, was followed by various allegations of ministerial impropriety levelled at the likes of Peter Mandelson, Geoffrey Robinson and Keith Vaz. And then there was the matter of the MP who happened to present a friend for a peerage just at the moment that he happened to received a 'loan' of £5000. And so it went on. Whether or not there is a Parliamentary Commissioner, the phenomenon of 'crony capitalism' appears to be little diminished.[70] One in five MPs still refuse to register their interests, in blatant contravention of one of the most strident recommendations of the Nolan

[67] For a discussion of the Nolan Committee report and its implications, see B Winetrobe, 'The Autonomy of Parliament', in Oliver & Drewry, above n 52, 27–28.

[68] See Winetrobe, *ibid*, 28–30.

[69] Oliver, above n 50, 553–56.

[70] A Doig, 'Sleaze Fatigue in "The House of Ill-Repute"' (2002) 55 *Parliamentary Affairs*, 394, and also, above n 66, 367–69.

Committee; and one that was duly enshrined in the *Guide to the Rules Relating to the Conduct of Ministers* produced by the new Committee on Standards and Privileges.[71]

And as soon as the media spotlight diminished, the House set about systematically undermining its new Commissioner, to such an extent that she abandoned her office in despair. The Speaker rather ungraciously celebrated the departure of a 'witch-hunter' and looked forward to the time when someone who was prepared to work rather more 'quietly' took her place.[72] The present comissioner is working very quietly indeed.

II DARKNESS

Something Rotten

Thomas Jefferson, one of the 'framers' of the American constitution, remarked that 'whenever a man has cast a longing eye on offices, a rottenness begins in his conduct'.[73] The insight can be set alongside Lord Acton's more famous observation, 'Power corrupts, and absolute power corrupts absolutely'. The extent to which our executive has, like our legislative indeed, fallen prey to what John Locke termed the 'temptations' of human 'frailty' can be seen in the 1,806 page report of the Scott Inquiry into the 'arms to Iraq' affair.[74] It provides a gruesome, if fascinating, prologue to any account of modern British government. 'The sight', as Adam Tomkins puts it, 'is not a pretty one'. The Inquiry revealed that the heart of our government was, indeed, rotten to the core. 'It is little wonder', Tomkins adds, 'that British government prefers secrecy to accountability and opts to keep itself under wraps as much as possible'. It 'would be indecent to expose such an ugly scene to the unprotected public'.[75]

Set within the context of government paranoia, and all the thrills and spills of spies and spooks, the Scott Inquiry set about investigating the sale of arms to Iraq; contrary to the Howe 'guidelines' which suggested that no arms should be sold to either Iraq or Iran if they were likely to

[71] M Rush, 'The Law Relating to Members' Conduct', in Oliver & Drewry, above n 52, 113.

[72] Doig, above n 66, 396–98.

[73] In P Ford (ed), *The Writings of Thomas Jefferson*, (Putnam, 1896), 7.380–81.

[74] J Locke, *Two Treatises on Government*, (London, Dent, 1989), 190.

[75] A Tomkins, *The Constitution After Scott: Government Unwrapped*, (Oxford UP, 1998), 1.

exacerbate the war in which they were engaged between 1980 and 1988. During the mid-1980s three junior ministers, William Waldegrave, Alan Clark and Lord Trefgarne, decided to 'reinterpret' these guidelines, in order to grant export licenses to arms companies who wished to trade with Iraq. This action was itself dubious. But the constitutional crux of the matter involved two particular questions. First, there was the question of whether the three ministers deceived Parliament in failing to disclose their 'reinterpretation'. Second, there was the cover-up, and the issue of Public Interest Immunity certificates; something to which we shall return shortly.

The kernel of 'Iraqgate' was located in the interpretation of the third of the Howe 'guidelines'. The original draft suggested that orders for arms should not be sanctioned if they 'would significantly enhance the capability of either side to prolong or exacerbate the war'. It was never intended that such a definition would be terribly precise, or constraining. As Alan Clark admitted, the 'guidelines' were 'an almost ideal Whitehall formula; imprecise, open to argument in almost every instance, guaranteed to generate debate'.[76] And so, when the guideline was recast by one of the ministers, so that orders would only be denied if they 'would be of direct and significant assistance to either country in the conduct of offensive operations', it was argued that this was merely a matter of reinterpretation, and so did not require disclosure in Parliament. The excuse was dismissed by Scott as 'not even remotely tenable'.[77] The original guideline appeared to embrace all arms; the second just those that might be thought to make a 'significant' difference, whatever that might be.

Moreover, when ministers were asked in Parliament about the status of the export guidelines, there was a consistent refusal to divulge information, generally based on the dubious assertion that such details were not, by convention, made public. If such a convention existed, and Scott was doubtful that it did, then it was something that should be 'urgently re-thought'.[78] And on the rare occasion that a minister could be persuaded to actually answer a particular question, he invariably did so in a way that Scott found to be 'inaccurate and potentially misleading', generally couched in terms that were intended to be 'presentationally convenient' rather than 'factually accurate'. All in all, the

[76] In N Lewis & D Longley, 'Ministerial Responsibility: The Next Steps', (1996) *Public Law*, 497.

[77] Tomkins, above n 75, 28–29, and Lewis & Longley, *ibid*, 495–98.

[78] Tomkins, above n 75, 31–32.

Report concluded, answers to parliamentary questions 'failed to inform Parliament of the current state of government policy'. Moreover, this 'failure was deliberate'.[79]

The question remains as to whether this deception was unconstitutional. We shall shortly take a closer look at the murky world of constitutional 'conventions'; 'rules' which, according to Dicey, fall somewhat short of legality. One such convention suggests that ministers should resign if they are found to have 'knowingly' misled Parliament. The obvious excuse, when caught lying, is to hide behind the 'knowingly' bit. Waldegrave, who redrafted the third 'guideline', clung to this like a drowning man clings to a lifebelt. Former Prime Minister James Callaghan was left to voice the question which was on everybody's lips; was Waldegrave a 'knave' or a 'simpleton'?[80] Either way, it is questionable whether he should have been permitted to stay in office.

It was not just a matter of ugly deception. There was also a startling degree of incompetence. It was clear that government and the intelligence agencies enjoyed, at best, a semi-detached relationship. Waldegrave admitted that ministers often made decisions when they 'did not actually have' any of the right information.[81] And then there was the recalcitrance, the whingeing and the bluster. As Scott observed, with something of an understatement, 'the process of extraction was sometimes difficult and often extended over a lengthy period'. Some key witnesses, such as Lord Howe, proved to be peculiarly reluctant to answer any questions, bleating loudly about how the Inquiry had not allowed him to have legal representation and so on. All the niceties of judicial process and evidence law, with which a judicious degree of obfuscation might have been achieved, were denied.[82] It was all so unfair.

And when the Report was finally published, the government immediately set about casting aspersions in the direction of its author; of such magnitude that Sir Stephen Sedley was minded to observe that the government's response 'illustrated how far we have travelled away

[79] Tomkins, *ibid*, 32–34, 99. For a similar conclusion, see I Leigh, 'Matrix Churchill, Supergun and the Scott Inquiry' (1993) *Public Law*, 640.

[80] Tomkins, above n 75, 41–45.

[81] Tomkins, *ibid*, 154, and generally 129–51.

[82] See Tomkins, above n 75, 8, and Lord Howe, 'Procedure at the Scott Inquiry' (1996) *Public Law*, 445–60. Howe was of the opinion that the Inquiry should have observed the Salmon 'principles', which included such matters as legal representation, of bring witnesses in support, and of having legal representatives cross-examine other witnesses.

from received notions of public probity'.[83] Former senior civil servants pompously wondered if judges could be expected to appreciate what it is like to be 'in the thick of things'; as if that could somehow excuse the attempt to secure the conviction of innocent men in order to cover-up ministerial deception.[84] And there was one final, supreme irony. The publication of the Scott report, intended to promote greater openness and accountability in government, was immediately suppressed by the government for eight days, in order to give ministers some time to work out what to do. It was then released on the day of the scheduled House of Commons debate, giving designated members of the opposition just three hours to formulate their responses.

There is an awful lot that should trouble us here, and this is before we encounter what is, from the perspective of constitutional law, perhaps the most troubling aspect of all; Public Interest Immunity certificates. Above all, perhaps, we should be troubled by Adam Tomkins's sobering observation, that whilst the events surrounding the Scott Inquiry might seem to be peculiar, in fact they are 'representative' of a 'malaise at the centre of British government'.[85] Jonathan Friedland reaches the same conclusion, 'Iraqgate was no one-off; darkness covers our public life'.[86]

In the Public Interest?

During the legal proceedings of the Matrix Churchill case, the government repeatedly issued Public Interest Certificates (PIIs). It was only because the sitting judge took the bold step of refusing to accept one such certificate that the wholly sorry business seeped out. Such certificates are issued in order to prevent the disclosure of supposedly intelligence-sensitive material. They are not supposed to be what Lord Bingham termed 'a trump card vouchsafed to certain privileged players to play when and as they wish'.[87] The weight of judicial history, however, suggests otherwise.

[83] S Sedley, 'The Common Law and the Constitution', in Lord Nolan & S Sedley (eds), *The Making and Remaking of the British Constitution*, (London, Blackstone, 1997), 28.

[84] See D Wass, 'Scott and Whitehall', (1996) *Public Law*, 462

[85] Tomkins, above n 75, 131. Ian Leigh reached a similar conclusion, above n 79, 648–49.

[86] J Friedland, *Bring Home the Revolution: The Case for a British Republic*, (London, Fourth Estate, 1998), 47.

[87] *Makanjula v Commissioner of Police of the Metropolis* [1992] 3 All ER 623.

In the case of *Duncan v Cammell Laird*, for example, in 1942, the House of Lords upheld the Admiralty's refusal to release documents relating to the death of ninety-nine submariners during naval tests. Viscount Kilmuir reinforced the fact that such a refusal was acceptable, provided the government declared that it was in the 'public interest'.[88] In *Conway v Rimmer*, the House of Lords at least asserted its jurisdiction to consider the veracity of the claim of 'public interest'. But it still retained a clear prejudice. Lord Reid concluded that:

> The business of government is difficult enough as it is, and no government could contemplate with equanimity the inner workings of the government machine being exposed to the gaze of those ready to criticize without adequate knowledge of the background and perhaps with some axe to grind.[89]

Of course, such decisions are always made with 'public interest' in mind. It is just that this interest is, with only the rarest of exceptions, taken to be the same as the interest of the government. Thus in the *Lewes Magistrates* case, the House of Lords decided that the 'public interest' lay in allowing police and magistrates to keep confidential documents relating to licensing applications.[90] The list of cases in which courts similarly declined to investigate too deeply how the 'public interest' might be served by promoting government secrecy is a long one.

A fine example of pedantry and pomposity can be found in Lord Denning's statements in *Harman*. Here, a solicitor acting for a prisoner shared information gleaned from Home Office papers with a journalist. Access to the papers had, on this occasion, been successfully gained through a court order. Although the papers were read out in court, the solicitor was held to be in contempt for having shared the disclosure outwith the immediate legal process. It was, of course, a supremely petty distinction. But Denning held forth:

> It was in the public interest that these documents should be kept confidential. They should not be exposed to the ravages of outsiders. I regard the use made by the journalists in this case of these documents to be highly detrimental to the good ordering of our society.

[88] *Duncan v Cammell Laird* [1942] AC 624.
[89] *Conway v Rimmer* [1968] AC 910.
[90] *R v Lewes JJ ex p Home Secretary* [1973] AC 388.

He continued:

> The danger of disclosure is that critics—of one political colour or another—will seize on this confidential information so as to seek changes in governmental policy, or to condemn it. So the machinery of government will be hampered or even thwarted.[91]

The problem with 'outsiders', of course, as Lord Denning knew only so well, is that they have axes to grind, predilections for democracy and accountability. The House of Lords, albeit by the narrowest of margins, upheld the contempt, suggesting, that the disclosure was actually an infringement of privacy. The reasoning, as John Griffith rightly concludes, was possessed of 'manifest absurdities'.[92]

There are, of course, occasions when the attempt to suppress disclosure of material fails. But they tend to be exceptional. One famous example is *A-G v Jonathan Cape*, which involved the putative publication of the diaries of a recently deceased former minister, Richard Crossman. On receiving a pre-publication copy of the diary manuscript, the Cabinet Secretary refused permission to publish on the grounds of a potential breach of the convention of Cabinet collective responsibility. When the *Sunday Times* began to publish extracts, the Attorney-General sought an injunction. On this occasion, the Lord Chief Justice decided not to oblige. Whilst he fully agreed that the 'public interest' might ordinarily be better served in protecting the confidentiality of Cabinet ministers than in facilitating open and accountable government, in this instance the lapse of time, nearly ten years, made publication less damaging to the principle of Cabinet responsibility.[93]

Another incidental success for the cause of open government was the *Ponting* case, which involved the disclosure, by a civil servant, of documents surrounding the sinking of the Argentine battleship, the *General Belgrano*, by British forces during the Falklands War. The documents cast severe doubt on the government line that the battleship posed an immediate threat to British naval ships, not least because it was apparent that the *Belgrano* was steaming away from the warzone as fast as its ageing turbines could take it. Ponting was charged under section 2 of the Official Secrets Act, with having disclosed an unauthorized 'communication'. Having been thwarted in his attempt to direct a verdict, the judge gave a stunningly biased summing-up to the jury

[91] *Home Office v Harman* [1981] 2 WLR 310.
[92] J Griffith, *The Politics of the Judiciary*, 4th ed (London, Fontana, 1997), 236.
[93] *A-G v Jonathan Cape* [1975] 3 All ER 484.

urging conviction. The jury ignored him.[94] It was, as Trevor Allan confirms, 'a legitimate repudiation by the jury of the judge's account of the law'.[95] It was also a small, though exhilarating, victory for liberty, democracy and the principle of open government.

Overall, however, with the occasional exception represented by the likes of *Jonathan Cape* and *Ponting*, legal history suggested that government ministers in the 'Iraqgate' affair had every chance of getting their PII certificates accepted in court, and thus hiding their duplicity. But they were to be rudely surprised. Four PIIs were issued during the trial, each intended to keep government documents evidencing ministerial deceit away from public view. Most important were documents that allegedly provided evidence that Clark had actually encouraged Matrix Churchill to export arms to Iraq. The government defence, as articulated by the Attorney-General, was that the four ministers who signed PIIs had a duty to do so, and could not 'pick and choose when to make a claim'. This, as Scott suggested, was either wrong in fact, as suggested by the House of Lords in the 1994 *Wiley* case or, if not, then certainly wrong in principle.[96]

Needless to say, the disingenuousness was pervasive. In an interesting, and entirely revealing, exchange, Scott asked one of those ministers who signed a PII, Tristan Garel-Jones, to explain his reasoning. In his PII, Garel-Jones had alleged that disclosure of certain documents 'would cause unquantifiable damage to the functions of the security and intelligence services'. When it was suggested that such damage might be negligible, and what precisely 'unquantifiable' was supposed to mean, the minister replied that it might mean 'unquantifiably large' or 'unquantifiably small'. The response was, as Scott concluded, 'risible.[97] Aside from this kind of semantic nonsense, the government further suggested that 'public interest' might amount to an interest in protecting the 'proper functioning of the public service'; a logic which managed to imply that the encouragement of ministerial candour could only be nurtured by persuading ministers that they could do pretty much anything they want without fear of being found out. The argument was, as Scott concluded, no less contemptible.[98]

[94] *R v Ponting* [1985] Crim LR 318.

[95] T Allan, *Law, Liberty and Justice: The Legal Foundations of British Constitutionalism*, (Oxford UP, 1993), 118–19.

[96] *R v Chief Constable of the West Midlands ex p.Wiley* [1995] 1 AC 274.

[97] Tomkins, above n 65, 180–81.

[98] Tomkins, *ibid*, 184–85.

On the matter of PIIs, aside from dismissing the argument that ministers were under some kind of 'duty' to issue certificates in the 'public interest', the Scott Report strongly concluded that;

> for the purposes of criminal trials, the balance must always come down in favour of disclosure if there is any real possibility that the withholding of the document may cause or contribute to a miscarriage of justice. The public interest factors underlying the PII claim cannot ever have a weight sufficient to outweigh that possibility.[99]

It should never have been in doubt. Two centuries ago, in *R v Hardy*, Chief Justice Eyre could be found saying precisely the same thing.[100] And as Scott concluded, the fact that those with axes to grind might relish the disclosure of government documents is 'part of the price that has to be paid for a democratic and open system of government'.[101]

Relics of a Past Age

The Scott Inquiry emphasised, then, not merely the acuity of Jefferson's insight, but also the apparent inability of our constitution to do much about it. In the broader sense, there are two aspects to the problem of executive despotism, aside from the seemingly irresistible tendency of our political leaders to 'rottenness'. First there is the root, and extent, of executive power. Second there is the absence of limits on this power.

The first aspect takes us into the realm of Crown prerogative, something which is notoriously ill-defined. Locke suggested that prerogative is 'nothing but the power of doing public good without a Rule'.[102] Dicey asserted that prerogative powers were merely the 'residue of discretionary or arbitrary power'; powers that history had bequeathed to government.[103] As Lord Reid rather whimsically admitted in the *Burmah Oil* case, it is 'not easy to discover and decide the law regarding the royal prerogative'. It is, simply, 'a relic of a past age'.[104] Lord

[99] Tomkins, above n 75, 190.

[100] *R v Hardy* (1794) 24 St Tr 199.

[101] R Scott, 'The Acceptable and Unacceptable Use of Public Interest Immunity', (1996) *Public Law*, 443, and also 444.

[102] J Locke, *Two Treatises on Government*, (London, Dent, 1989), 199.

[103] Dicey, *An Introduction to the Law of the Constitution*, (London, Macmillan, 1959), 424–25.

[104] *Burmah Oil Company v Lord Advocate* [1965] AC 99, 101.

Diplock tried to cut through the indeterminacy in *BBC v Johns*, declaring that the Crown simply 'personifies the executive government of the country'.[105] It is regrettable that we emerge from all this little the wiser; for whilst government may enjoy certain powers enacted under statute, the real 'efficient secret' of modern government is located here, deep in the murky world of Crown prerogative.

Needless to say, the genealogy takes us back into the realm of constitutional mythology, and more particularly into the various corporeal metaphors that have been commonly used to describe monarchy. The metaphorical distinction between 'private' and 'public' bodies was central to medieval theories of monarchy.[106] Edmund Spenser, author of the *Faerie Queene*, duly observed that Elizabeth 'beareth two persons, the one of the most royall Queene or Empresse, the other of a most virtuous and beautifull Lady'. Elizabeth's famous address to her troops at Tilbury in 1588 was made in this spirit. She had, she informed them, the 'body' of a woman, as well as the 'heart of a king, aye, and a king of England too'.[107]

The prerogative powers flow from this kaleidoscope of corporeal metaphor and myth.[108] The prerogatives relating to the 'private' person have remained with the monarch. Most are trivial, some absurd, some rather more insidious. Amongst the trivial can be found the handing out of 'honours' and other trinkets. Amongst the absurd can be found the royal prerogative regarding whales caught along the coast; something which fascinated Blackstone.[109] Amongst the more insidious is the special tax regime enjoyed by the Queen and her nearest and dearest; a prerogative notoriously approved in *Madras Electric Supply Corporation*.[110] The iniquity of this latter prerogative is barely alleviated by the recently negotiated system of voluntary donations in lieu of

[105] *BBC v Johns* [1965] Ch 79.

[106] For the original account, see H Kantorowicz, *The King's Two Bodies: A Study in Medieval Political Theology*, (Princeton UP, 1957). For a recent restatement, see M Loughlin, 'The State, the Crown and the Law', in M Sunkin & S Payne (eds), *The Nature of the Crown: A Legal and Political Analysis*, (Oxford UP, 1999), 51–56.

[107] E Waller, *Edmund Spencer: A Literary Life*, (Basingstoke, Macmillan, 1994), 101.

[108] For a broad overview, see HWR Wade, 'The Crown, Ministers and Officials: Legal Status and Liability', in Sunkin & Payne, above n 106, 23–32.

[109] In his *Commentaries*, Blackstone commented that being a 'royal fish, the head belongs to the King while the tail belongs to the Queen'. The reason, historically, was that the division would furnish the Queen's wardrobe with whalebone. But given that the whalebone is to be found in the head, the division was, Blackstone concluded, 'whimsical'. See Blackstone, *Commentaries* 1.1.8, quoted in Tomkins, 'Crown Privileges', in Sunkin & Payne, above n 106, 172.

[110] *Madras Electrical Supply Corporation v Boarland* [1955] AC 667.

tax. The Queen still contributes dramatically less than she would if she was subject to the normal tax regime.[111]

Other prerogatives occupy a kind of twilight zone, existing somewhere between the private person and the public office, the trivial and the insidious. One such example, to which we shall return, is the appointment of Prime Ministers. Another is the dissolution of Parliament. In each case, the powers are circumscribed by entrenched conventions; something which does not, however, make the mechanics of the process any less arcane, ridiculous and in terms of democratic principle, offensive. The potential for monarchical interference in the appointment of Prime Ministers remains, whilst only half a century ago Palace officials were happy to assert that the prerogative of dissolution remained 'entirely personal to the Sovereign'.[112]

The situation of Crown prerogatives is all the more unsatisfactory in the light of their essentially allusive and indeterminate nature; measured, as Edmund Spenser suggested, only by the 'line of conscience' of each monarch.[113] The 1947 Crown Proceedings Act sought to bring a measure of coherence to the situation, providing for individual actions against the Crown in contract and tort. Section 21, however, precluded the remedies of injunction and specific performance in civil proceedings against either of the Crown's persons, 'public' or 'private'.[114] The situation where the mystical prerogative of 'perfection' should be allowed to exempt both the person of the monarch and the government from all appropriate remedies for unlawful actions has, as Rodney Brazier rightly concludes, 'stained our constitutional fabric' for far too long.[115]

Courts have occasionally tried to make some sense of it all, whilst monarchs have persistently tried to resist any judicial encroachment on prerogative. James I's famous spat with Lord Chief Justice Coke, to which we shall return in the final chapter, oscillated around the matter of prerogative. A century and a half later, George III's ministers forced the issue once again. On this occasion, however, in *Entick v Carrington*, the Lord Chief Justice famously condemned the issue of general warrants under prerogative as 'subversive of all the comforts of

[111] For a commentary, see Tomkins, above n 109, 176–88.

[112] Hennessy, above n 3, 60–61.

[113] E Spenser, *Faerie Queene* book 5, 1.7.4, in *Complete Poetical Works*, (Oxford UP, 1980), 278.

[114] T Cornford, 'Legal Remedies Against the Crown and its Officers Before and After *M*', in Sunkin & Payne, above n 106, 245–57.

[115] R Brazier, 'Constitutional Reform and the Crown', in Sunkin & Payne, above n 106, 346.

society'. It was, the triumphant radical presses declared, a 'decision which gives every well-wisher to the Constitution of England cause to rejoice', as well as giving a sharp 'lesson to all ministers' that they should not seek to interfere with 'our happy laws'.[116]

Entick, however, remains famous precisely because it was exceptional. It is only relatively recently that courts have ventured to challenge the exercise of prerogative powers. In *De Keyser's*, decided in 1920, the court held that if there was a parliamentary statute which addressed the conditions under which a government might act, then the government could not seek to subvert that statute by claiming to act under prerogative.[117] The rationale for this case, of course, lay in a determination to promote the cherished principle of parliamentary sovereignty. The *Northumbria Police Authority* case revisited the same issue, the relation between statute and prerogative, sixty-nine years later. Here, a rather hesitant Court of Appeal approved the broad principle of the *De Keyser's* case, but not before Lord Justice Purchas could confirm that it was 'unlikely' that a court would want to intervene if the prerogative was being exercised for the 'benefit or protection of the individual'. Lord Justice Nourse admitted that the law relating to prerogatives would continue to be 'piecemeal'.[118]

In the *CCSU* case, which we will revisit in the next chapter, the House of Lords again asserted its ability to review prerogative, even if it once again refused to dispute its particular exercise.[119] But the most determined recent assertion of judicial competence in the exercise of prerogative can be found in Lord Justice Simon Brown's suggestion in *Smith*, that 'only the rarest cases will today be ruled strictly beyond the court's purview', these being 'cases involving national security properly so-called and where in addition the courts really do lack the expertise or material to form a judgment on the point at issue'.[120] There is,

[116] See P Thomas, *John Wilkes*, (Oxford UP, 1996), 86–87, and F Prochaska, *The Republic of Britain 1760–2000*, (London, Allen Lane, 2000), 3–4, and also A Bradley, 'Police Powers and Prerogative', (1988) *Public Law*, 301, suggesting that *Entick* remains a compelling authority for courts taking a sceptical approach to 'new assertions of prerogative'.

[117] *A-G v De Keyser's Royal Hotel* [1920] AC 508.

[118] *R v Secretary of State for the Home Department ex p.Northumbria Police Authority* [1989] QB 26.

[119] *Council of Civil Service Unions v Minister for the Civil Service* [1985] AC 374. For a commentary on this aspect of the case, see B Hadfield, 'Judicial Review and the Prerogative Powers' in Sunkin & Payne, above n 119, 214–19.

[120] A view that was approved in the Court of Appeal. See *R v Ministry of Defence ex p Smith* [1995] 4 All ER 427, and also [1996] 1 All ER 257.

perhaps, a glimmer of hope here. But it is only a glimmer. Prerogative remains, in the words of one MP, a 'chilling example' of 'the way in which our democracy is deficient'.[121]

The stark implications of prerogative are perhaps best seen in Privy Council decisions regarding the death sentence. In the 1996 *Reckley* case the Privy Council refused to intervene to review the exercise of the prerogative of mercy in case appealed from the Bahamas.[122] In *Lewis*, however, decided five years later, the Privy Council reversed its decision, holding that the exercise of the prerogative must be in accordance with principles of natural justice.[123] There is something very wrong in a system of justice which reduces human life to the whims of a jurisprudence that is rooted in the relics of medieval constitutional fantasy.

The Obligations of Conscience

The second problem with executive power, which was again emphasised by the 'Iraqgate' Inquiry, is the lack of effective constraint. There is, as we shall see in due course, the realm of judicial review, which can on occasion constrain the exercise of administrative powers. But otherwise, rather too much depends upon trusting to luck, and hoping that members of the executive will observe the various conventions which purport to limit their activities. It is what Peter Hennessy terms the 'good chaps' theory of government.[124]

The most famous of these conventions, the conventions of 'responsibility', relate to the Cabinet. Of course, like so much of our constitution and government, there is no clear statement of what the Cabinet is supposed to do; which is why there is no clear statement of what it is not supposed to do either. As one contemporary critic has recently confirmed, it 'is impossible to definitely state the role of the Cabinet and what its functions are'.[125] Former Cabinet ministers tend to come to rather different, indeed sometimes strikingly polar, opinions. Clement Attlee thought that it was the only institution that stood

[121] John Garrett, quoted in S Payne, 'The Royal Prerogative', in Sunkin & Payne, above n 106, 77.

[122] *Reckley v Minister of Public Safety no.2* [1996] AC 527.

[123] *Lewis v A-G of Jamaica* [2001] 2 AC 50. In reaching this decision, the Privy Council followed the decision of the Divisional Court in *R v Secretary of State for the Home Department ex p Bentley* [1994] QB 349.

[124] Hennessy, above n 3, 57, 64, 136, 187.

[125] G Thomas, *Prime Minister and Cabinet Today*, (Manchester UP, 1998), 192.

between England and despotism. Lord Hailsham, however, famously opined that the elision of Prime Ministerial and Cabinet government actually militated towards 'elective dictatorship'. His complementary comments, that the Cabinet, as the epitome of 'civilized government', also described a distinctively 'British political genius', merely confirms the apparently irreducible ambiguity of the institution.[126]

As we have seen, Bagehot placed the Cabinet at the centre of British government. Ivor Jennings, similarly, stated that the 'Cabinet is the core of the British constitutional system', integrating 'what could otherwise be a heterogeneous collection of authorities exercising a vast variety of functions'.[127] More recently, it has become commonplace to suggest that the rise of the cult of Prime Minister has rather rewritten Bagehot's 'buckle', reducing the relative power of the Cabinet. In his introduction to Bagehot's *English Constitution*, back in 1963, Richard Crossman suggested that the Cabinet was taking on the appearance of being one of the 'dignified' rather than 'efficient' elements of the constitution.[128] But this merely deflects rather than addresses the overarching concern.

And the indeterminacy of what the Cabinet is supposed to be and to do, is compounded by the collateral indeterminacy regarding the conventions that are supposed to govern it. Jennings famously suggested that conventions 'provide the flesh which clothes the dry bones of the law'. They make 'the legal constitution work; they keep it in touch with the growth of ideas'. More controversially, he then went on to suggest that there was 'no distinction of substance or nature' between laws and conventions; a conclusion which was dramatically at variance with Dicey's.[129] Other academic definitions abound. Geoffrey Marshall tended towards the idea of rules that create some kind of 'obligation'.[130] Joseph Jaconelli prefers a still firmer notion of conventions as 'rules' rather than mere 'habits'.[131] Colin Munro, in comparison, emphasises the differentiated nature of conventions, some clearly more

[126] In Hennessy, above n 3, 94–117.

[127] I Jennings, *Cabinet Government*, (Cambridge UP, 1936), 1.

[128] R Crossman, 'Introduction' to W Bagehot, *The English Constitution*, (London, Fontana, 1963), 54.

[129] I Jennings, *The Law and the Constitution*, (London, Hodder & Stoughton, 1959), 81, 117.

[130] G Marshall, *Constitutional Conventions: The Rules and Forms of Political Accountability*, (Oxford UP, 1984), 11–12.

[131] J Jaconelli, 'The Nature of Constitutional Convention', (1999) 19 *Legal Studies*, 28–32, 45–46.

solid than others, and by implication more important. Of course, this barely takes us any closer to a precise definition, as he readily concedes.[132] In *Jonathan Cape*, Lord Widgery famously held that a 'true convention' is an 'obligation founded in conscience only'.[133] We are little the wiser.

If constitutional definition remains elusive, the political value of Cabinet conventions was prosaically admitted by Lord Salisbury a century ago; they provide a means by which Prime Ministers can control colleagues.[134] This is particularly the case with regard to the convention of 'collective responsibility', which is supposed to commit all members to speak with one voice on matters of policy. If any minister feels unable to accept the Cabinet position, he or she is supposed to resign. There are two issues here. First, there is the obvious, but often overlooked, question of quite why ministers should be obliged to resign just because they have an independent mind. Second, there is the inconsistency of practice. Sometimes ministers resign, sometimes they do not. During the recent Iraq war, one minister, Robin Cook, resigned because he could not support the Cabinet position. Another, who appeared to share similar misgivings, Clare Short, somehow managed to quell her conscience and stay in office. It is all a bit hit and miss; the mists of convention rolling into the murky fogs of 'pollitricks' and personal ambition. As Tony Benn suggested as long ago as 1979, there is no better example of the mythic nature of our constitution than the belief that the convention of collective responsibility actually convinces anyone that the Cabinet is united of purpose.[135]

The second Cabinet convention is that of 'ministerial responsibility'. This convention, it is suggested, holds 'that Ministers are responsible for the general conduct of government, including the exercise of many powers legally vested in the Monarch; and ultimately through Parliament and parties, to the electorate'.[136] The importance of the principle was broadly reaffirmed by the Scott Inquiry, which stressed in particular the responsibility of ministers to be openly accountable for the actions of their departments. The classical understanding of the

[132] C Munro, *Constitutional Studies*, (London, Butterworths, 1999) particularly 81–87.

[133] *A-G v Jonathan Cape* [1976] QB 765.

[134] In I Jennings, *Cabinet Government*, (Cambridge UP, 1959), 281, and C Brady, 'Collective Responsibility of the Cabinet: An Ethical, Constitutional or Managerial Tool' (1999) 52 *Parliamentary Affairs*, 214–15 and 218–19.

[135] A Benn, 'Democracy in the Age of Science', (1979) 50 *Political Quarterly*, 18–19.

[136] G Marshall & G Moodie, *Some Problems of the Constitution*, (London, Hutchinson, 1971), 37.

convention further holds that ministers are responsible, not just for their personal actions, but also for actions of those who work in their departments.

Occasionally ministers do resign in pursuance of this principle. Back in 1954, the Minister of Agriculture, Sir Thomas Dugdale, resigned over the Crichel Down 'affair', when the government failed to honour a commitment to return compulsorily acquired land to its rightful owner. Lord Carrington likewise accepted responsibility for the failure of the Foreign Office to predict the Argentine invasion of the Falkland Islands in 1982, and duly resigned as Foreign Secretary. In this context, it has been suggested that the convention of individual responsibility actually spawns a convention of resignation.[137] If it does, it is a conspicuously weak convention. As Peter Hennessy has confirmed, the Carrington resignation is a peculiarly rare instance of integrity.[138]

In recent times, ministers have preferred a distinction between 'policy' and 'operational' failure; a convention which is supposed to govern the original convention. Successive Conservative Home Secretaries, James Prior, Kenneth Baker and Michael Howard, deployed this distinction in order to deny responsibility for serial break-outs from maximum security prisons. Such failures were deemed to be 'operational'. Of course, as one particularly robust director of the Prison Service suggested, the 'policy' failure to provide sufficient resources underlay the supposedly 'operational' failures.[139] It is, needless to say, impossible to cleanly distinguish the two; which is, after all, precisely why the distinction was dreamt up in the first place. As the Treasury and Civil Service Committee observed, 'If Crichel Down is dead and Ministers are not accountable to Parliament for some actions of their officials, then who is?'[140]

The reality of the conventions of ministerial responsibility today is rather more prosaic. Ministers sometimes resign in order to further their career. The bizarrely theatrical resignation of Michael Heseltine as Defence Secretary over the Westland 'affair' in 1986 comes into this category. More generally, however, they resign when the Prime Minister, troubled by the vicissitudes of public opinion, tells them to.

[137] For this idea, see S Finer, 'The Individual Responsibility of Ministers', (1956) 34 *Public Administration*, 393–94.

[138] Hennessy, above n 6, 415.

[139] A view that was subsequently reinforced by the Learmont Report into prison security. See D Woodhouse, 'The Reconstruction of Constitutional Accountability', (2002) *Public Law*, 75–76.

[140] In C Turpin, *British Government and the Constitution*, (Butterworths, 2002), 458.

As Rodney Brazier rightly concludes, ministers can get away with anything unless it is the kind of thing that 'sells newspapers'.[141] The resignation of Stephen Byers as Trade and Industry Secretary in 2002 provided a fine example of ministers desperately clinging to office until the Prime Minister finally put them, and everybody else, out of their misery. And what bothers Prime Ministers, and public opinion, is not competence, but careless talk, careless sex and careless corruption. A recent ministerial list of the lying, the rude, the over-sexed and the grasping is extensive; Jonathan Aitken, Nicholas Ridley, Edwina Currie, Peter Mandelson time and again, Cecil Parkinson, Nicholas Fairbairn, Michael Mates, Patrick Nicholls, Ron Davies, David Mellor, Neil Hamilton, Keith Vaz, Tim Yeo, Geoffrey Robinson, and the lords Brayley, Lambton and Jellicoe. And this is just the ones that got caught.

Locke's prophesy resonates once again; the 'temptations' of human 'frailty' cannot, it seems, be easily resisted. Of course, those matters that relate primarily to private life are not really matters of ministerial accountability at all, at least not in the constitutional sense.[142] But it all adds up to an unedifying picture. Moreover, as Trevor Allan has argued, it further reinforces the sense that judicial review, rather than watery conventions of responsibility, is the only effective means of holding ministers to account.[143] The coruscating criticism of the convention of ministerial responsibility in the Scott Inquiry carried the same implication.[144]

Interestingly, in the wake of the Scott Report, the House of Commons adopted a resolution on ministerial accountability in 1997; one of the rare instances in which a convention transmuted into a rather more solid state. The resolution focussed on the particular responsibility to provide information to Parliament, in the process clarifying the distinction between 'responsibility' and 'accountability'. Ministers, the government submitted, are 'accountable' for everything that takes place in their departments. But they are not personally 'responsible'. This distinction is little more tenable that that which was supposed to lie between 'policy' and 'operational' matters. It is, as Diana Woodhouse has observed, simply another strategy by which

[141] See R Brazier, 'It is a Constitutional Issue: Fitness for Ministerial Office in the 1990s', (1994) *Public Law*, 440.

[142] See R Scott, 'Ministerial Accountability', (1996) *Public Law*, 414–15.

[143] Allan, above n 95, 184–85.

[144] See Scott, 'Accountability', particularly 424–26.

ministerial 'blame' might be diluted. Ministers, she rightly concludes, should simply be responsible for what goes on, and what goes wrong, in their departments.[145]

III AN ELECTIVE DICTATORSHIP?

First Amongst Equals

Of all the beasts who roam our constitutional landscape the biggest of all is the Prime Minister, the *primus inter pares* of the Cabinet, in the words of one commentator, our 'surrogate monarch', the effective head of legislative and executive, and state.[146] It is the Prime Minister, nourished by the seemingly inexhaustible powers of Crown prerogative, whose growl makes underlings shiver, recalcitrant ministers come into line, and supine MPs gibber on the backbenches.[147] It is he or she who wins and loses elections, and thus makes or breaks careers. It is he or she who decides whether the nation is at war or at peace.[148] As John Mackintosh observed, back in 1962, in simple terms, when all is said and done, 'the country is governed by the Prime Minister'.[149]

The historic origins of the office of Prime Minister, which gradually emerged during the eighteenth century, were not auspicious. Contemporary constitutional culture suggested that the 'prime' minister was merely the 'first amongst equals', the first minister of the King's Cabinet of ministers. Such was the degree of popular contempt for all the king's ministers that Robert Walpole, generally reputed to be the first 'first' minister, denied that he was at all. The *Grub Street Journal* defined a 'prime' minister as someone with 'all the essential power of a monarch, without the pomp'. The *Craftsman* was even less impressed, aligning the office with that of 'an arbitrary Viceroy or deputy tyrant'.[150] No 'prime' minister actually confessed to being a Prime

[145] See D Woodhouse, 'Ministerial Responsibility: Something Old, Something New', (1997) *Public Law*, 269–71, 277–78, and 'Accountability', 77–90. The same sentiment can be found in Lord Nolan, 'The Executive', in Lord Nolan & S Sedley (eds), *The Making and Remaking of the British Constitution*, (Blackstone, 1997), 44–48.

[146] J Friedland, *Bring Home the Republic: The Case for a British Republic*, (Fourth Estate, 1998), 172.

[147] See Brazier, above n 115, 350–51.

[148] Hennessy, above n 3, 90.

[149] J Mackintosh, *The British Cabinet*, (Stevens, 1962), 451.

[150] See Hennessy, above n 6, 38–46, and I Ward, *A State of Mind?: The English Constitution and the Popular Imagination*, (Sutton, 2000), 115–16.

Minister, at least in the context of official business, until Disraeli in the 1870s.[151]

The constitutional status of the Prime Minister is typically uncertain. Not that many Prime Ministers have appeared to be too bothered or too inclined to expound on the subject. Modern Prime Ministerial autobiographies evade the question with a striking regularity. A century ago, Herbert Asquith suggested that the 'office of Prime Minister is what its holder chooses and is able to make of it'; a view echoed by another incumbent, Harold Wilson, who concluded that 'No.10 is what the Prime Minister of the day makes of it'. Yet another incumbent, Stanley Baldwin, likened it to being 'stuck in a glue pot'; an observation that probably said at least as much about Baldwin as it did the office of Prime Minister. Prime Ministers, it seems, just are. The office of Prime Minister is what they do.[152]

There are, once again, a handful of conventions that surround the office. One of the more famous attaches to the process of appointing Prime Ministers. The monarch is supposed to invite the leader of the largest party in the Commons to form a government. Rough logic suggests that this leader should be best able to do so; though the controversy that surrounded Edward Heath's ungainly attempt to cling to office by forming a minority administration after the 1974 election suggests just how rough the logic really is.[153] The Prime Minister is also, by convention, First Lord of the Treasury, and Minister for the Civil Service. A further convention suggests that the Prime Minister should sit in the House of Commons, rather than the House of Lords. The last peer to be Prime Minister was Lord Salisbury who left office a century ago, in 1902. In 1963, the Earl of Home disclaimed his peerage prior to becoming Prime Minister. Of course, all Prime Ministers, no matter how incompetent or unpopular, can expect to be offered a peerage on their retirement.

The Prime Minister also enjoys various powers of appointment. Aside from choosing the Cabinet, Prime Ministers appoint security chiefs, Cabinet Secretaries, Civil Service Commissioners and Parliamentary Ombudsmen. The Prime Minister also plays a role in selecting bishops and making senior military appointments. Such powers of appointment are either derived from convention, or, through

[151] Hennessy, above n 3, 78–79.

[152] Hennessy, above n 6, 3, 17, 54.

[153] The events of 1974, according to Hennessy, revealed just how 'dicey' the convention really is. See Hennessy, above n 6, 21.

convention, from the Crown prerogative. And so too are honours, the 'area', as Hennessy terms it, 'of greatest magic and mystery' in the Prime Ministerial gift.[154] The Queen bestows honours on those suggested by the Prime Minister; just as the Prime Minister permits the Queen to bestow honours on all her best friends and relatives. And as a thank you for all this, and to seal their pact of mutual benevolence and dependence, the Prime Minister and the Queen have weekly chats. Here they discuss all the pressing issues of domestic and international concern. It is all very polite. The Queen listens politely, and the Prime Minister then inserts suitably polite paragraphs into his or her autobiography saying just how polite she was.[155] And so the wheels of government are oiled.

It is often said that the power of Prime Ministers are fully constrained by constitutional convention. Lest we should feel tempted to believe that this is so, and sufficient, we should, perhaps, recall the aside of one former Prime Minister, James Callaghan. When challenged as to the veracity of the particular convention of collective Cabinet responsibility, Callaghan responded, 'I certainly think the doctrine should apply', and then added 'except in cases where I announce that it does not'.[156] The powers that Prime Ministers wield, mostly derived from the 'mystical but mighty' powers of prerogative, are enormous, the constitutional constraints upon their office negligible.[157] This should concern us.

And the power is getting ever greater. It is commonly agreed that the present Prime Minister is the most powerful yet.[158] Peter Hennessy suggests that the Blair premiership is 'Napoleonic' in style, and 'more extreme than ever now'.[159] Tony Benn has gone so far as to suggest that 'There is currently Prime Ministerial diktat. It is not presidential government but monarchical government, where Parliament is used as a rubber stamp, merely convened at the Prime Minister's pleasure'.[160] On assuming power in 1997, Prime Minister Blair advised his MPs that

[154] Hennessy, above n 6, 74–75.

[155] A good, and unsurprising, example can be found in Margaret Thatcher's paean to the Queen's 'formidable grasp of current issues and breadth of experience'. See M Thatcher, *The Downing Street Years* (Harper Collins, 1993), 18.

[156] Quoted in Turpin, above n 140, 219.

[157] See Hennessy, above n 6, 6–9, 139.

[158] For a broad account, see Rawnsley, *Servants*, particularly viii, 5–13.

[159] P Hennessy, 'The Blair Style of Government: An Historical Perspective and an Interim Audit', (1998) 33 *Government and Opposition*, 5, and above n 6, 477–78, 507.

[160] In Brady, above n 134, 215.

their role was not to be independent thinkers or servants of their constituencies, but to be 'ambassadors for the government', and, by implication, for him.[161]

And the same seems to be the case with regard to the Cabinet. The age of Cabinet government, the defining characteristic of post-war governments, had passed by 1963, when Richard Crossman noted the 'final transformation of Cabinet government into Prime Ministerial government'.[162] Clement Attlee declined to end Cabinet meetings until all parties had talked themselves into agreement. 'A monologue', he famously observed, 'is not a decision'.[163] Today, Cabinet meetings rarely last more than half an hour. Within months of Blair's arrival in Downing Street, *The Times* concluded that the 'long predicted demise of the Cabinet as a central organ of government has finally occurred'.[164] As one senior civil servant has observed, the Prime Minister 'doesn't like argument', and it is for this simple reason that 'Cabinet these days is just a series of self-congratulatory remarks'.[165]

And neither, as Hennessy observes, is the present Prime Minister too keen on 'spending his hours at Westminster'.[166] Policy is not decided in Cabinet or in Parliament. A Cabinet of would-be assassins and successors is too dangerous a place to discuss much, a Parliament of largely anonymous juveniles, too ridiculous. Major policy initiatives are more likely to be decided by an inner coterie of mates and spin-doctors. The proposal to abolish the office of Lord Chancellor was not ventured in Cabinet, and neither was the suggestion that one of the Prime Ministers closest chums should be invited to run a brand new Department of Constitutional Affairs instead.

In the context of the evident increase in Prime Ministerial authority it has been suggested that recent occupants of No 10 Downing Street more obviously resemble Presidents than first ministers. There is an echo here of Bagehot's observation, that in our 'disguised republic' the House of Commons is 'the assembly which chooses our president'.[167] Rather more recently, the accusation was levelled against Margaret Thatcher, but has become ever more resonant under successive Blair

[161] Rawnsley, above n 158, 30.
[162] Hennessy, above n 6, 56.
[163] See Hennessy, above n 6, 147, and also 150–51, 159.
[164] Hennessy, above n 159, 4, 11, and above n 6, 481–83.
[165] In Paxman, above n 12, 216.
[166] Hennessy, above n 6, 550–51.
[167] W Bagehot, *The English Constitution*, (Cambridge UP, 2001), 44, 94.

administrations.[168] According to Peter Riddell, though the word 'Presidency' is never actually 'uttered publicly by any of the Blair inner circle', it 'is often used by them privately'. 'There has', he adds, 'been a deliberate attempt to change the way Downing Street and the Cabinet Office work to allow the Prime Minister to exercise more control over the Whitehall machine'.[169] It was even reported that Chancellor Gordon Brown envisaged his role as being that of 'Prime Minister' to Blair's 'President'.[170]

The appointment of unelected 'cronies' to senior ministerial offices, resembling the practice of American Presidents, reinforces the sense that the office of Prime Minister has assumed presidential overtones. Of course, the idea that senior ministers should be drawn from the House of Lords is not new. It was common practice during the age of Whig oligarchy. And previous ministers, such as Lord Carrington who was Foreign Secretary during the first Thatcher administration, have been appointed from the House of Lords. But the habit of first picking mates, then giving them life peerages, and then finally making them ministers, is rather more novel; though present proposals for a selected second Chamber, selected in large part by the Prime Minister of the day, suggests that it will become more familiar over time. The new Secretary of State for Constitutional Affairs, Lord Falconer, may or may not be the right man for the job; but he enjoys not the slightest tincture of democratic legitimacy.

If the practice of the Blairite premiership carries distinctively presidential connotations, the presidential, even quasi-monarchical, 'image' is even more apparent. All the essential strategies deployed by Fairy Kings and Queens down the centuries are present; the carefully choreographed naturalness, the pretended personal affinity, the measured 'intimacy' between monarch and supine subject, the attempt to project youthfulness and virility. And then there is the added inflection, demanded by the media of the twenty-first century, the sheer 'blokiness'; the father who announces the birth of a child coffee-cup in hand, the party political broadcasts from kitchen tables with sleeves rolled up, just a little, not too much.[171] Trollope's Lady Glencora understood

[168] For the suggestion regarding the Thatcher premiership, see M Foley, *The Rise of the British Presidency*, (Manchester UP, 1993), 263, and also Hennessy, above n 6, 398–407.

[169] In Hennessy, above n 159, 10.

[170] In Hennessy, above n 159, 14–15.

[171] A Finlayson, 'Elements of the Blairite Image of Leadership', (2002) 55 *Parliamentary Affairs* 590, 596–97.

the game; 'when a man wants to be Prime Minister he has to submit to vulgarity'.[172]

As they have for centuries, people want to identify with icons more than ideologies. If the second Queen Elizabeth is a sorry shadow of the first, her 'first' minister is altogether more up for the challenges of governing Fairyland. Blair, as Andrew Rawnsley has noted, is an enthusiastic and 'consummate political actor', one who utterly dominates the stage.[173] Where Gloriana progressed round her Fairyland, today's Prime Minister descends upon the sitting rooms of England in carefully staged political broadcasts and photo opportunities.[174] The idealised image of a presidential Premier, surrounded by a coterie of ministerial and other 'cronies' has led Tom Nairn to suggest that it all bears a comparison with 'a quasi-courtly regime straight out of the pages of a seventy-year-old novel from the Hapsburg Empire'.[175] It is not a happy comparison. In this context there is a very real pertinence to Peter Hennessy question:

> Surely as a political nation we did not struggle to replace the single executive represented by the seventeenth-century sovereign by a more collective form of cabinet governance only for it to mutate once more into an elected monarchy?[176]

A World of Invisible Powers

Pondering the power of the Prime Minister and the Cabinet, Lord Hailsham famously expressed his concern regarding the emergence of an 'elective dictatorship'; a concern that noticeably vanished once he ascended to power himself.[177] The danger was, of course, clearly portrayed in Bagehot's *Constitution*, and it has been revisited by various constitutional commentators over the intervening decades. A century ago, Frederick Maitland warned against a complacent acceptance of the 'supralegal, suprajural plenitude of power concentrated in a single

[172] A Trollope, *The Prime Minister*, (Penguin, 1994), 164.

[173] A Rawnsley, *Servants of the People: The Inside Story of New Labour*, (Hamish Hamilton, 2000), 62.

[174] Finlayson, above n 171, 593.

[175] Nairn, above n 49, 24.

[176] Hennessy, above n 159, 19.

[177] See D Shell, 'Labour and the House of Lords: A Case Study in Constitutional Reform', (2000) 53 *Parliamentary Affairs*, 290.

point at Westminster'.[178] The same sentiment can be found in Wade's later injunction:

> It must not be forgotten that the inevitable consequence of the supremacy of Parliament in the legislative field is that there can be no check upon the unscrupulous use of power by a Government which finds itself in command of a majority in the House of Commons.[179]

This is the 'mask' of despotic anarchy; the fiction that the executive is answerable to the legislative, and the legislative is answerable to the people. The last occasion that Parliament actually forced the resignation of a government was 1979. The people get to elect their legislators whenever the Prime Minister says they can.

The problem is one of balance. The relationship between legislature and executive is not that of equals. The power of government to rule Parliamentary business is enshrined in Standing Order 14.1, which confirms that 'Save as provided in this order, government business shall have precedence at every sitting'. The appointment of a Cabinet member as the Leader of the House reaffirms the power of government to determine what Parliament does and how it is run.[180] Regardless of the technical niceties, government tells Parliament what to do, and Parliament does it.

Parliament does enjoy the constitutional power to scrutinize legislation introduced by government. But much of this power is negated by the convention which prescribes proportional representation on parliamentary committees. The only government that is likely to suffer any serious inconvenience in committee is a minority one. The same is true in the Commons. Only minority governments, or governments with slender majorities, are likely to be troubled by backbench discontent. The present government has forced through a number of statutes against the wishes of a sizeable contingent of its own MPs, including the 2000 National Air Traffic Services and the 2001 Anti-terrorism, Crime and Security bills. Given a decent majority, government can largely do as it wishes; ensuring that its own legislation passes, and making sure that any other legislation only passes if it so chooses. At present, a government can expect to secure the passage of between forty and sixty bills each session, dependent upon the extent of delay-

[178] In D Nicholls, *The Pluralist State* (Macmillan, 1994), 31.

[179] Wade, 'Introduction' to A Dicey, *An Introduction to the Law of the Constitution*, (Macmillan, 1959), xxiii.

[180] For a discussion of this anomaly, see Winetrobe, above n 67, 19–26.

ing strategies deployed by the opposition. In the past, the House of Lords might have been expected to provide some kind of opposition, particularly to Labour governments. Proposed reforms to the House, vesting the powers of appointment in the executive, are likely to dilute even this limited constraint.

This, once again, should trouble us. According to Dennis Kavanagh, the 'central issue in British politics has not been how to curb the elective dictatorship but how to capture it', for 'the formal concentration of political authority in Britain is remarkable'.[181] The Scott Inquiry revealed just how true this is. Forty years ago, the former Cabinet minister and diarist Richard Crossman made the same point. 'Ministers', he observed, 'aren't bothered by Parliament, indeed they're hardly ever there'. The 'executive', he added, 'rides supreme in Britain and has the minimum trouble from the legislature'.[182]

The lack of accountability is patent, and it is becoming ever more so, with the advance of more and more 'quangos' and now more recently 'Next Steps' agencies; the latter established on the assumption that efficient local governance is much more important than accountable or democratic local governance.[183] It is suggested that this regime of quasi-autonomous bodies better reflects the demands of the modern 'regulatory state'; a state in which, as one apologist has conceded, any 'personal sense of responsibility makes no sense'.[184] In terms of open government, however, it all leaves much to be desired.[185] It also confirms the acuity of Raphael Samuel's observation, that Britain is a 'society honeycombed with invisible powers', such that:

> Here government is typically—even obsessively—secretive. The system of representation is not transparent but opaque; decision-making is not an

[181] D Kavanagh, *Thatcherism and British Politics: the End of Consensus?*, (Oxford UP, 1986), 285.

[182] R Crossman, *Diaries*, (Jonathan Cape, 1975–7), 2.130–31.

[183] Two-thirds of all civil servants are now employed in Next Steps agencies. For an overview, see M Freedland, 'The Crown and the Changing Nature of Government', in Sunkin & Payne, above n 106, 111–33. We will revisit this issue in the final chapter.

[184] M Moran, 'The Rise of the Regulatory State in Britain', (2001) 54 *Parliamentary Affairs*, 31.

[185] See, for example, Lord Nolan, above n 145, 41–45, M Smith, 'Reconceptualizing the British State: Theoretical and Empirical Challenges to Central Government', (1998) 76 *Public Administration*, particularly 59–65 and also M Flinders, 'Governance in Whitehall', (2002) 80 *Public Administration*, particularly 70–1. For earlier discussions of these issues, see R Rhodes, 'The hollowing out of the state: the changing nature of the public service in Britain' (1994) 65 *Political Quarterly*, 138–51, B Hogwood, 'The Machinery of Government 1979–1997', (1997) 45 *Political Studies*, 704–15.

> event but a process. Judges do not make law in Britain, they only follow precedent. Policy emerges from administrative necessity, rather than from legislative enactment. Nobody is responsible in Britain for anything.[186]

Secrecy, unaccountability, anonymity, a lack of responsibility which might properly be termed irresponsibility. It is not what a liberal democratic community is entitled to expect of its government, or its constitution.

Talking Points

And it was not how things were supposed to be; an impotent Parliament masking a corrupt and despotic executive. It was certainly not what the architects of the 'Great and Glorious' revolution prescribed. At the heart of John Locke's second *Treatise on Government*, the defining account of the 'revolution principles' of 1689, could be found a principle, originally derived from Aristotle, of the separation of powers.[187] According to Locke the 'separation' of legislative, executive and 'federative' powers is a necessary prerequisite for all 'well-ordered commonwealths', providing a necessary barrier to the temptations of 'human frailty' so 'apt to grasp at power'.[188] It is this principle which is missing in our modern experience of government; and it is a critical absence.

Locke's principle was reaffirmed in Blackstone's *Commentaries*. Whilst Parliament can 'do everything that is not naturally impossible', Blackstone advised that it is 'highly necessary for preserving the balance of the constitution, that the executive power should be a branch, though not the whole, of the legislative'. 'The total union' of the executive and legislative powers, he continued:

[186] R Samuel, 'Ethics and the Strike', *New Society* 28.2.1985.

[187] Locke's *Treatise* was famously described by Sir Frederick Pollock, in his 1922 *Essays in Law*, as 'probably the most important contribution ever made to English constitutional law by an author who was not a lawyer by profession'. For a more recent commentary on Locke's separation thesis, see N Barber, 'Prelude to a Separation of Powers', (2001) 60 *Cambridge Law Journal*, particularly 59–66, and for a wider discussion of its implications, E Barendt, 'Separation of Powers and Constitutional Government' (1996) *Public Law*, 599–619.

[188] Locke, *Treatises*, 190. By 'federative', Locke meant that power which related in particular to matters of security and public interest. Today, 'federative' powers are generally assumed to be part of the wider executive competence.

> would be productive of tyranny; the total disjunction of them, for the present, would in the end produce the same effects, by causing that union against which it seems to provide. The legislature would soon become tyrannical, by making continual encroachments, and gradually assuming to itself the rights of executive power.[189]

Those who argue the case for a 'partial' separation of powers do so in honour of Locke and Blackstone.[190]

Later in the eighteenth century, the doctrine of the separation of powers would be vigorously propounded across the Atlantic, by the likes of Thomas Jefferson who recommended a federal model of separated competences precisely because the 'way to have good and safe government, is not to trust it all to one, but to divide it among the many'.[191] And a century later, Harold Laski would deploy it against the Diceyan orthodoxy, suggesting that the 'secret of liberty is in the division of powers'.[192] More recently it has resurfaced as a central tenet of Trevor Allan's defence of a balanced 'constitutional state' properly 'grounded in law'. If a constitution is to be so balanced, according to Allan, then 'legislative supremacy must ultimately be limited by the principle of the separation of powers'.[193] And it is in this spirit that Sir Stephen Sedley has recently suggested that a principle of the separation of powers, taken to describe a series of 'distinct but interlocking spheres of constitutional competence', should be reinvested at the heart of our constitution.[194]

The principle of the separation of powers has attracted occasional judicial approval. Alluding to the various constitutions of former colonies in *Hinds v the Queen*, Lord Diplock opined that:

> All of them were negotiated as well as drafted by persons nurtured in the tradition of that branch of the common law of England that is concerned with public law and familiar in particular with the basic concept of separation of legislative, executive and judicial power as it had been developed in the unwritten constitution of the United Kingdom.[195]

[189] Blackstone, *Commentaries on the Law of England* (Walker, 1826), 1.2.160–61, 153–54.

[190] Barendt, above n 187, 608–9.

[191] In G Hart, *Restoration of the Republic: The Jeffersonian Ideal in 21st Century America*, (Oxford UP, 2002), 82.

[192] H Laski, *The Foundation of Sovereignty and Other Essays*, in P Hirst, (ed), *The Pluralist Theory of the State*, (London, Routledge, 1993), 37.

[193] Allan, above n 95, 69, 264.

[194] S Sedley, 'The Sound of Silence: Constitutional Law Without a Constitution', (1994) 110 *Law Quarterly Review*, 271. See also, Sedley, 'Law and Public Life' in Nolan & Sedley, above n 83, 60.

[195] *Hinds v the Queen* [1977] AC 212.

And it was Diplock again, stressing the importance of a collateral principle of judicial independence, who affirmed in *Duport Steel v Sirs* that:

> at a time when many more cases involve the application of legislation which gives effect to policies that are the subject of bitter public and parliamentary controversy, it cannot be too strongly emphasised that the British Constitution, though largely unwritten, is firmly based upon the separation of powers: Parliament makes the laws, the judiciary interprets them.[196]

Formal support was voiced by Lord Templeman in *M v Home Office*, stating that 'Parliament makes the law, the executive carry the law into effect and the judiciary enforce the law'.[197] And similar sentiments can be found in Lord Mustill's opinion in the *Fire Brigades Union* case.[198]

But such statements are, on the whole, in the minority. Dicey's dismissal of the principle of separated powers has retained its force. Of course, as Locke observed, there is no necessary tension between separated powers and parliamentary sovereignty; so long as such sovereignty is limited to legislative power.[199] As far as Locke was concerned, whilst sovereign power might be nominally transferred to a parliament as part of a social 'contract', a 'supreme power' remained in the citizenry to 'remove or alter the legislative, when they find the legislative act contrary to the trust reposed in them'.[200] For this reason any check on parliamentary sovereignty was rather less of a threat. Indeed, it was to be welcomed; for no legislative power can be 'absolutely arbitrary', at least not in a free society.[201]

As we have already seen, however, Whig historiography recast the 'Great and Glorious' revolution in terms of Parliamentary supremacy rather than a separation of powers, and in time Dicey would entrench this historiography in the aspic of 'unitary' sovereignty. Generations of lawyers have dutifully digested Dicey's dicta, dismissing, as de Smith commented, the principle of the separation of powers as a 'tiresome talking point'.[202] In *Halsbury's Laws of England*, Sir William Holdsworth declared that Locke's doctrine had never 'to any great extent corresponded with the facts of English government'.[203]

[196] *Duport Steel v Sirs* [1980] 1 All ER 541.

[197] *M v Home Office* [1994] 1 AC 395.

[198] *R v Secretary of State for the Home Department ex p.Fire Brigades Union* [1995] 2 AC 513.

[199] As, more recently, does Allan. See *Law*, 269–70.

[200] Locke, *Treatises*, 167–69, 179, 192.

[201] Locke, *Treatises*, 184–87.

[202] S de Smith, 'The Separation of Powers in New Dress', 12 *McGill LJ* 1966, 491.

[203] *Halsbury's Laws of England* (Butterworths, 1952), 6.385.

However, as we have already seen, the supposed supremacy of the principle of parliamentary sovereignty is no longer so credible. There are various forms of legislation that appear to bind future Parliaments; most obviously the Acts of Union, the 1972 European Communities Act, and the statutes of dominion, to which might now be added the statutes of devolution and the 1998 Human Rights Act. It is within this context that we are urged to think of a constitutionalism that is 'beyond' unitary conceptions of sovereignty.

And it is in this context that we can revisit the supposition that a modern liberal constitution could, and should, be better balanced. It is a liberating thought. For, as Locke urged, if Parliament is indeed the only institution that can bind itself, then it is truly despotic. And if it pretends to be supreme as well, then it is tyrannical too; for the purpose of pretended legislative supremacy, today at least, is to mask the uglier reality of an even greater tyranny, that of unconstrained executive power. Historical whimsy is no excuse for such a grotesque corruption of the liberal democratic principles of government and constitution. A modern constitution should be better constructed, and better equipped to constrain the excesses of government. The separation and balance of powers is the pivotal component of such a constitution. We shall revisit this proposition in the final chapter. First, however, we must take a closer look at another critical relationship in the Anglo-British constitution; that which exists between the executive and the judiciary.

3

Renaissance

IN HIS *GULLIVER'S Tales*, published in 1726, Jonathan Swift's eponymous hero informs the King of Brobdingnag that judges 'are persons appointed to decide all controversies of property, as well as for trials of criminals, and picked out from the most dexterous of lawyers who have grown old or lazy'. All in all, he concluded, 'in all points out of their own trade', England's 'breed' of judges and lawyers:

> Were usually the most ignorant and stupid generation amongst us, the most despicable in common conversation, avowed enemies to all knowledge and learning, and equally disposed to pervert the general reason of mankind in every other subject of discourse, as in that of their own profession.[1]

Such scepticism is healthy. We should always treat those who assume the power to govern us or adjudge us with a sceptical eye.

At the same time, we enter the twenty-first century with an emasculated legislature and an over-mighty executive. Accordingly, there is a renewed interest in the role of the judiciary, and in its dormant capacity to provide a necessary check and balance in our constitution. Diana Woodhouse has argued that the final decades of the last century saw 'a steady shift in power from politicians to judges', whilst Dawn Oliver prophesies a coming age of 'increased judicial activism'.[2] In the same vein, the former Permanent Secretary to the Lord Chancellor's Department has recently suggested that 'In the century now opening, the judges are clearly going to have an increased role in our constitution.'[3] Robert Stevens suggests that this evolution can be cast in terms of a shift in jurisprudential culture, from a 'parliamentary democracy' to a 'constitutional democracy', from a constitution nominally shaped by politicians to one nominally secured by judges.[4] The statistics are

[1] J Swift, *Gulliver's Travels*, (London, Penguin, 1985), 296–98.

[2] D Woodhouse, 'The Law and Politics: More Power to the Judges—and to the People?' (2001) 54 *Parliamentary Affairs*, 223, and D Oliver, *Constitutional Reform in the UK*, (Oxford UP, 2003), 385.

[3] T Legg, 'Judges for the New Century', (2001) *Public Law*, 62.

[4] R Stevens, *The English Judges: Their Role in the Changing Constitution*, (Oxford, Hart, 2002), 148.

themselves revealing. There were 149 judicial review cases in 1980. In 1997 there were 2,753.[5] And then there is the impact of the new Human Rights Act. According to Jeffrey Jowell, taken together, the assumed powers of 'judicial' review and the 1998 Act can be more properly, and more honestly, termed 'constitutional'.[6]

If this is so, then it asks considerable questions of another of the great myths of our constitutional order; that of judicial independence. As Robert Stevens suggests, the idea of judicial independence has always leant more to 'rhetoric' than to reality; something that has become ever more apparent during the last 'challenging' decade or so.[7] It has even been suggested that we are presently living in an era of judicial 'antagonism', an era in which the judiciary has begun to reassert certain principles of a distinctive 'common law' constitutionalism, such as the rule of law and the separation of powers, in defiance of executive despotism. Whilst we should always keep Swift's observations firmly in mind, we should also approach the idea of a more antagonistic judiciary with a measured degree of enthusiasm.

I MORE FAIRYTALES

Hugging the Coast

According to the Home Secretary in David Hare's recent and critically acclaimed play, *Murmuring Judges*, the principle of the independence of the judiciary is 'perhaps the most important bulwark against chaos this country has'; an observation tempered by the fact that he immediately attempts to pervert it.[8] The principle was set in the historical aspic of the Act of Settlement which accompanied the arrival of William III. It provided that 'judges commissions' should 'be made *quamdiu se bene gesserint* and their salaries ascertained and established; but upon address of both houses of Parliament it may be lawful to remove them'. In his *Commentaries*, Blackstone duly recorded that:

[5] In C Foster, 'The Encroachment of the Law on Politics',(2000) 53 *Parliamentary Affairs*, 342.

[6] J Jowell, 'Beyond the Rule of Law: Towards Constitutional Judicial Review' (2000) *Public Law*, 682–83.

[7] R Stevens, 'A Loss of Innocence?: Judicial Independence and the Separation of Powers' (1999) 19 *Oxford Journal of Legal Studies*, 365, 367. See also J Griffith, *The Politics of the Judiciary*, (London, Fontana, 1997), 326–28.

[8] D Hare, *Murmuring Judges*, (London, Faber and Faber, 1994), 56.

> In the distinct and separate existence of the judicial functions in a peculiar body of man, nominated indeed, but not removable at pleasure, by the Crown, consists our main preservation of the public liberty; which cannot subsist long in any state, unless the administration of common justice be in some way separated as well from the legislative as from the executive power.

'Nothing' he confirmed 'is to be more avoided, in a free constitution, than uniting the province of a judge with that of a minister of state'.[9] When Lord Chancellor Mackay tabled proposals for reform of the legal profession in 1989, it was in this spirit that Lord Chief Justice Lane could dismiss the proposals as being 'sinister', and Lord Ackner argue that 'political considerations, political dogma and doctrine' had overridden a respect for judicial independence and integrity.[10]

The myth of judicial independence is, as we have already seen, related to that of the separation of powers.[11] As Lord Diplock famously affirmed in *Duport Steel v Sirs*, 'Parliament makes the laws, the judiciary interprets them.[12] It was a sentiment revisited more recently by Lord Nolan in *M*:

> The proper constitutional relationship of the executive with the courts is that the courts will respect all acts of the executive within its lawful province, and that the executive will respect all decisions of the court as to what its lawful province is.[13]

More recently still, in a speech made in the House of Lords in 1996, a year before he took office as Lord Chancellor, Lord Irvine claimed that the constitution 'is firmly based upon the separation of powers', a doctrine which, he added, 'is a crucial but delicate component of our unwritten constitution'.[14]

The collateral impact of the conjoined principles of the separation of powers and the independence of the judiciary is the hoary myth that judges should not make the law. Rather, as Dicey suggested, they are supposed to interpret the law as set down by Parliamentary statute.[15] The orthodox view was crisply articulated by Lord Chancellor Bacon at the beginning of the seventeenth century. The duty of a judge, Bacon

[9] Quoted in Stevens, above n 7, 375.
[10] Griffith, above n 7, 53–56.
[11] For a discussion of what he terms the 'traditional view' of judicial independence, and its 'myth', see Griffith, above n 7, 290–94.
[12] *Duport Steel v Sirs* [1980] 1 All ER 541.
[13] *M v Home Office* [1992] 1 QB 314–15.
[14] D Williams, 'Bias; the Judges and the Separation of Powers', (2000) *Public Law*, 47.
[15] See Stevens, above n 4, 16.

affirmed, is to 'interpret law, and not to make law or give law'.[16] Three centuries later, in the *Earl of Norfolk Peerage Case*, Lord Halsbury affirmed that 'to alter' the law 'or even to modify it is the function of the Legislature and not of your Lordships' House'.[17] In *Arlidge*, decided just eight years later in 1915, Lord Shaw likewise suggested that courts should not even seek to enforce due process in executive decision-making, for if the 'judiciary should presume to impose its own methods on administrative or executive officers' it 'is a usurpation'.[18]

This attitude has passed down the judicial generations. In 1944, the then Master of the Rolls, Lord Greene, commented that 'The function of the legislature is to make the law, the function of the administration is to administer the law and the function of the judiciary is to interpret and the enforce the law. The judiciary is not concerned with policy'.[19] The classical idea of what judges do, and do not do, was articulated in Lord Devlin's suggestion that whilst judges are now expected to do more than simply follow precedent, 'creative' or 'dynamic' lawmaking requires 'a surer political touch than a judge is likely to have'. For this reason, he added, judges must not be tempted to engage in programmes of 'social justice', but must instead 'operate' within the pervasive 'consensus'.[20] As Devlin suggests, the role of judges is simply to 'interpret' the statute.[21]

And the preferred mode of interpretation has been generally 'literal', a matter of ascertaining the precise meaning of a statute from within the prescribed words of the statute. In *Magor and St Mellons RDC*, Lord Simonds declared that 'The duty of the courts is to interpret the words that the legislature has used; these words may be ambiguous, but, even if they are, the power and duty of the court to travel outside them on a voyage of discovery are strictly limited'.[22] He would not, he confirmed in a later case, be 'led' by any 'undiscerning zeal for some abstract kind of justice to ignore our first duty', that of interpreting Parliamentary statutes and enforcing existing common law precedent.[23] The same navigational metaphor was used thirteen years earlier

[16] F Bacon, *The Essays*, (London, Penguin, 1985), 222–25.
[17] *Earl of Norfolk Peerage Case* [1907] AC 12.
[18] *Arlidge* [1915] AC 137–38.
[19] W Greene, 'Law and Progress', (1944) 94 *Law Journal*, 349.
[20] P Devlin, *The Judge*, (Oxford UP, 1979), 2, 10–11.
[21] *Ibid*, 14.
[22] *Magor and St Mellons RDC v Newport Corp* [1952] AC 191.
[23] *Midland Silicones v Scruttons* [1962] AC 467–68.

by Lord Wright, this time in the context of common law reasoning. English judges, he suggested, had always preferred to proceed 'from case to case, like the ancient Mediterranean mariners, hugging the coast from point to point and avoiding the dangers of the open sea of system and science'.[24]

It is only recently, in the cases of *Pepper v Hart* and *McGuckian*, that courts have been prepared to venture just a little way from the coast. In *Pepper*, the House of Lords held that courts could look beyond the narrow remit of the statute in question, at least so far as ministerial commentaries in Parliament, in order to ascertain interpretive meaning if it was, on the face of the statute, somewhat obscure.[25] This approach was then approved by Lord Steyn in *McGuckian*, observing that 'during the last 30 years there has been a shift away from the literalist approach to progressive methods of construction'. He continued, 'When there is no obvious meaning of a statutory provision the modern emphasis is on a contextual approach designed to identify the purpose of a statute and give effect to it'.[26]

Fairytales

In due deference to the Diceyan theory of Parliamentary sovereignty that underpins it, the 'classical' *ultra vires* doctrine of judicial review limits courts to reviewing executive action if it appears to have been conducted outwith the limits established by statute. It is, as Mark Elliott puts it, the 'central tenet of the *ultra vires* principle' that 'all limits on statutory discretionary power derive from the intention of Parliament'.[27] In other words, courts do not review Parliamentary statutes; the statutes inhere their own capacity for review. The ability of courts to review the exercise of this power is thus circumscribed by the doctrine of Parliamentary sovereignty. There is, as we shall see, an alternative idea of judicial review, based on residual common law authority to constrain government, and there are principles such as reasonableness and proportionality. But the classical *ultra vires* doctrine continues to enjoy the support of commentators such as Elliot, and also

[24] Wright, 'The Study of Law', (1938) 54 *Law Quarterly Review*, 186.
[25] *Pepper v Hart* [1993] AC 593.
[26] *IRC v McGuckian* [1997] 3 All ER 817.
[27] M Elliott, 'The Demise of Parliamentary Sovereignty?: The Implications for Justifying Judicial Review', (1999) 115 *Law Quarterly Review*, 120–23.

Christopher Forsyth who concludes that it continues to have the 'crucial role' of providing the ultimate 'constitutional justification for judicial review'. In this way, it does not 'challenge', but rather 'fulfils the intention of Parliament.[28]

The classical view has recently received judicial approbation in cases such as *ex p Page*, and more recently *ex p Pierson* and *Boddington*.[29] For Lord Browne-Wilkinson, the purpose of judicial review, very simply, is to check the government, and by implication, ensure that the paramount will of Parliament is observed. In the *Fire Brigades Union* case he again emphasised that 'The constitutional history of this country is the history of the prerogative powers of the Crown being made subject to the overriding powers of the democratically elected legislature as the sovereign body'.[30] The role of the courts is to ensure that the will of Parliament, as expressed in legislation, is followed; no more and no less. Or so the logic goes.

The problem, of course, is that interpretation of statute, whether by an administrative body or a court, is invariably political to some degree. The very act of interpretation invites opinion and prejudice. Indeed, it needs it. Otherwise there would be no such thing as judgement, merely a restatement of what the statute reads. So much was famously admitted by the Canadian Supreme Court in *R v S*. The 'reasonable person', the Court held, cannot 'expect that judges will function as neutral ciphers'. 'It is apparent', the Court continued, 'that triers of fact will be properly influenced in their deliberations by their individual perspective on the world in which the events in dispute in the courtroom take place.'[31]

Lord Reid made a similar confession in his famous observation made as long ago as 1972:

> There was a time when it was thought almost indecent to suggest that judges make law—they only declare it. Those with a taste for fairy tales seem to have thought that in some Aladdin's cave there is hidden the Common law in all its splendour and that on a judge's appointment there descends on him knowledge of the magic words Open Sesame.

[28] C Forsyth, 'Of Fig-Leaves and Fairytales: The Ultra Vires Doctrine, the Sovereignty of Parliament and Judicial Review', (1996) 55 *Cambridge Law Journal*, 136–37.

[29] *R v Lord President of the Privy Council ex p Page* [1993] AC 701–2; *R v Secretary of State of the Home Department ex p Pierson* [1998] AC 575; *Boddington v British Transport Police* [1998] 2 WLR 655.

[30] *R v Secretary of State for the Home Department ex p.Fire Brigades Union* [1995] 2 ALL ER 244.

[31] *R v S (RD)* (1997) 118 CCC (3d) para 119.

'But', Reid concludes, 'we do not believe in fairytales any more'.[32] Or so we should hope.

And then, rather more recently, there is Lord Browne-Wilkinson's admission in the *Kleinwort Benson* case that:

> The theoretical position has been that judges do not make law or change law: they discover and declare the law which is thought the same. According to this theory, when an earlier decision is overruled the law is not changed; its true nature is disclosed, having existed in that form all along . . . In truth judges make and change law. The whole of the common law is judge-made and only by judicial changes in the law is the common law kept relevant in a changed world.[33]

Pepper v Hart presents itself as a compelling example of this kind of evolution. Another, equally renowned, is the case of *R v R*, in which the House of Lords created, or perhaps merely refined, the common law of marital rape. The common law, as Lord Keith asserted, must be 'capable of evolving in the light of changing social, economic and cultural developments'.[34]

If the English constitution is indeed described, at least in substantial part, by the common law, then the English constitution is something that is intrinsically judge-made. Even Dicey acknowledged that 'Our constitution is a judge-made constitution, and it bears on its face all the features, good and bad, of judge-made law'.[35] In the *National Federation of the Self-Employed* case in 1982, Lord Diplock likewise admitted that 'most of English public law' had been 'made by the judges' and 'by judges can be changed'. And so, he continued, has English law evolved, shaped by judges:

> over the years to meet the need to preserve the integrity of the rule of law despite changes in social structure, methods of government and the extent to

[32] Lord Reid, 'The Judge as Law Maker', (1972) 12 *Journal of the Society of Public Teachers of Law*, 22.

[33] *Kleinwort Benson v Lincoln City Council* [1998] 4 All ER 513.

[34] *R v R* [1991] 3 WLR 771. Until the decision in *R v R* husbands enjoyed a common law immunity from accusations of having raped their wives. It was an immunity that Glanville Williams, one of the most revered 'authorities' on criminal law, thought entirely understandable. Judges, he opined, should be sympathetic towards husbands who, now and again, need to 'use their strength' in order to persuade an unwilling wife to provide a little sexual satisfaction. Thankfully the House of Lords did not favour such a repellent attitude. See G Williams, 'The Problem of Domestic Rape', (1991) *New Law Journal*, 205–6. For an interesting overview of *R v R* and the context, see N Naffine, 'Erotic Love in the Law of Rape', (1994) 57 *Modern Law Review*, 10–37.

[35] A Dicey, *An Introduction to the Study of the Law of the Constitution*, (London, Macmillan, 1959), 196.

> which the activities of private citizens are controlled by governmental authorities, that have been taking place, sometimes slowly, sometimes swiftly, since the rules were originally propounded.[36]

The business of judging is the business of voicing opinions and prejudices, whether they be those of the community or those of the judges, or, in reality, those that judges like to think are held in the community. The myth that judges should not appear to make the law is closely related to the myth that their judgments are impartial. Both are absurd. Both are vigorously defended.

The Case of the Lucky Dictator

The myth of impartiality was famously stipulated by Lord Hewart in *McCarthy*. Justice should not only be done 'but manifestly and undoubtedly be seen to be done'.[37] Everything about the judicial process is about maintaining this appearance of impartial justice. As Lord Devlin admitted, the 'judge who gives the right judgement while appearing not to do so may be thrice blessed in heaven, but on earth is no use at all'.[38] A limited common law rule against bias developed in cases such as *Dimes* which held that judges who held a pecuniary interest in a case were automatically disqualified from sitting in it.[39] Outside of this pecuniary interest, however, everything was trusted to luck and good intentions.

And then came the case of the lucky dictator. In September 1999, Augusto Pinochet Ugarte, was arraigned before the Bow Street Magistrates on an application for extradition to Spain on charges of torture and conspiracy to torture. Pinochet was one of the most brutal fascist dictators of the last part of the twentieth century, in turn President of the governing Junta and then Head of State of Chile between 1973 and 1990. He was also a valued friend of various senior members of successive Conservative governments. Most importantly, he was a compulsive shopper, and it was on one of his many shopping visits to London that he was arrested. Opinions regarding Pinochet

[36] *R v IRC ex p National Federation of the Self-Employed* [1982] AC 639–40.
[37] *R v Sussex Justices ex p McCarthy* [1924] KB 259.
[38] Devlin, above n 20, 3.
[39] *Dimes v Proprietors of Grand Junction Canal* (1852) HL cas759. For a commentary on this series of early authorities, see A Olowofoyeku, 'The *Nemo Judex* Rule: The Case Against Automatic Disqualification', (2000) *Public Law*, 457.

were strongly held and passionately argued. Former Conservative ministers and Knightsbridge shopkeepers were appalled at his arrest; pretty much everyone else was elated.

During Pinochet's rule 1,102 people disappeared and 2,095 were executed or died under torture; and that is just the figure recorded by the Chilean Truth and Reconciliation Commission. The real figures are likely to have been rather higher. And Pinochet was a cosmopolitan kind of dictator. It was not just Chileans who were tortured and murdered. So were citizens of the UK. Not that successive UK governments seemed too concerned; the Attorney-General rejecting permission for the Association of Relatives of the Disappeared to seek a private prosecution against Pinochet as late as 1998. The Spanish authorities, however, seemed to be rather more troubled by the fate of their citizens, and it was the warrant of a Spanish investigating magistrate that was passed to Interpol in late 1998, and which then wound its way to Bow Street a year later.[40]

Pinochet's lawyers immediately recognised that the case carried considerable political, as well as legal, ramifications, and asked the Home Secretary to exercise an executive authority to cancel the warrant and to discharge the aging torturer. The Home Secretary declined, pontificating nobly on the fact that Pinochet should not be exempted from the ordinary course of the law. Pinochet's lawyers also issued a writ of *habeas corpus*, which was adjourned to the Divisional court, along with an application for judicial review of the Home Secretary's decision to refuse to cancel the warrant. The Divisional Court focused on the question of state immunity, and whether the alleged actions could fall under the heading of the normal 'state functions' of the Chilean head of state. And, they concluded, whilst torture might be regrettable, it could indeed fall under the heading of state functions.[41]

An appeal to the House of Lords was immediately launched, on the legal point of what the proper interpretation and scope of state immunity should be. An array of human rights bodies intervened alongside the Crown Prosecution Service, which was acting on behalf of the Spanish authorities. The House took torture to be the paradigm offence, and heard a multitude of arguments drawn from public international and human rights law. A powerful argument was based on the 1984 UN Convention on Torture, which placed signatories under an obligation

[40] F Webber, 'The Pinochet Case: The Struggle for the Realization of Human Rights', (1999) 26 *Journal of Law and Society*, 528–31.

[41] *Ibid*, 531–32.

to prosecute or extradite alleged perpetrators. The Convention had been incorporated into domestic British law in the 1988 Criminal Justice Act. The 1978 State Immunity Act, however, affirmed that former heads of state enjoyed special exemptions from criminal responsibility for acts performed as state 'functions'. The question was whether torture was an exempted 'function'. And the House decided by a majority of 3 to 2 that it was not. Lord Nicholls suggested that torture was a universal crime, and could not be confined by any alleged 'state' immunity.[42]

The matter was not, however, over. Pinochet's lawyers submitted a complaint to the Lords' judicial committee alleging bias. It transpired that Lord Hoffmann, one of the sitting judges in the House of Lords hearing, was a director of Amnesty International, one of the bodies that had intervened in the action against Pinochet. It was suggested that he should, accordingly, have discharged himself from hearing the case. The committee agreed that there was a potential bias, and so in December 1999 the court in *Pinochet 2* set aside the original decision and ordered a fresh trial before a panel in which Hoffmann was not present.[43]

Pinochet 3 accordingly arrived before a newly constituted House of Lords in March 1999. Whilst the House reaffirmed that torture was an international crime over which it had jurisdiction, it decided that the tense in which section 2 of the 1989 Extradition Act was written prevented its application to any acts alleged to have taken place before 1989.[44] On the basis of this essentially specious distinction, Pinochet was duly discharged. The Home Secretary wrung his hands before the camera, and decided to allow an apparently ailing Pinochet to leave immediately. Pinochet departed in his wheelchair, and then arrived a few hours later in Santiago where he skipped happily, and unaided, down the aircraft steps, to be welcomed by a handful of his admiring cronies.

The *Pinochet* cases revealed many things, not least the attention which judges are inclined to give to the tense in which statutes are written, regardless of the extent to which this might confound the clear intent of both domestic and international law. It also revealed an almost pathological concern for the appearance of judicial indepen-

[42] *R v Bow Street Magistrates ex p Pinochet Ugarte* [1998] 3 WLR 1456.
[43] *R v Bow Street Magistrates ex p Pinochet Ugarte* [1999] 2 WLR 272.
[44] *R v Bow Street Magistrates ex p Pinochet Ugarte* [1999] 2 WLR 827.

dence from bias. The suggestion that Hoffmann was genuinely biased is untenable. But it is the appearance of bias that mattered. Above all, the *Pinochet* cases reveal the law to be an ass. The idea that a judge should be precluded from sitting in a case simply because he is prepared to offer his overt support to the principle of human rights, and to do so by supporting a renowned human rights organisation, is absurd. All in all, as *The Economist* concluded, the resolution of the *Pinochet* litigation was deeply unsatisfactory, 'muddled' and 'bizarre'.[45]

Conceivable and Inconceivable Bias

The story does not end here. In the months that followed *Pinochet*, a mass of cases were begun on the grounds that various judges had been biased.[46] In response, the floodgates were firmly shut in the later 1999 decision in *Locabail*. Here, a specially instituted court of senior judges held that there must be a 'real likelihood or danger' of bias, rather than a 'reasonable suspicion'.[47] The immediate implication is that 'real likelihood' requires something rather more tangible than the mere 'appearance' of bias. Interestingly, this approach had already been advanced in the 1994 case *ex parte Dallaglio*, where Sir Thomas Bingham had even suggested that Hewart's aphorism was 'no longer, it seems, good law'.[48] The court in *Pinochet 2*, however, clearly thought differently. Only after Pinochet was allowed to escape justice has the judiciary finally agreed that the mere appearance of bias is no longer sufficient to quash decisions.

And there is a second, and no less troubling, implication that flows from the *Locabail* ruling. The court also went out of its way to reduce the danger of potential actions alleging bias by demarcating a number of what it deemed to be 'inconceivable' factors. In other words, allegations that judges might be biased on the grounds of their race, sex or sexual orientation, age, religion or even class, were deemed to be 'inconceivable'. Alongside is an array of potential prejudices that are deemed to 'ordinarily unchallengeable', including political associations, membership of charitable bodies, and educational background. The distinction between conceivable and inconceivable factors is

45 In Stevens, above n 7, 109.
46 K Malleson, 'Safeguarding Judicial Impartiality', (2002) 22 *Legal Studies*, 53.
47 *Locabail v Bayfield Properties* [2000] 2 WLR 883.
48 *R v Inner West London Coroner ex p Dallaglio* [1994] 4 All ER 162.

tenuous in the extreme. As Kate Malleson rightly wonders, is it 'conceivable' that a Roman Catholic judge can give a ruling, unconstrained by personal theological beliefs, in cases regarding euthanasia or abortion?[49]

Nearly a century ago, Lord Justice Scrutton readily confided that the idea of impartiality is 'rather difficult to attain in any system'. He continued:

> I am not speaking of conscious impartiality; but the habits you are trained in, the people with whom you mix, lead to your having a certain class of ideas of such a nature that, when you have to deal with other ideas, you do not give as sound and accurate judgments as you would wish.[50]

Rather more recently, Lord Browne-Wilkinson admitted that the 'features of current judicial reasoning' are:

> First, the actual decision is based on moral, not legal factors. Second, these moral reasons are not normally articulated in the judgment. Third, the morality applied in any given case is the morality of the individual judge.[51]

Such honesty is refreshing. But it should also give us pause to consider once more Gulliver's denunciation of the 'breed'. The nature of the modern judiciary might be very different from that which Swift ridiculed two centuries ago. But, equally, it would be naïve to ignore the reality of endemic and institutionalised social and political prejudice in today's judicial caste. According to Hare's Mr.Justice Cuddeford in *Murmuring Judges* the legal profession is little more than a gentlemen's club, a remote and socially exclusive one:

> Remember, all the time judging brings you in touch with ordinary people. In our courts. We see them every day. Ordinary, common-as-muck individuals. Some of them quite ghastly, I promise you that. This makes us alert to public opinion. We're closer to it, perhaps, than you think.[52]

Again, we are dealing with caricature here. But it is not fantasy. This cultivated image of other-worldliness was given voice by a real-life member of the senior judiciary, Lord Parker, who commented that a judge 'is not supposed to know anything about the facts of life until

[49] Malleson, above n 46, 59.

[50] Scrutton, LJ, 'The Work of the Commercial Courts', (1921) 1 *Cambridge Law Journal*, 8.

[51] Lord Browne-Wilkinson, 'The Impact of Judicial Reasoning', in B Markesinis (ed), *The Impact of the Human Rights Bill on English Law* (Oxford, 1998), 21.

[52] Hare, above n 8, 54–55.

they have been presented in evidence and explained to him at least three times'.[53]

Judges, as Lord Devlin admitted, are 'men' chosen for their office because they 'do not seriously question the *status quo*'. He continued, 'No doubt judges, like any other body of elderly men who have lived on the whole unadventurous lives, tend to be old-fashioned in their ideas'. This, however, is not a matter of concern, merely a simple 'fact of nature which reformers must accept'.[54] But it is not. In his seminal *Politics of the Judiciary*, John Griffith concluded that the modern judiciary has 'acquired a strikingly homogenous collection of attitudes', a 'unifying attitude of mind, a political position, which is primarily concerned to protect and conserve certain values and institutions'. They 'are the product of a class and have the characteristics of that class'.[55] This matters, not just because judges are 'placed in positions where they are required to make political choices', but because 'their interpretation of what is in the public interest and therefore politically desirable is determined by the kind of people they are and the position they hold in our society'.[56]

The dominance of 'elderly men' in the modern judiciary is not natural. It is contrived. Feminist commentators, such as Clare McGlynn, have graphically described the misogynistic composition of the judiciary; something which makes the famously female figure of blindfolded justice a rather obvious and rather 'sad irony'.[57] Only recently has the first female Lord of Appeal in Ordinary been appointed, and only three out of thirty-six Lords Justice of Appeal are women.[58] All in all less than ten percent of all judges in the English High Court are female. And with the institutional misogyny comes the institutional racism. Less than one per cent of judges are from ethnic minorities. Needless to say these statistics are lower still for higher judicial appointments.

Back in 1992, Lord Chief Justice Taylor acknowledged that the 'present imbalance between male and female, white and black in the

[53] In B Hale, 'Equality and the Judiciary: Why Should We Want More Women Judges?', (2001) *Public Law*, 503.

[54] Devlin, above n 20, 8, 15.

[55] Griffith, above n 7, 7, 295, 338.

[56] Griffith, above n 7, 336.

[57] C McGlynn, *The Woman Lawyer: Making the Difference*, (London, Butterworths, 1998), 171.

[58] The *Daily Mail* greeted the news of the first female Lord of Appeal in Ordinary with the sage warning that the appointee, Brenda Hale, was a 'dangerous feminist'.

judiciary is obvious'. Things, he promised, would change.[59] They have not. The recent Campbell Commission for Judicial Appointments, which reported in 2002, concluded that the present judiciary is 'overwhelmingly white, male and from a narrow social and educational background', and added, 'Statistics suggest that the make-up of the judiciary does not reflect that of the potential pool of applicants from which it could be drawn, which raises questions about equality of opportunity'.[60]

The entire process of appointment lies at the root of contemporary anxieties regarding the 'conceivable' bias of our judiciary. For centuries, appointments were, as Gavin Drewry noted, shrouded in a 'notorious culture of secrecy', part of the prerogative fiat of the Lord Chancellor in his capacity as a member of the executive.[61] As Helena Kennedy has pithily concluded, the system of 'secret soundings' resembles nothing more than a form of juristic 'cloning'.[62] Public school, Oxbridge educated white male judges seem to prefer the appointment of more public school, Oxbridge educated white male judges. As Lord Bridge confessed as recently as 1992, when selecting a new judge, he and his colleagues in the senior judiciary looked for 'chaps like themselves'.[63] The case for an independent judicial appointments commission has long been argued. As David Pannick concluded, such a commission 'could hardly fail to improve on the unarticulated criteria, acts of God, and secret processes of nature which currently govern judicial appointments'.[64] Lord Chancellor Irvine, like his predecessors, rebuffed such criticisms, arguing that judicial appointments were based on 'merit'. This is, of course, another myth.[65] Those who are deemed meritorious have flourished in a system that is endemically discriminatory.

Sir Sydney Kentridge has recently regretted the present 'fashion for general criticism of the judiciary', something which he suggests, rather vaguely, has 'to do with the Millenium'. 'Our judges' Kentridge continues, are accused of being 'mostly white middle-class, middle-aged

[59] Lord Taylor, *The Judiciary in the Nineties*, Richard Dimbleby Lecture, 1992), 9.
[60] *Guardian* 8.10.02, 9.
[61] G Drewry 'Judicial appointments', (1998) *Public Law*, 4.
[62] In McGlynn, above n 57, 183. For a similar observation, see Griffith, above n 7, 22.
[63] In McGlynn, above n 57, 178.
[64] D Pannick, *Judges*, (Oxford UP, 1987), 69. See also McGlynn, above n 57, 182–84.
[65] Legg, above n 3, 67, and S Kentridge, 'The High Court of Justice: Selecting the Judges', (2003) 62 *Cambridge Law Journal*, 59 admitting that 'merit' is rather 'difficult' to define.

males', and therefore they are 'said to be out of touch with ordinary life, and not representative of our diverse population'.[66] That is because, in simple terms, far too many are. A modern society deserves a modern, properly accountable and representative judiciary. Brenda Hale's conclusion is unarguable, a 'system of justice will be the richer for diversity of background and experience', and likewise, it 'will be poorer, in terms of appreciating what is at stake and the impact of its judgments, if all its members are cast in the same mould'.[67]

Much will depend upon the anticipated new judicial appointments commission. But much too depends upon a cultural shift in the judicial mindset. Most importantly, there is a pressing need for honesty. Judges make political and moral decisions. It is an unavoidable responsibility. In this sense they are endemically biased, and it makes no sense to pretend otherwise. As Lord MacMillan confessed:

> The judicial oath of office imposes on the judge a lofty duty of impartiality. But impartiality is not easy of attainment. For a judge does not shed the attributes of common humanity when he assumes the ermine. The ordinary human mind is a mass of prepossession inherited and inquired, often none the less dangerous because unrecognised by their possessor. Few minds are as neutral as a sheet of plate glass, and indeed a mind of that quality may actually fail in judicial efficiency, for the warmer tints of imagination and sympathy are needed to temper the cold light of reason if human justice is to be done.[68]

The marriage of reason and sympathy, to which Lord MacMillan alluded, is of especial pertinence. It speaks to the possibility of a new kind of judiciary; one that can be properly entrusted with the responsibility to oversee the recasting of a revitalised English constitution.

II ENEMIES WITHIN AND WITHOUT

The Renaissance of Judicial Review

The doctrine of judicial review, as Lord Templemen famously declared, was an 'invention' of judges in order 'to secure that decisions are made by the executive or a public body according to law even if the

[66] Kentridge, *Ibid*, 56.

[67] See Hale, above n 53, 504.

[68] In B Wilson, 'Will women judges really make a difference?', (1990) 28 *Osgoode Hall Law Journal*, 508–9.

decision does not otherwise involve an actionable wrong'.[69] It has recently been suggested that the doctrine is presently experiencing something of a 'renaissance', one that can be aligned with the broader renaissance of the 'common law' constitution.[70] The sentiment can be found in Lord Steyn's recent suggestion that judges do not 'decide cases in a vacuum', but rather observe the governing constitutional principles within the deeper context defined by the political imperatives of liberal democracy, of 'values of justice, liberty, equality and humanity'.[71] It has also been stridently reaffirmed by Trevor Allan, whose defence of the 'common law' constitution will be revisited in the final chapter.[72]

Whereas the 'classical' doctrine of judicial review, founded on the orthodox doctrine of *ultra vires*, is dedicated to preserving the myth of parliamentary sovereignty, the 'common law' alternative puts rather more stock in the principle of the rule of law. The reason being, as Lord Bridge held in *Morgan-Grampian*, that the 'maintenance of the rule of law is in every way as important in a free society as the democratic franchise'.[73] Lord Woolf has spelt out the implications:

> If Parliament did the unthinkable, then I would say the courts would also be required to act in such a manner which would be without precedent . . . I myself would consider there were advantages in making it clear that ultimately there are even limits on the supremacy of Parliament which it is the courts' inalienable responsibility to identify and uphold. They are limits of the most modest dimensions which I believe that any democrat would accept.[74]

The classical doctrine of judicial review is further dependent on another of the defining myths of English public law, that of the 'reasonable man' advanced by Lord Greene in the *Wednesbury* case in 1948. Outwith the doctrine of *ultra vires*, Greene suggested that courts might only intervene against an administrative decision of the executive when discretionary powers had been effected in a manifestly 'unreasonable' fashion. Driven by the desire to limit the potential juris-

[69] *Mercury Energy v Electricity Corporation of New Zealand* [1994] NZLR 388.

[70] Both references in Stevens, above n 4, 67, 69.

[71] Lord Steyn, 'The Weakest and Least Dangerous Department of Government', (1997) *Public Law*, 85.

[72] See T Allan, *Law, Liberty and Justice: The Legal Foundations of the British Constitution*, (Oxford UP, 1993), 173, and also 183–210, and 237–64.

[73] *X v Morgan-Grampian* [1991] AC 48.

[74] Lord Woolf, 'Droit Public—English Style', (1995) *Public Law*, 57–58.

diction of the courts, Greene was keen to emphasise that matters of policy were not themselves 'the concern of judges save in so far as the manifest object of the statute, as appearing on its face, may provide a context pointing to one interpretation rather than another'.[75]

It is beyond this conceptual 'torpor', as Sir Stephen Sedley has recently termed it, that judges are now hesitantly beginning to move.[76] First, there has been a clear determination to widen competence. In both *Lain*, in which Crown prerogative was held to be reviewable, and *Anisminic*, where specific statutory exclusion was ignored, the courts asserted their overriding jurisdictional capacity in terms of the rule of law.[77] Second, there has been an increasing determination to deal in terms of 'fairness' rather than mere 'reasonableness'. An early expression could be found in *Ridge v Baldwin* in 1964, in which judicial review was aligned with principles of natural justice.[78]

More recently, however, the case for 'fairness' has been impelled by the experience of European legal integration.[79] A good example here is *Doody*, in which it was held that interested parties have a basic right to know the reasons for decisions made by administrative bodies.[80] Lord Woolf cites *Doody*, and the wider European experience, as pivotal in the process of widening the 'empire' of judicial review beyond the *ultra vires* doctrine.[81] Sir John Laws has reached a similar conclusion.[82] According to Murray Hunt, it represents a revolutionary 'phase' in the development of a broad 'common law human rights jurisdiction' in English public law.[83]

The impact of European integration on the classical doctrine of judicial review can be seen in two distinct areas. The first is the matter of remedies. Traditionally, domestic courts have refused to make

[75] *Associated Provincial Picture Houses Ltd v Wednesbury Corporation* [1948] 1 KB 223. For a commentary on the political context, see Griffith, above n 7, 104–5.

[76] S Sedley, 'The Common Law and the Constitution' in Lord Nolan & S Sedley (eds) *The Making and Remaking of the British Constitution* (London, Blackstone, 1997), 19. See also Sir John Laws's observations, in his 'The Limitations of Human Rights', (1998) *Public Law*, 261–62.

[77] *R v Criminal Injuries Compensation Board ex parte Lain* [1967] 2 QB 864; *Anisminic v Foreign Compensation Commission* [1969] 2 AC 147.

[78] *Ridge v Baldwin* [1964] AC 40.

[79] C Hilson, 'The Europeanization of English Administrative Law: Judicial Review and Convergence', (2003) 9 *European Public Law*, 126–29.

[80] *R v Secretary of State for the Home Department ex p.Doody* [1993] 3 WLR 154.

[81] Woolf, above n 74, 58–67.

[82] Laws, above n 76, 258–59, 265.

[83] M Hunt, *Using Human Rights Law in English Courts* (Oxford, Hart, 1997), particularly 162–74.

available the remedies of injunctions and damages against public bodies; a refusal reasserted as lately as 1982 in the seminal case of *O'Reilly v Mackman*.[84] In European Community law, however, such remedies must be enforced by courts as and when appropriate. The result is a clear discrepancy between the availability of remedies in domestic and Community law; a discrepancy which was described by Lord Donaldson in the *M* case as being 'anomalous' and 'wrong in principle', and by Lord Woolf as 'unhappy'.[85]

The second area is the advance of an alternative principle of proportionality which might better equip courts to ensure 'fairness' in administrative decision-making.[86] Whereas the *Wednesbury* principle requires the judge to search for the mythical reasonable man, proportionality instead demands that they should balance the respective interests of government and citizen. The approach received Lord Justice Sedley's approval in *Interbrew*, and Lord Steyn's in *ex p Daly*.[87] It has been argued that the distinction between the reasonableness and proportionality tests is slight.[88] In *Smith*, Sir Thomas Bingham suggested that the balancing test required by the principle of proportionality could be interpreted as ensuring that, in weighing up the different interests at play, the decision reached was 'reasonable'.[89] Lord Slynn made a similar observation in *Alconbury*; 'Trying to keep the *Wednesbury* principle and proportionality in separate compartments seems to me to be unnecessary and confusing'.[90]

There is, then, an affinity between the 'renaissance' of a common law conception of judicial review and the demands imposed by European legal integration. Sir John Laws suggests that a reshaped *Wednesbury* principle will exemplify 'the rule of reason as a fundamental principle'

[84] *O'Reilly v Mackman* [1983] 2 AC 237.

[85] *M v Home Office* [1992] 4 All ER 139; *In Re M* [1993] 3 WLR 448. For a discussion of *M* in the European dimension, see I Ward, *A Critical Introduction to European Law*, (London, Butterworths, 2003), 126–28.

[86] See G de Burca, 'Proportionality and *Wednesbury* unreasonableness: The influence of European legal concepts on UK Law', (1997) 3 *European Public Law*, 561–6, and also I Leigh & Lt Lustgarden, 'Making Rights Real: The Courts, Remedies, and the Human Rights Act', (1999) 58 *Cambridge Law Journal*, 517–18, and also Laws, above n 76, 261–62.

[87] *Interbrew v Financial Times* [2002] EMLR 24; *R v Home Secretary ex p Daly* [2001] 2 WLR 1622.

[88] See Hilson, above n 79, 131–36.

[89] *R v Ministry of Defence ex p.Smith* [1996] QB 554.

[90] *R (Alconbury Developments) v Secretary of State for the Environment, Transport and the Regions* [2001] 2 WLR 1389.

of a distinctive common law constitution, one that is necessarily evolutionary.[91] In doing so, he reaches back to cases such as *Rookes*, in which Lord Chief Justice Coke held that administrative action 'ought to be limited and bound with the rule of reason and law'.[92] Paul Craig deploys a similarly historical methodology in order to recommend an idea of judicial review that 'expresses the proper relationship between the rule of law and sovereignty, and best captures the practice of the courts'.[93] But the affinity finds its most compelling expression in Lord Steyn's observations in *ex p Pierson*, that 'Parliament does not legislate in a vacuum. It legislates for a European liberal democracy founded on the principles and traditions of the common law. And courts may approach legislation on this initial assumption.'[94] Such an attitude may well, as Jeffrey Jowell suggests, represent a 'provocative challenge to traditional British constitutional doctrine'.[95] But that should not detract from its desirability.

The Politics of Review

As the law of judicial review has evolved, it has become ever more obvious that the courts are engaged in an overtly political venture; a venture which must, therefore, undermine the fiction of absolute judicial independence, as well as the thought articulated as recently as 1982 by Lord Brightman in *ex p Evans*, that 'judicial review is concerned not with the decision but with the decision-making process'.[96]

Examples of the irreducibly political nature of this engagement abound. Two particularly good ones are the *Tameside* and *GLC* cases. It is the resolution of cases like these which, according to John Griffith, leads to the inexorable conclusion that in many judicial review cases 'judges rely almost entirely on their own sense of justice or on their own personal conception of what is best'.[97] In *Tameside*, the House of

[91] J Laws, 'Wednesbury', in Forsyth & Hare (eds), *The Golden Metwand and the Crooked Cord*, (Clarendon, 1998), particularly 196–201.

[92] *Rookes Case* (1598) 5 Co Rep 99.

[93] P Craig, 'Competing Models of Judicial Review', (1999) *Public Law*, 428, 438–39, 443–44.

[94] *R v Secretary of State for the Home Department ex p.Pierson* [1998] AC 575.

[95] J Jowell, 'Of Vires and Vacuums: The Constitutional Context of Judicial Review', (1999) *Public Law*, 448, 459.

[96] *R v Chief Commissioner of North Wales Police ex p.Evans* [1982] 1 WLR 1173.

[97] Griffith, above n 7, 112, and also 336.

Lords was required to rule between two countervailing political ideologies, the very different education policies of a Conservative council and a Labour government. In deciding that the former, in refusing to implement government policy, had acted reasonably, the House of Lords could not fail but make an intensely political decision.[98]

Similarly, in *GLC* courts were again required to decide between alternative political ideologies, between a Labour controlled Greater London Council, which wanted to levy a charge on all boroughs in order to supplement public transport, and a Conservative local authority which refused to do so. According to both the Court of Appeal and the House of Lords, the GLC, and the transport executive which it oversaw, were under a fiduciary duty to accord with ordinary business practices. A reduced fares scheme was held to be contrary to such practices, and so could not be enforced. The decision was nakedly political, entirely dependent upon loose notions of what business practice was supposed to be. In reaching its decision, the court had clearly chosen to ignore the assumed democratic mandate of the GLC. Of course, the existence of a similar mandate held by the Bromley borough council merely underlined the necessarily political and tendentious role that the courts were obliged to assume.[99]

But perhaps the most striking examples of the political implications of judicial review can be found in the area of industrial relations law; precisely the area which so troubled Dicey a century ago, and from which the modern law of judicial review is derived.[100] Amongst the more famous of the early cases was *Quinn v Leathem*, in which the House of Lords constructed a union threat to boycott a meat supplier as a form of conspiracy to injure, and *Taff Vale Railway*, in which it was held that trade unions could be sued for losses sustained by employers during strike periods.[101] But the most famous of all was undoubtedly *Roberts v Hopwood*, in which the House of Lords struck down a minimum wage established by a local Council.[102] Here Lord Wrenbury anticipated the *Wednesbury* doctrine, opining that dis-

[98] *Secretary of State for Education v Tameside MBC* [1976] 3 WLR 641.

[99] *R v GLC ex p Bromley LBC* [1983] 1 AC 768. For a commentary, see Griffith, above n 7, 126–33.

[100] For a good overview of this area of public law, see K Ewing, 'The Politics of the British Constitution', (2000) *Public Law*, 414–28

[101] *Quinn v Leathem* [1901] AC 495; *Taff Vale Railway Co.v Amalgamated Society of Railway Servants* [1901] AC 426.

[102] *Roberts v Hopwood* [1925] AC 578.

cretionary powers must be used 'reasonably'.[103] The icon of reason cannot, however, mask the political reality of decisions in cases such as *Roberts*, and the reality here, as Harold Laski observed, is that the House of Lords had revealed itself to be 'the unconscious servant of a single class in the community'.[104]

Forty years later, the same accusation could be levelled at the decision in *Rookes v Barnard*, in which it was held that strikes could be adjudged unlawful if in breach of contract.[105] The various decisions that emanated from Lord Donaldson's National Industrial Relations Court (NIRC) during the 1970s, most famously *Heaton*, were just as notorious.[106] So, too, were a series of decisions at the end of the same decade given by Lord Denning's Court of Appeal; all of which were to be reversed in the House of Lords. In *Hearn*, *NWL* and *McShane*, Denning had sought to enforce statutory limitations on trade union immunities, chiefly by deploying a narrow understanding of what action 'in furtherance' of a trade union could be.[107] The matter was then revisited in *Duport Steel v Sirs*, in which private steel companies sought injunctions to prevent the Iron and Steel Confederation from widening public sector industrial action to the private sphere in order to put pressure on the government. The Court of Appeal duly obliged on the ground that any extended strike action represented a distinct dispute, and could not be interpreted as being 'in furtherance' of the original dispute, as defined in the Industrial Relations Act. The House of Lords, however, decided that there was no real distinction between the two alleged disputes.[108] Ultimately, in cases such as these, all a court can do is pick an ideology and favour it.[109]

Increasingly draconian industrial relations law has sought to enforce a greater degree of consistency. It is within this context that courts have, in cases such as *Marina Shipping*, ruled 'secondary' strike action unlawful under section 17 of the 1980 Employment Act.[110] The political nature of such decisions is plain. As Lord Wedderburn emphasised, it enforces a particular political vision of industrial relations, with

[103] *Roberts v Hopwood* [1925] AC 613.
[104] Stevens, above n 4, 23.
[105] *Rookes v Barnard* [1964] AC 1129.
[106] See Griffith, above n 7, 75–77.
[107] *BBC v Hearn* [1977] 1 WLR 1004; *NWL v Woods* [1979] 1 WLR 1294; *Express Newspapers v McShane* [1979] 2 All ER 360.
[108] *Duport Steel v Sirs* [1980] 1 All ER 529.
[109] Griffith, above n 7, 311–13.
[110] *Marina Shipping v Laughton* [1982] 2 WLR 569.

labour 'cut up into atomized units of which the boundaries are by law coterminous with the employers' definitions of employment units in both private and public sectors'.[111] Cases such as *Thomas* and *Clarke*, in which the courts have levied swingeing fines against unions that continued to organise strike actions prohibited either by statute or by the courts, reinforce this conclusion.[112] So, too, does *Associated Newspapers*, in which the House of Lords held that employers could offer what amounted to an incentive to employees who agreed to opt out of collective bargaining procedures.[113]

There are occasions when the courts have taken a broader attitude to industrial relations disputes. Famously, in *ex p Vardy*, the divisional court upheld an injunction against the British Coal Corporation on the grounds of irrationality following its decision to close thirty-one of the remaining fifty deep mine collieries.[114] In *Middlebrook Mushrooms*, meanwhile, the Court of Appeal refused to issue an injunction preventing union organised leafleting outside certain superstores. Such activity, the Court decided, did not interfere with any contractual relationship between employers and employees.[115] But such instances tend to be rare. Courts have, in general, sought to enforce industrial relations law, regardless of the depth of its ideological charge. In doing so, they have been forced to enjoin a nakedly political endeavour.

Enemies Without

Government has always feared the enemy within, whether it be striking workers or crowds milling in fields outside Manchester waiting to listen to radical orators. And it has always liked to pretend that 'God' and the 'Law' is on its side. For far too long, this pretence has gone unchallenged. Yet, the fear of the enemy within is nothing compared to the fear of the enemy without. Governments need bogey-men to fascinate and to terrorise the public imagination, and they need courts that are willing to play along with the fantasy.

[111] Wedderburn, 'Labour Law Now: A Hold and a Nudge' (1984) 13 *Industrial Law Journal*, 73.

[112] *Messenger Newspapers v NGA* [1984] IRLR 397; *Thomas v NUM* [1985] 2 WLR 1081; *Clarke v Heathfield* [1985] ICR 203, and 606.

[113] *Associated Newspapers v Wilson*, joined with *Associated British Ports v Palmer* [1995] 2 WLR 354.

[114] *R v British Coal Corporation ex p Vardy* [1993] ICR 720.

[115] *Middlebrook Mushrooms v TGWU* [1993] ICR 612.

Of course, wartime is peculiarly fraught, lending itself to the grossest abuse of civil liberties, such as those accepted by the House of Lords in *Liversidge v Anderson* half a century ago.[116] Paranoia in time of peace is rather less excusable. Sadly, though, it is no less common. And courts have, with rare exceptions, done little to counter it. Observations such as Lord Denning's in *Hosenball* in 1977, are all too common. Denning felt moved to observe that 'In some parts of the world national security has on occasion been used as an excuse for all sorts of infringements of individual liberty. But not in England'; an observation that was immediately qualified by his refusal to intervene if there was 'a conflict between the interests of national security on the one hand and the freedom of the individual on the other'. The balance here, he concluded, 'is not for the court of law', but for the government.[117] The paradox, and the complacency, is stark.

There has been no better recent example of this complacency, and this paranoia, than the notorious 'Spycatcher' saga in the mid 1980s.[118] As John Griffith suggests, when it comes to exposing the 'political bias of some of the most senior members of the judiciary in the most blatant way', the 'Spycatcher' saga 'towers' above the jurisprudential landscape.[119] Proceedings in 'Spycatcher' were opened in Australia, where the Attorney-General succeeded in gaining an *ex parte* order to stay publication of the memoir of a former MI5 agent. Proceedings then continued in the UK, where he secured a similar order against certain British newspapers.[120] The matters of temporary and permanent injunctions ran together throughout much of the litigation. In April 1987, matters were spiced up when the *Independent* newspaper published allegations taken from the 'Spycatcher' manuscript. The Attorney-General brought proceedings for contempt, and found a sympathetic Court of Appeal. By now, however, the *Sunday Times* had begun serialising the book, and so the *Independent* and certain other newspapers duly applied for the discharge of their particular injunction. Sir Nicholas Browne-Wilkinson agreed, commenting:

> It is frequently said that the law is an ass. I, of course, do not agree. But there is a limit to what can be achieved by orders of the court. If the courts were

[116] *Liversidge v Anderson* [1942] AC 206.

[117] *R v Secretary of State for Home Affairs ex p.Hosenball* [1977] 1 WLR 166.

[118] For a accessible, and compelling, account of the proceedings, see Griffith, above n 7, 223–32.

[119] Griffith, above n 7, 298–99.

[120] *A-G v Guardian Newspapers and the Observer* [1989] 2 FSR 23.

> to make orders manifestly incapable of achieving their avowed purpose, such as to prevent the dissemination of information which is already disseminated the law would to my mind indeed be an ass.

The Court of Appeal, however, immediately allowed the appeal. The Master of the Rolls, Sir John Donaldson, was rather less troubled with the thought that the law might appear to be an ass, and decided that the publication of the book available pretty much everywhere else in the western world, did not necessarily mean that it had passed into the 'public domain'. The injunction was modified so as to preclude the publication of specific information concerning the security services. The House of Lords, by the narrowest of margins, supported the Court of Appeal.[121]

As is so often the case in such circumstances, much the most compelling statement was given in dissent, this time by Lord Bridge, who said:

> Freedom of speech is always the first casualty under a totalitarian regime. Such a regime cannot afford to allow the free circulation of information and ideas among its citizens. Censorship is the indispensable tool to regulate what the public may and what they may not know. The present attempt to insulate the public in this country from information which is freely available elsewhere is a significant step down that very dangerous road.

In the end, the substantive matter reached the courts at the end of 1987. The Attorney-General's request for an injunction was rejected at each stage, with the House of Lords finally holding that publication of the book could not damage the 'public interest' to any greater degree than the effective circulation of its contents already had.[122] In a final petty gesture, the Attorney-General sought damages for the original alleged contempt of the temporary injunction, prior to its discharge. The Court of Appeal upheld the action, but refused to permit damages.[123] It was an appropriately ridiculous end to an absurd saga perpetuated by a government that was clearly motivated by nothing more than paranoia, and then, increasingly, spite.

The fantastic conjunction of imagined enemies within and supposed enemies without was realised, once again in suitably fantastic form, in the notorious *CCSU*, or 'GCHQ', case in 1984. In this case, the government introduced new working practices for civil servants at GCHQ,

[121] *A-G v Guardian Newspapers and Others* [1987] 1 All ER 1248.
[122] *A-G v Guardian Newspapers and Others* [1988] 3 WLR 776.
[123] *A-G v Newspaper Publishing* [1989] FSR 457.

practices which included a prohibition on membership of trade unions. They did so, perhaps not surprisingly, without consulting the unions. The House of Lords held that it needed evidence that national security was at risk, and received the scantiest of vague assertions. But it was enough. The actions of the government, though in stark contravention of principles of natural justice and legitimate expectations, was accepted. In his leading judgment Lord Diplock clung tenaciously to the doctrine of 'reasonableness', and would only review an executive action which was 'so outrageous in its defiance of logic or of accepted moral standards that no sensible person who had applied his mind to the question could have arrived at it.'[124] According to Sir Stephen Sedley, the *CCSU* case is one of the starkest examples of an innate judicial 'quietism', one which is, moreover, nourished by the 'self-congratulatory myth' that the doctrine of judicial review can alone protect individual liberties.[125]

Two decades after *CCSU*, despite the much-vaunted 'renaissance' in judicial review, judicial attitudes to the fate of alleged enemies, both within and without, remains just as supine. In the recent *Rehman* case, which involved the deportation of someone who, it was admitted, posed no immediate threat to the security of the UK, Lord Hoffmann alluded to the terrorist attacks of September 2001, observing:

> I wrote this speech some three months before the recent events in New York and Washington. They are reminders that, in matters of national security, the cost of failure can be high. This seems to me to underline the need for the judicial arm of government to respect the decision of ministers of the Crown on the question of whether support for terrorist activities in a foreign country constitutes a threat to national security. It is not only that the executive has access to special information and expertise in these matters. It is also that such decisions, with serious potential results for the community, require a legitimacy which can be conferred only by entrusting them to persons responsible to the community through the democratic process. If the people are to accept the consequences of such decisions, they must be made by persons whom the people have elected and whom they can remove.[126]

Unfortunately, it is precisely at moments such as this that strong judicial principle is most necessary. As Diana Woodhouse rightly

[124] *In re the Civil Service Unions* [1984] 3 All ER 935; *CCSU* [1985] AC 410.

[125] S Sedley, 'The Sound of Silence: Constitutional Law Without a Constitution', (1994) 110 *Law Quarterly Review*, 277–78, 281–82.

[126] *Home Secretary v Rehman* [2002] 1 All ER 122.

concludes, the 'bottom line is that human rights are more in need of protection in bad times than in good'.[127]

The 1998 Human Rights Act poses an immediate challenge to existing regulations, and attitudes, regarding the imagined enemy without. The decision of the Special Immigration Appeals Commission in *A*, in which the 2001 Anti-Terrorism, Crime and Security Act was declared to be incompatible with section 4 of the Human Rights Act, is intriguing.[128] But there has, as yet, been no sign that the government is prepared to bring domestic anti-terrorism legislation into line with the ordinary principles of the European Convention; something that has been consistently demanded by the European Court of Human Rights in cases such as *Brogan* and *Malone*.[129] The 2001 statute, moreover, was passed despite its clear infringement of precisely the same provisions.

Antagonism

Lord Irvine has recently warned against the 'unprecedented antagonisms' that appear to have arisen between the executive and the judiciary in the area of judicial review.[130] But it is more antagonism, not less, that is really needed. The 'renaissance' of judicial review has, thus far, feinted to deceive. There is still a long way to go before the principle of the rule of law can truly be said to apply to government as much as it does to the private citizen, whilst judicial attitudes towards perceived enemies both within and without can hardly be said, so far at least, to reveal an overly liberal attitude to the defence of civil liberties. But if governments feel antagonised by the courts, then there is at least reason to hope.

The truth is that we live in a world in which politics is rather more about Hobbesian conceptions of power than it is Aristotelian idylls of

[127] D Woodhouse, 'The Law and Politics: In the Shadow of the Human Rights Act', (2002) 55 *Parliamentary Affairs*, 269. The same sentiment can be found in Lord Steyn, 'Human Rights: The Legacy of Mrs Roosevelt', (2002) *Public Law*, 474.

[128] *A and Others v Secretary of State for the Home Department*, discussed in F Klug and C O'Brien, 'The first two years of the Human Rights Act', (2002) *Public Law*, 653. For a discussion of the doubts of Joint Select Committee on Human Rights see D Bonner & C Graham, 'The Human Rights Act 1998: The Story So Far', (2002) 8 *European Public Law*, 179–83.

[129] *Brogan v UK* 11 EHRR 117; *Malone v UK* 13 EHRR 448.

[130] In Williams, above n 14, 46.

consensus. Politics is a dirty business. It breeds antagonism. A notorious recent example of such antagonism between the judiciary and the executive was provided by the 'Pergau Dam' case, where a court struck down the government's attempt to use use foreign aid and developmental packages to promote business, rather than actually aid anyone who needed it. 'It seems to me', Lord Justice Rose caustically concluded, 'that if Parliament had intended to confer a power to disburse money for unsound developmental purposes, it could have been expected to say so expressly'.[131] It is one thing to have a politically contentious decision reversed in the courts; it is quite another to be ridiculed in the process.[132]

Equally illustrative are the serial spats between the courts and successive Home Secretaries over various matters generally relating to criminal justice and detention and asylum procedures. Conservative Home Secretary Michael Howard was repeatedly frustrated by the courts, not just in his efforts to reform sentencing, but also in his attempt to reform the criminal injuries compensation scheme. In striking down the latter initiative, in the *Fire Brigades Union* case, Lord Mustill observed that it had, in 'recent years', become apparent that 'minimum standards of fairness' were being flaunted by decision-making bodies. Accordingly, he continued:

> To avoid a vacuum in which the citizen would be left without protection against a misuse of executive powers the courts have had no option but to occupy the dead ground in a manner, and in areas of public life, which could not have been foreseen 30 years ago. For myself I am quite satisfied that this unprecedented role has been greatly to the public benefit.[133]

When the same Home Secretary then advanced the idea of a 'two strikes and you're out' penal policy, of the kind adopted in certain states of the US, Lord Chief Justice Taylor was happy to denounce such a scheme as 'inconsistent with doing justice' and a 'bonanza for prison architects'.[134] Other judges joined the fray. Lord Nolan thought the sentencing proposals were 'unnecessary and unjust', whilst Lord

[131] *R v Secretary of State for Foreign Affairs ex p World Development Movement* [1995] 1 WLR 386.

[132] For a defence of the judicial ruling in the *Pergau Dam* case, see Sedley, above n 76, 22–23.

[133] *R v Secretary of State for the Home Department ex p.Fire Brigades Union* [1995] 2 All ER 244, [1995] 2 AC 513.

[134] See Stevens, above n 4, 52, and M Loughlin, *Sword and Scales: An Examination of the Relationship between Law and Politics*, (Oxford, Hart, 2000), 46–49.

Donaldson suggested that they implied a deep distrust on behalf of the executive towards the courts.[135] *The Times* intimated that the case of 'Howard v the Judges' was one of the most significant constitutional engagements of the era.[136] In the words of one right-wing commentator, Boris Johnson, a 'new generation' of judges was 'coming up' and 'what especially enrages the Government is that their judgments tend to go in the liberal direction'.[137] Whilst some senior members of the judiciary seemed to relish baiting the Home Secretary, others, with perhaps a mind to future responsibilities, sounded a note of caution. Lord Irvine advised the House of Lords that in 'exercising their powers of judicial review, the judges should never give grounds for the public to believe that they intend to reverse government policies which they dislike'.[138]

Whilst the merry excesses of the Howard 'era' may have passed, the arrival of the 'new' Labour government has only marginally reduced the tension. The present Home Secretary, David Blunkett, has crossed swords with the judiciary on a number of occasions. At the Labour Party conference in 2001, Blunkett warned against the use of judicial review as a mechanism for checking government. It was, he grandly informed the awed delegates, 'justice we seek, not just the primacy of jurisprudence'.[139] His clash with the one retiring judge, Popplewell, revisited the vexed subject of sentencing policy. According to Popplewell, Blunkett was guilty of ostentatious 'whining', driven by the perpetual urge to chase 'populist gimmicks'. Blunkett preferred to think of it as 'decent common sense', and countered with the assertion that judges like Popplewell did 'not live in the real world'; or at least not in one familiar to senior Cabinet ministers.[140]

More recently Blunkett has raged against judicial interpretation of existing asylum law, and particularly Section 55 of the Nationality, Immigration and Asylum Act, which holds that support can be withdrawn from an applicant if the application for asylum was not 'made as soon as reasonably practicable'. Certain judges have refused to accept the draconian interpretation claimed by the Home Secretary, and enforced the Section 55.5 provision that the Act must not be inter-

[135] Griffith, above n 7, 51–52.
[136] Stevens, above n 4, 73.
[137] *Ibid*, 70.
[138] In Williams, above n 4, 50.
[139] Stevens, above n 4, 131.
[140] *Guardian* 15.5.03, 1.

preted in contravention of the European Convention. After one particular rebuff, the Home Secretary went on record as saying, 'Frankly, I'm fed up with having to deal with a situation where parliament debates issues and judges then overturn them.' Democracy itself, the Home Secretary pompously continued 'is under threat'.[141] It certainly is; but the danger represented by puffed-up politicians is just as great as that posed by antagonistic judges. In this context it is perhaps to be regretted that the Court of Appeal decided to retreat from reviewing asylum policy in the recent 'Oakington' case.[142] The spectre of the enemy without suddenly trying to get in was, it seems, just too terrible.

Of course, antagonism can come in various forms. One of the more oblique is the activity of judges on certain tribunals of inquiry. It is certainly no coincidence that accusations of antagonism have emerged alongside the serial judicial inquiries which have repeatedly condemned various aspects of executive action; from the Nolan and Scott Inquiries, to the Macpherson Inquiry into the Lawrence murder enquiry and the Phillips Inquiry into the government handling of the BSE scare. Current suggestions that judicial inquiries should be used more 'sparingly and selectively' speak to the lingering hope that the mask of judicial independence might be reset.[143] Judges, it is argued, should not be engaged in the dirty world of politics. They should not be placed in positions that might necessitate their antagonising the legislative or the executive. But why not? There is no compelling reason why politicians, or political cronies, would be any better suited to chairing inquiries.

Our political 'culture', as Sir Stephen Sedley has suggested, is becoming ever 'more muscular'.[144] In this context there is much to be said for annoying ministers and civil servants. It is the price that the rule of law demands of those who aspire to govern us. As Lord Chief Justice Wilmot informed the jury in the *Wilkes*, as long ago as 1769, 'The law makes no difference between great and petty officers. Thank God, they are all amenable to justice'.[145] What should worry us is not the occurrence of such antagonism, but its rarity. As Lord Steyn has rightly

141 *Guardian* 25.2.03, 17.

142 *R (Shayan and Others) v Secretary of State for the Home Department* [2001] EWCA Civ.1512. For an overview, see D Woodhouse, 'The Law and Politics: In the Shadow of the Human Rights Act', (2002) 55 *Parliamentary Affairs*, 260–61, 263–64.

143 See, for example, G Drewry, 'Judicial Inquiries and Public Reassurance' (1996) *Public Law*, 371–72.

144 Sedley, above n 76, 22.

145 *Wilkes v Lord Halifax* (1769) 19 St Tr 1406.

suggested, 'It is when there is a state of perfect harmony between the judges and the executive that citizens need to worry'.[146]

III A BRAVE NEW WORLD?

A Field Day for Crackpots?

The 1998 Human Rights Act arrived, as one commentator observed, 'wholesale from on high'.[147] It was part of the promise of 'new' Labour, and had been tested on those traditional guinea-pigs of political and constitutional innovation, the Scots. Nothing too untoward had happened north of the border, despite Lord McCluskey's suggestion that a human rights statute would inevitably prove to be 'a field day for crackpots' and a 'pain in the neck for judges'. Meanwhile, the idea that the Act should be extended to the entire country had, as Conor Gearty suggests, 'grown from an eccentric liberal side-show into a central part of our contemporary political culture'.[148]

The immediate origins of the Act were very obviously European.[149] Lord Slynn even argued that the 1972 Act has anyway rendered the European Convention good law in the UK.[150] Writing in 1992, Sir Nicholas Browne-Wilkinson suggested that the experience of European integration had already 'infiltrated' a culture of rights into English law.[151] Senior judges and commentators alike argued the case for formal incorporation of the Convention.[152] Unsurprisingly, therefore, the 1998 Act sought to incorporate most of the Convention. And so, accordingly, both the Convention 'rights' and the jurisprudence of

[146] Steyn, above n 71, 93.

[147] F Klug, *Values for a Godless Age: The Story of the United Kingdom's New Bill of Rights*, (London, Penguin, 2000) 24.

[148] C Gearty, 'The Human Rights Act 1998 and the Role of the Strasbourg Organs: Some Preliminary Reflections', in G Anderson (ed), *Rights and Democracy: Essays in UK-Canadian Constitutionalism*, (London, Blackstone, 1999), 169–70, and also Stevens, above n 4, 112.

[149] For an overview, see J Young, 'The Politics of the Human Rights Act', (1999) 26 *Journal of Law and Society*, particularly 29–34, and in a prospective sense, D Beyleveld, 'The Concept of a Human Right and Incorporation of the European Convention on Human Rights', (1995) *Public Law*, 577–98.

[150] The point is made, and strongly argued, In Beyleveld, 'Incorporation', 589–98.

[151] Sir N Browne-Wilkinson, 'The Infiltration of a Bill of Rights', (1992) *Public Law*, 405.

[152] See, for example, T Bingham, 'The European Convention on Human Rights: Time to Incorporate', (1993) 109 *Law Quarterly Review*, 398–400, Woolf, above n 74, 69–80, and Beyleveld, above n 150, 595–98.

the Strasbourg court, including the 'margin of appreciation' which gives domestic courts a certain latitude in the interpretation of these rights, enjoy a more direct force in Anglo-British public law.[153]

All the rights that are familiar to such conventions are present; the rights to life, to found a family, to privacy, and so on. And with them come all the familiar problems of interpretation. But the real problem lies with the absences and omissions. There is, for example, a signal failure to incorporate the Preamble to the Convention, which reaffirms an explicit and 'profound belief in those fundamental freedoms which are the foundations of justice and peace in the world'.[154] Not only does this omission detract from the sentiment of the Act, but so too does it deny domestic courts a valuable guide to the rationale of the rights themselves.[155]

A second problem relates to the absence of 'horizontal' applicability.[156] A horizontally applicable act would permit individuals to hold both government and private bodies, including corporations, to account. As it is, everything depends on what might be deemed a public body, and thus far, in cases such as *Poplar Housing* and the *Leonard Cheshire Foundation*, courts have been reluctant to provide any definitive guidance.[157] Moreover, the situation is confused further by the willingness of courts, in celebrated cases such as *Douglas v Hello Magazine* and *Venables*, to anyway extend Convention rights, particularly the right to privacy, to legal actions between purely private parties. In *Douglas*, Lord Justice Keene suggested that a court is itself 'a public authority' and thus 'cannot act in a way which is incompatible with a Convention right', something that vested a duty to interpret and develop 'common law, even where no public authority is party to the litigation'.[158] The suggestion echoed that made by the Lord Chancellor as he introduced the Bill in the House of Lords.[159]

[153] For a discussion of this implication, see I Leigh & L Lustgarten, 'Making Rights Real: The Courts, Remedies, and the Human Rights Act', (1999) 58 *Cambridge Law Journal*, 510, 514–17, and also, T Jones 'The Devaluation of Human Rights Under the European Convention' (1995) *Public Law*, 430–49.

[154] Indent 4.

[155] Gearty, above n 148, 173–74.

[156] For a discussion of this issue, see M Hunt, 'The Horizontal Effect of the Human Rights Act', (1998) *Public Law*, 423–43.

[157] *Poplar Housing and Regeneration Community Association v Donoghue* [2001] 4 All ER 604; *R v Leonard Cheshire Foundation* [2002] EWCA Civ.366.

[158] *Douglas v Hello Magazine* [2001] 2 WLR 992. See also *Venables v New Group Newspapers* [2001] 1 WLR 2341.

[159] F Klug and C O'Brien, 'The first two years of the Human Rights Act', (2002) *Public Law*, 657.

As a matter of principle, of course, there is no reason why such semantic games should be necessary, save for the essentially mythic determination to maintain the pretended distinction between public and private law.[160] But there is a very obvious political one. If citizens could hold government directly to account, it could have an immediate, and telling, impact upon executive prerogative. No one in the executive, it seems, was particularly thrilled by this thought. This brings us to another critical omission, that of effective remedies. Instead of incorporating Article 13 of the Convention, which requires the provision of effective remedies, section 3.1 of 1998 Act requires domestic courts to interpret legislation in a way that is compatible with the Convention in 'so far as it is possible to do so'. Although Section 6.1 says that it is 'unlawful for a public authority to act in a way which is incompatible with a Convention right', the omission of a fully effective remedy for correcting such unlawful acts is of enormous importance. As Sir Stephen Sedley has pointedly observed, 'rights without remedies are of little value'.[161]

The alternative to the formal incorporation of Article 13 is the section 4 provision, that judges can make 'declarations of incompatibility' if an existing or indeed fresh piece of legislation appears to conflict with a Convention right. Parliament can then, if it sees fit, revisit that legislation and amend it, or even repeal it. According to Lord Chancellor Irvine, it strikes 'the right balance between the judiciary and Parliament', for 'incorporation' of the Convention 'must not disturb Parliament's supremacy'.[162] Thus far, there have been a handful of declarations, concerning, for example, fixed penalties imposed on a 'no-fault' basis for carriers found to have transported illegal immigrants, and the incompatibility between certain sections of the 1983 Mental Health Act with Article 5 of the Convention.[163] The earth is not moving.

It may be that existing domestic legislation is already fully in accord with the basic provisions of European human rights law. Or it may be that the various strategic omissions in the 1998 Act have succeeded in

[160] S Sedley, *Freedom, Law and Justice*, (London, Sweet & Maxwell, 1999), 22–25.

[161] *Ibid*, 3.

[162] See Lord Irvine, 'The Development of Human Rights in Britain under an Incorporated Convention on Human Rights', (1998) *Public Law*, 225, and A Barnett, *This Time: Our Constitutional Revolution*, (London, Vintage, 1997), 21–.

[163] *International Transport Roth v Secretary of State for the Home Department* [2002] EWCA Civ.158; *R v Mental Health Review Tribunal* [2001] 3 WLR 5112.

deadening the effect of incorporation.[164] The statistics are suggestive. So far, only about 15% of cases in which it was alleged that a Convention right has been infringed have been successful.[165] As we have already noted, neither government nor courts have been inclined to deploy it against legislation that purports to deal with terrorism or national security. Whilst the Act has been cited on a number of occasions in various courts, it has hardly heralded a juristic revolution. The courts seemed to have accepted the Lord Chancellor's urgent injunction to cast aside any actions that might be deemed fanciful. The adage of the baby and the bath-water springs to mind.

Indeed, critics have suggested that decisions in early cases such as *Alconbury* were a conscious attempt at 'Strasbourg proofing'.[166] In *Alconbury* the House of Lords swiftly overturned a Divisional Court judgment had held that the Department of the Environment, Transport and the Regions was not an 'independent and impartial' authority, as required by Article 6, when engaged in considering planning decisions. As Lord Hoffmann put it, 'the Human Rights Act of 1998 was no doubt intended to strengthen the rule of law, but not to inaugurate the rule of lawyers'.[167] The courts have tended to follow the spirit of *Alconbury* in a variety of cases, from banning travel abroad for suspected football hooligans in *Gough*, to upholding the validity of social banning orders in *ex p McCann*, to refusing to injunct newspapers from reporting the sexual exploits of professional footballers in *A v B*.[168]

All in all, as Lord Hoffmann predicted, the anticipated impact of the of the Act had 'been greatly exaggerated'.[169] For this reason, unsurprisingly, initial criticism has tended to be negative. According to James Young, the 1998 Act is little more than a 'lawyer's provision for lawyers', whilst Tom Campbell suggests that it appears to be at the

[164] For an overview of the sovereignty issue, see D Feldman, 'The Human Rights Act 1998 and Constitutional Principles', 1999) 19 *Legal Studies*, 185–91, and also Leigh & Lustgarten, above n 153, 536–42.

[165] Woodhouse, above n 127, 254, and Klug & O'Brien, above n 159, 649–50.

[166] See L Clements, 'The Human Rights Act—A New Equity or a New Opiate: Reinventing Justice or Repackaging State Control?' (1999) 26 *Journal of Law and Society*, 76–77.

[167] *R (Alconbury Developments) v Secretary of State for the Environment, Transport and the Regions* [2001] 2 All ER 929. For a commentary see, I Loveland, 'Alconbury in the House of Lords', *New Law Journal* 18.5.2001, 713.

[168] *Gough v Chief Constable of Derbyshire* [2001] 4 All ER 289; *R (ex p McCann) v Crown Court at Manchester* [2001] 4 All ER 264; *A v B* [2002] 1 All ER 449.

[169] Lord Hoffmann, 'Human Rights and the House of Lords', (1999) 62 *Modern Law Review*, 161.

'modest end of the range of alternatives'.[170] The absence of effective remedies is rightly condemned by many.[171] As we leave the bare bones of the 1998 Act, puzzled perhaps by its rather emaciated condition, it is perhaps worth recalling the comments of Prime Minister Blair, made just a year after coming to office. 'A decent society is not actually based on rights', he averred. 'It is based on duty'.[172] The sense of muted enthusiasm for rights, even from its putative political champions, is tangible.

Rights and Wrongs

Historically, the English have never been terribly comfortable with the idea of rights, certainly not those that are proclaimed to be somehow 'natural'. Having listened to Blackstone's lectures on the subject, Jeremy Bentham dismissed the idea of 'natural rights' as 'nonsense on stilts'. In his *Principles of Morals and Legislation*, Bentham identified this particular 'nonsense' as typical of the 'suspicious fancy' with which English common lawyers clothed their metaphysical jurisprudence.[173] His pupil, John Austin, was just as dismissive. In his *Province of Jurisprudence Determined*, he denounced the idea of natural rights as 'stark nonsense', part of the 'muddy speculation' that shrouded the history of English constitutional law.[174] And Dicey was, unsurprisingly, hugely sceptical, declaring that the Habeas Corpus Acts, whilst they 'declare no principle and define no rights' were 'for practical guidance worth a hundred constitutional articles guaranteeing individual liberty'. He admitted that there were three kinds of common law 'right'—to 'personal freedom', to 'discussion' and to 'public meetings'; but did so with precious little enthusiasm.[175]

Constitutional history reveals the occasional judicial foray in support of putative civil 'rights'. Lord Atkin's dissent in *Liversidge* is justly famous:

[170] See Young, above n 149, 37, and T Campbell, 'Human Rights: A Culture of Controversy', (1999) 26 *Journal of Law and Society*, 7.

[171] See K Ewing, 'The Human Rights Act and Parliamentary Democracy', (1999) 62 *Modern Law Review*, 84–6.

[172] Klug, above n 147, 59.

[173] J Bentham, *An Introduction to the Principles of Morals and Legislation*, (London, Methuen, 1982), xxxvi, 4, 17–20.

[174] See J Austin, *The Province of Jurisprudence Determined*, (Cambridge UP, 1995), 19–20, 38–57, 73, 154.

[175] Dicey, above n 35,199.

> I view with apprehension the attitude of judges who on a mere question of construction when face to face with claims involving the liberty of the subject show themselves more executive minded than the subject . . . It has always been one of the pillars of freedom, one of the principles of liberty for which on recent authority we are now fighting, that the judges are no respecters of persons and stand between the subject and any attempted encroachments on his liberty by the executive, alert to see that any coercive action is justified in law. In this case I have listened to arguments which might have been addressed acceptably to the Court of King's Bench in the time of Charles I.[176]

In general, however, as recent cases such as *CCSU* reveal, English judges have shared Bentham's scepticism.[177] The mood was captured in Denning's sniffy dismissal, in *Becker*, of the idea that 'disgruntled prisoners' might have rights.[178]

It is this history of scepticism, if not hostility, that has prompted so much debate about the need for a 'culture' of rights to complement the 1998 Act. Ushering the statute through Parliament, the Home Secretary announced that it would 'bring about the creation of a human rights culture in Britain'.[179] It would, he later added, be a culture founded on 'considerations of common humanity'.[180] The implication was drawn out by Lord Howe who observed that an effective culture of rights will 'depend at least as much upon an enlightened public opinion' as 'upon anything the law might design'.[181] In the same vein, Tom Campbell has argued that a 'human rights culture may be political rather than legal in nature, preferring debate to litigation'.[182] The rather narrower legalistic implications were also predicted by Lord Irvine who welcomed the prospect of a new 'culture in judicial decision making where there will be a greater concentration on substance rather than form'.[183]

All in all, enthusiasts of the idea of rights, and statutes of rights, have welcomed what Francesca Klug terms the 'new spirit of the age'.[184] Helena Kennedy, for example, celebrates the arrival of the Act with the

[176] *Liversidge v Anderson* [1942] AC 206.

[177] For a commentary on rights in the context of the *CCSU* case, see Sedley, above n 125, 277–78, 281–82.

[178] *Becker v Home Office* [1972] 2 QB 407.

[179] Klug, above n 147, 7, 49.

[180] Klug, above n 147, 66.

[181] G Howe, 'Sovereignty, Democracy and Human Rights', (1995) 66 *Political Quarterly*, 137.

[182] Campbell, above n 170, 25.

[183] Irvine, above n 162, 236.

[184] Klug, above n 147, 6–7.

observation that it represents 'a different *Zeitgeist*, a shift in the legal tectonic'.[185] Sir Stephen Sedley sees it as leading 'English law' into 'what is certainly a new phase, possibly a new era', whilst Lord Steyn advances the thought that the incorporation of the Convention has 'generally accelerated the constitutionalisation of our public law'.[186] The thought that the Act might supplement a wider recasting of our constitution, one that reinvests dormant conceptions of liberty and rights, is striking; for reasons that we will investigate shortly.

The cultural idea of rights is, of course, quintessentially liberal. It found expression in the great Enlightenment defences of rights, such as Tom Paine's *Rights of Man* and Immanuel Kant's *Metaphysics of Morals*. According to both Paine and Kant, civil rights are derived from natural rights. As Paine averred, the 'origin of rights' can be traced to the 'origin of man' himself, they 'appertain to man by right of his existence'; and they are universal too, enjoyed by all, equally.[187] Kant, too, described a 'principle of innate freedom', one that inheres an 'innate equality, that is, independence from being bound by others to more than one can in turn bind them'.[188] Civil rights, accordingly, were valid only so far as they approximated to the metaphysical principles of natural rights. It was for this reason that Paine was so caustic in his dismissal of the Bill of Rights, 'more properly called a bill of wrongs'.[189]

Contemporary liberal defences of rights have revealed a greater determination to accommodate Aristotelian conceptions of the 'good community'. John Rawls advanced his idea of an 'overlapping consensus' as a means by which the political morality of a community can accommodate the differing morality of individual citizens.[190] Ronald Dworkin has similarly argued that political rights must be set within a 'constellation of principles', and it is the duty of the judge to interpret these rights within that particular 'constellation'.[191] This approach has found a compelling recent echo in Sir John Laws suggestion that a human rights 'culture' can only be forged in the 'crucible of a life

[185] Klug, above n 147, *Values*, xi.

[186] Sedley, above n 160, 19, and Lord Steyn, 'The Case for a Supreme Court', (2002) 118 *Law Quarterly Review*, 385.

[187] T Paine, *The Rights of Man*, (London, Penguin, 1984), 65–66, 68.

[188] I Kant, *The Metaphysics of Morals*, (Cambridge University Press, 1991), 63.

[189] Paine, above n 187, 193.

[190] J Rawls, *Political Liberalism*, (New York, Columbia University Press, 1993), 164–72, 213–15.

[191] R Dworkin, *Taking Rights Seriously*, (London, Duckworth, 1977), 42–44, 55–57, and *Law's Empire*, (Oxford, Hart, 1986), 50–55, 151–52, 167–75, 243.

shared with others', and is the reflection, above all, of a 'shared morality, which defines the 'good' community.[192]

The sceptical voice, of course, remains. The critic of liberalism is a critic of rights. 'Critical' legal scholars such as Peter Gabel and Duncan Kennedy have railed against rights as 'illusions' and 'myths', designed to furnish individuals with a false sense of security against both the ravages of government and the realities of social inequality and injustice.[193] In like vein, Jonathan Morgan has suggested that the 1998 Act is a 'nakedly' political instrument', one that promotes a 'particular, radical, liberal social agenda'.[194] There is also a collateral criticism of disutility. Human rights statutes, it is suggested, bring out the Pangloss in all of us; like Voltaire's protagonist, we naturally assume that because we have been gifted a set of rights we must indeed live in the 'best of all possible worlds'. Doom-mongers such as Allan Hutchinson castigate the 'attenuated discourse of rights-talk' that will necessarily accompany the 1998 Act. It will, he alleges, come to represent a 'huge step backwards on the path to truly democratic government'.[195]

On occasion, moreover, the Act may also prove to be less than progressive. In *R v A*, for example, the House of Lords held that a statutory provision designed to prevent rape victims from having to suffer the trauma of cross-examination on their past sexual history was overridden by the right to a 'fair trial'.[196] And then there is the matter of indeterminacy, the conflict of different rights. In the recent case of *D*, for example, a health authority sought permission not to resuscitate a terminally ill patient, against the wishes of the parents who cited the Article 2 right to life, as well as the Article 3 right not to be 'subjected to torture or to inhuman or degrading treatment or punishment'. The court held that such permission could be granted, in order to allow the patient to die with dignity, a reversal of the parents' understanding of Article 3.[197]

The ethical landscape is a treacherous one, and notorious cases such as *Shaw v DPP* and *Knuller*, and more recently *Brown*, suggest that the judiciary tends to prefer a distinctly conservative conception of morality; of the kind that found notorious expression on the opening page of

[192] J Laws, 'The Constitution: Morals and Rights', 627, 635.

[193] See, for example, P Gabel & D Kennedy, 'Roll Over Beethoven', (1984) 36 *Stanford Law Review* 1984, 33–36.

[194] J Morgan, 'Law's British Empire', (2002) 22 *Oxford Journal of Legal Studies*, 734.

[195] A Hutchinson, 'Supreme Court Inc', in Anderson, above n 148, 30, 44.

[196] *R v A* [2001] 3 All ER 1. See also, Morgan, above n 194, 742.

[197] *A National Health Service Trust v D* [2000] 2 FCR 577.

Lord Devlin's essay *The Enforcement of Morals*, with its denunciation of 'homosexuality' as 'a miserable way of life', one that it is 'duty of society', and its judges, 'to save any youth from being led' into.[198] The 'culture' of rights that should complement the 1998 Act will need to evidence a rather greater tolerance. Human rights are as much about understanding the human as they are about effecting the right.[199]

Above all, the arrival of the Act will immerse courts, more and more, in the hardest of 'hard cases'. It will demand, as Lord Irvine acknowledged, an 'explicitly moral approach to decisions and decision-making'.[200] In the tragic case involving the separation of Siamese twins, *Re A*, the presiding judge confessed that the moral questions involved, the possible killing of one child in order to save the other, were 'excruciatingly difficult'.[201] At some point the most sophisticated of human rights statutes reaches its limits.

A Brave New World?

One of the last veils to be lifted from the image of judicial independence was the Kilmuir 'rules', intended to forestall extra-judicial utterances. According to their eponymous originator:

> The overriding opinion, of myself and my colleagues, is the importance of keeping the judiciary in this country insulated from the controversies of the day. So long as a judge keeps silent his reputation for wisdom and impartiality remains unassailable: but every utterance which he makes in public, except in the course of his judicial duties, must necessarily bring him within the focus of criticism.[202]

It was a testament to the absurd, to the belief that the myth of judicial impartiality might be maintained by pretending that judges were devoid of opinion.

The 'rules' were finally lifted in 1987. Since then it has become rather easier to read the judicial mind. And what has become particularly

[198] *Shaw v DPP* [1961] 2 WLR 897; *R v Knuller* [1972] 3 WLR 143; *R v Brown* [1993] 2 All ER 75, and P Devlin, *The Enforcement of Morals* (Oxford UP, 1968), v.

[199] C Douzinas, *The End of Human Rights: Critical Legal Thought at the Turn of the Century*, (Hart, 2000), 1–4, 17–19, 121–31. For a similar view, see S Toope, 'Cultural Diversity and Human Rights', (1997) 42 *McGill Law Journal*, 171.

[200] Klug, above n 147, 33.

[201] In Woodhouse, above n 2, 227–28.

[202] Griffith, above n 7, 42.

striking is the extent to which a number of senior members of the judiciary have welcomed the possibilities that the 'renaissance' in judicial review and the Human Rights Act introduce. The welcome articulated by three such members, Sir Stephen Sedley, Sir John Laws and Lord Steyn, is particularly striking; not least because each aligns this 'renaissance' with the idea of a broader recasting of a distinctive 'common law' constitutionalism.

Sir Stephen Sedley, for example, suggests that 'the common law itself has both the capacity and the obligation to move in the next generation towards a principled constitutional order'. After all, English constitutional law has always comprised a 'common law ocean dotted with islands of statutory provisions', and nothing has changed.[203] The 'main crucible of modern constitutional law', according to Sedley, is the kind of common law constitutionalism that was championed by judges such as Lord Chief Justice Coke and later Lord Chief Justice Wilmot who supported John Wilkes's assertion that the rule of law underpinned the very idea of an English constitution.[204] In simple terms, the residue of sovereignty lies, as Wilkes argued, in the people. It does not lie, as Dicey subsequently countered, in Parliament.[205] It is, ultimately, Sedley concludes, a matter of rethinking the meaning of democracy:

> A democracy is more than a state in which power resides in the hands of a majority of elected representatives: it is a state in which individuals and minorities have an assurance of certain basic protections from the majoritarian interest, and in which independent courts of law hold the responsibility for interpreting, applying and—importantly—supplementing the law laid down by Parliament in the interests of every individual, not merely the represented majority.[206]

The arrival of the Human Rights Act adds a very obvious impetus to the recasting of the constitution in these terms. For Sedley, the idea of rights resonates with a very English, and very liberal, political theory, of the kind that reached its apogee in the 'possessive individualism' of John Stuart Mill's 'harm principle'.[207]

[203] Sedley, above n 125, 273.
[204] Sedley, above n 125, 287, 291, and above n 76, 12–14, 37.
[205] S Sedley, 'The Constitution in the Twenty-first Century' in Nolan & Sedley, above n 76, 85.
[206] Sedley, above n 76, 25.
[207] S Sedley, 'Human Rights: a Twenty-First Century Agenda', (1995) *Public Law*, 386, 391.

Sir John Laws has similarly invoked Mill's principle, arguing that a 'good constitution must vouchsafe legal arrangements to secure that no one's freedom of action is curtailed, save on grounds justified by the need to protect the rights and freedoms of others'.[208] At the same time, he has also immersed himself in the rather more metaphysical world of Kantian 'higher-order' law. In this world, the primary responsibility of judges is not merely to protect individual rights, but to check government. 'Ultimate sovereignty rests', accordingly, 'in every civilised constitution, not with those who wield governmental power, but in the conditions under which they are permitted to do so'. It follows, therefore, that the 'constitution, not the Parliament, is in this sense sovereign'. There are certain 'fundamental principles' which underpin the 'imperative of democracy', and which are derived not just from the 'sovereign autonomy of the individual', but from a 'description' of the 'moral nature' of humanity itself. Government must govern in accordance with these principles. A 'good constitution', Laws concludes, is one in which the authority of any political institution, even a parliament, is subservient to the 'fundamental' rights which pertain to a human being.[209]

Dicey would be appalled at such sentiments. He would have been little more enamoured by Sedley's similarly resonant conclusion, that the UK must develop a new 'juridical culture'; one which 'does not imagine that the poorest citizen is made equal to the richest corporation simply by according both the same rights; one which does not co-opt the powerless into the opposition of the powerful to the state'; one 'which perceives the role of power in determining who gets to drink first and longest at the well'; and one 'which understands above all that in every society fundamental human rights, to be real, have to steer towards outcomes which invert those inequalities of power that mock the principle of equality before the law'.[210]

Finally, the wider constitutional implications of the Act have also been vividly advanced by Lord Steyn. The Act, Steyn suggests, 'cannot exist in a constitutional vacuum', but rather must 'fit into a constitutional structure of democratic character'.[211] Parliament, as he noted in *ex p Pierson*, does not 'legislate in a vacuum', but rather 'legislates for

[208] Laws, above n 192, 627.

[209] J Laws, 'Law and Democracy', (1995) *Public Law*, 81–87, 92–93, above n 96, and also above n 192, 624–27, 635.

[210] Sedley, above n 207, 400.

[211] Steyn, above n 207, 480, 482.

a European liberal democracy based upon the principles and traditions of the common law'.[212] The 'rule of law', alongside a properly secured separation of powers, must be reinvested at the heart of a distinctive 'principle of constitutionalism'. Such a principle is a:

> political theory as to the type of institutional arrangements that are necessary in order to support the democratic ideal. It holds that the exercise of government power must be controlled in order that it should not be destructive of the very values which it was intended to promote. It requires of the executive more than loyalty to the existing constitution. It is concerned with the merits and quality of constitutional arrangements.[213]

It is a conclusion that chimes with Laws' recent suggestion in *Roth* that the Anglo-British constitution is presently at 'an intermediate stage between parliamentary supremacy and constitutional supremacy'.[214] It is in this context that Laws has also suggested, in *Thoburn*, that judges must now think in terms of a hierarchy of statutes; appreciating the relative status of 'ordinary' statutes and 'constitutional' statutes.[215] The latter species of statute, of which the Human Rights Act is perhaps the most obvious example, assume a particular or, as he put it in *Prolife Alliance*, 'autonomous', authority.[216] The sense of evolution, of fundamental constitutional change, is striking; and it is a change that is being advanced, not just in academic journals, but in English courtrooms.

Of course, the 'brave new world' charted by the likes of Sedley, Laws and Steyn has attracted its sceptics. John Griffith is right to note the variable history of the English judiciary in promoting a progressive politics.[217] And the democratic question remains pertinent:

> The trouble with the higher-order law is that it must be given substance, be interpreted, and be applied. It claims superiority over democratically elected institutions; it prefers philosopher-kings to human politicians; it puts its faith in judges whom I would trust no more than I trust princes.[218]

212 *R v Home Secretary ex p.Pierson* [1998] AC 575.

213 Steyn, above n 71, 87–88.

214 *International Transport Roth v Secretary of State for the Home Department* [2002] EWCA Civ 158 para 71.

215 *Thoburn v Sunderland City Council* [2001] EWCH Admin 934 para 62.

216 *Prolife Alliance v BBC* [2002] EWCA Civ 297 para 34.

217 J Griffith, 'The Brave New World of Sir John Laws', (2000) 63 *Modern Law Review*, 163. See also, Oliver, above n 2, 21–25.

218 Griffith, *ibid*, 165. The same broad sentiment can be found in R Ekins, 'Judicial Supremacy and the Rule of Law', (2003) 119 *Law Quarterly Review*, 144 and R Mullender, 'Parliamentary Sovereignty, the Constitution and the Rule of Law', (1998) 49 *Northern Ireland Legal Quarterly*, 138–66.

An over-mighty judiciary can indeed pose as great a danger to individual rights and liberties as an over-mighty executive. But this scepticism is founded upon an emaciated idea of representative democracy, one that has created a modern caste of grotesquely over-mighty executive princes. So long as our constitution remains unbalanced, and our system of governance endemically corrupt, then there is something to be said for a judiciary that is prepared to be just a little antagonistic.

4

England and its Empires

THE PREAMLE TO the 1533 Act in Restraint of Appeals proclaimed an English constitution that was established in 'divers sundry old authentic histories and chronicles', and which vested in the king a legitimacy that was 'institute and furnished by the goodness and sufferance of Almighty God with plenary, whole and entire power, pre-eminence, authority, prerogative and jurisdiction to render and yield justice and final determination of all manner' of legal dispute. The Act further proclaimed an English 'empire', in effect much of Wales and a bit of Ireland. The break with Rome is the great caesura in English history; our re-engagement with European *res publica* the defining political event of the present generation.

According to the revered legal historian, Frederick Maitland, the 1533 Act was, quite simply, the most 'momentous' event in English constitutional history.[1] More recently, Norman Davies has similarly suggested that the Henrician statutes of reformation founded the modern 'Anglo-British state'.[2] They defined the future of the 'chosen people' and their successive Fairy Kings and Queens. For countless generations to come, the English would live their lives as if 'in the pages of the Bible'.[3] Edmund Spenser's *Faerie Queene* proclaimed a distinctive crusading people, doing God's work, building empires and slaughtering the ungodly. The Redcrosse Knight, who ventures forth to slay all manner of beasts, ogres and Frenchmen, does so in the express service of the 'new Hierusalem, that God has built' for those 'that are chosen his'.[4] Another of the great Elizabethan poet-chroniclers, Sir Philip Sidney, described the English in his *Arcadia* as an elect and 'only' people, governed both by 'justice and providence'.[5]

[1] F Maitland, *Roman Canon Law in the Church of England*, (London, Methuen, 1898), 92.

[2] N Davies, *The Isles: A History*, (Basingstoke, Macmillan, 1999), 452–53.

[3] P Collinson, *The Birthpangs of Protestant England*, (Basingstoke, Macmillan, 1988), 7–10.

[4] E Spenser, *Complete Poetical Works*, (Oxford UP, 1980), 1.9.53, 1.10.19, 57, 61.

[5] 'Old Arcadia', in P Sidney, *A Critical Edition of the Major Works*, (Oxford UP, 1989), 8/30–32, 29/23–24, 33/23–24, 358/2–359/7.

Half a millennia later, however, the 'chosen people' seem, in Davies's words, to be 'manifestly bewildered'; abandoned by God, divested of their empires, both 'outer' and 'inner', tempted once again by the European *res publica*, but troubled by it too.[6] Half a century ago, US Secretary of State Dean Acheson famously observed that 'Great Britain has lost an empire, and has not yet found a role'. It is still the case. Rather more recently, David Cannadine has confirmed that we now live in a 'diminished, post-imperial' Britain, and we do so in considerable discomfort.[7] For some the apparent demise of the English and their empire is a matter of little regret. 'Damn you England', declared the playwright John Osborne, a generation ago. 'You're rotting now, and quite soon you'll disappear'.[8] For others, however, the bitterness was tinged with sorrow. A wistful Noel Coward bemoaned 'The slow decline of our island race', its empire allowed to slip away whilst God's chosen people were 'engrossed' in their 'football pools'.[9] The 'united' Kingdom, its empire and its constitution; all suddenly seem rather arcane. The sense that the internal organs of the Anglo-British constitution are themselves riddled with disease has been complemented by the growing realisation that the outer façade is just crumbling away. All that awaits is to put the body in the ground.

I A NEW WORLD ORDER

The Best of All Possible Worlds?

A decade ago, the American philosopher, Francis Fukuyama notoriously announced the 'end of history'. According to Fukuyama, there was a 'remarkable consensus' that the 'ideal' of liberal democracy could not be 'improved upon'.[10] History had simply worked itself

[6] The idea of an 'inner' empire, described by the fictions of the 'united' Kingdom, and an 'outer' empire, depicting the rather grander trans-continental ventures, was first deployed by the renowned Victorian historian Sir John Seeley, and has been more recently redeployed by Norman Davies. See Davies, above n 2, 866–67, and also 990 commenting on our 'bewildered' state.

[7] D Cannadine, *In Churchill's Shadow: Confronting the Past in Modern Britain*, (Oxford UP, 2002), 21, 26.

[8] In J Paxman, *The English: A Portrait of a People*, (London, Michael Joseph, 1998), 233.

[9] In Cannadine, above n 7, 276.

[10] F Fukuyama, *The End of History and the Last Man*, (London, Penguin, 1992), xi–xx, 13–18, 31.

through, and alighted upon the best form of government. It was, to borrow Voltaire's ironic assertion, the 'best of all possible worlds'.[11] In his 1991 State of the Union address, US President George Bush had heralded the emergence of a 'new world order'. It was his 'big idea', one that he cast in terms of an era of coming 'peace and security, freedom and the rule of law'. It seemed to chime with the end of the Cold War, and the first Gulf War too, with the tearing down of the Berlin wall, and the opening up of global markets with the completion of the Uruguay round of the GATT (General Agreement on Tariffs and Trade).

The idea of a 'new world order' cannot be readily extricated from that of globalization. It is an order of vast transnational economic regimes; NAFTA, ASEAN, the World Trade Organisation (which superceded GATT), the European Community and Union, and so on. The global 'village', as it has been rightly suggested, has been constructed 'from the economic ground up'.[12] And its reach is vast, and thoroughly destabilizing, affecting us all in different ways, disrupting received senses of time and space. According to Thomas Friedman, 'All politics is now global. Not every country may feel itself part of the globalization system, but every country is directly or indirectly being shaped and affected by this system'.[13] Boaventure Santos has spoken of an overlapping relation of the global and the local, of 'globalized localism', meaning the globalization of local phenomena, and 'localized globalism', meaning changes in local conditions in response to global pressures.[14] International relations scholars have coined the phrase 'glocalism' in order to give this rather bewildering experience a shorthand expression. But the reality defies simplification. The 'new world order' seems to have shrunk the globe, just as it appears to have become more powerful and more intrusive than ever.

The paradoxes abound. For the 'new world order' is also, potentially at least, rather less stable and more fragmentary. It is haunted, as Benjamin Barber prophesised, by two 'specters'. The first is the 'retribalization of large swaths of humankind by war and bloodshed: a threatened Lebanonization of nation states in which culture is pitted against culture, people against people, tribe against tribe'. The second

[11] Voltaire, *Candide*, (London, Penguin, 1947).

[12] S Rosow, 'Globalisation as Democratic Theory', (2000) 29 *Millenium*, 29.

[13] T Friedman, *The Lexus and the Olive Tree*, (Anchor, 2000), 76.

[14] B Santos, *Towards a New Common Sense: Law, Science and Politics in Paradigmatic Transition*, (London, Routledge, 1995), 263.

'is being borne in on us by the onrush of economic and ecological forces that demand integration and uniformity and that mesmerize the world with fast music, fast computers, and fast food'. There was, he noted with some prescience, a real danger in living in 'one McWorld tied together by technology, ecology, communications, and commerce'. 'The planet', he concluded, 'is falling precipitately apart and coming reluctantly together at the very same moment'.[15]

The geo-political implications of globalization are vast. George Soros fears the onset of a new 'totalitarianism', an era of unconstrained global capitalism crushing the aspirations of liberal democratic politics, based as they are in smaller, generally national, communities.[16] As Will Hutton suggests, globalization appears to be just another form of Hobbesian politics, an 'exercise of raw power'.[17] And it is not optional. In similar vein, Stephen Gill refers to a pervasive, malignant spirit of 'commodification' that seeks to crush countervailing notions of community and localised sources of culture.[18] The 'spectres' of modernity as the controversial French philosopher Jacques Derrida terms them, are the harbingers of 'violence, inequality, exclusion, famine'.[19] Philip Allott puts it eloquently; 'With the globalization of mass culture, the many of humanity are adrift in a sea of collective fantasy, sleepwalking in a waking dream, formed and manipulated by the few who manage the great systems of mental production, the mass reality industry'.[20] More and more, we find our lives propelled by external dynamics, by the myriad forces of globalization; forces over which we appear to have limited democratic control.

And along the way, the 'old' world order, of autonomous nation-states, appears to have been crushed. In pronouncing the collateral 'end of the nation-state', Keniche Ohmae famously advised that 'in terms of the global economy, nation-states have become little more than bit actors', their power now dispersed amongst consumers and trans-national corporations, global institutions and regional 'states'. The

[15] B Barber, 'Jihad v McWorld', (1992) *The Atlantic*, 53.

[16] In B Barber, 'Can Democracy Survive Globalization?' (2000) 35 *Government and Opposition*, 299.

[17] In A Giddens and W Hutton, 'In Conversation', in A Giddens and W Hutton (eds), *On the Edge: Living with Global Capitalism*, (London, Jonathan Cape, 2000), 41.

[18] S Gill, 'Globalisation, Market Civilization and Disciplinary Neoliberalism', (1995) 24 *Millenium*, 402–10.

[19] J Derrida, *Specters of Marx*, (London, Routledge, 1994), 56–75, 85.

[20] P Allott, 'Reconstituting Humanity—New International Law', 3 *European Journal of International Law*, 233.

'old world', he concluded, has quite simply 'fallen apart'.[21] The idea of a countervailing process of global integration and disintegration is further reinforced by cold statistics. In 1975, for example, total foreign investments worldwide amounted to just $23bn. By 1997, that figure was $644bn. By the end of the 1990s, daily currency exchanges amount to around $1.5 trillion; a vast 'virtual economy' that exists only in the minds of its currency trading junkies.

The Anglo-British state is rooted in this 'old world'. And it is most certainly falling apart; as John Dearlove argues, reduced to nothing more than 'a complex of governance structures'. In the 'new world order', there is 'little left for' an identifiably 'British politics'.[22] The constitutional pretences of Fairyland may continue, but in reality its impact upon our everyday lives is becoming ever more marginal. And nowhere is this more obvious than in the Britain's fraught relationship with the 'new' Europe. In a very real sense, the 'new' Europe is the flagship of a 'new' world order.[23] According to George Soros, along with the 'future of Europe', lies the 'validity of the concept of an open society'.[24] It is an interesting thought, not least because so much contemporary discussion of a new global politics oscillates around classical ideas of a revitalized *ius humanitatis*. William Twining, for example, argues that there must be a 're-mapping' of public law, one that properly 'emphasises the complexities and elusiveness of reality, the difficulties of grasping it, and the value of imagination and multiple perspectives in facing these difficulties'.[25] Michael Sandel similarly invokes a 'cosmopolitan ideal' that 'rightly emphasises the humanity we share and directs our attention to the moral consequences that flow from it'.[26]

[21] K Ohmae, *The End of the Nation State and the Rise of Global Capitalism*, (London, HarperCollins, 1996), 7, 12, 15–16, 80–85.

[22] J Dearlove, 'Globalisation and British Politics', (2000) 20 *Politics*, 112, 117.

[23] W Hutton, *The World We're In*, (Boston, Little Brown, 2002), 10–18, 48, 312, 365.

[24] G Soros, 'The Global Financial Adventure', in A Giddens & W Hutton (eds), *On the Edge: Living with Global Capitalism*, (London, Jonathan Cape, 2000), 329.

[25] W Twining, *Globalization and Legal Theory*, (London, Butterworths, 2000), 140, 152, 172–74.

[26] M Sandel, *Democracy's Discontent: America in Search of a Public Philosophy*, (Cambridge, Mass, Harvard UP, 1960, 341.

An Ever Closer Union

Much appears to depend upon the fate of the 'new' Europe. Of course, it is only 'new' in one sense. The idea of a unified European *res publica* is centuries old. So, too, is the thought that it might be founded on a common market. Resurrecting this aspiration, Article 2 of the Treaty of Rome expressed the desire to:

> promote throughout the Community a harmonious development of economic activities, a continuous and balanced expansion, an increased stability, an accelerated raising of the standard of living and closer relations between its Member States.

Three points must be noted. First, the Community was created to make money. As the Preamble to the Treaty rather grandiloquently implied, the creation of economic wealth, the 'pooling of resources', was the best way 'to preserve and strengthen peace and liberty' in Europe. Second, the Rome Treaty sought to describe a Europe of nation-states. Third, the Community was merely founded. It was not settled. There was an implicit expectation that a process of integration would constantly reshape the 'new' Europe.[27]

There was also an implicit assumption that it would be shaped by lawyers. Article 220 (ex 164) of the Rome Treaty established a Court of Justice, and it is this court which has forged the rules by which the market operates. The first such rule is the supremacy of Community law.[28] In the seminal case of *Costa v ENEL*, in 1964, the Court stated that:

> By contrast with ordinary international treaties, the EEC Treaty has created its own legal system which on entry into force of the Treaty became an integral part of the legal systems of the Member States and which their courts are bound to apply. By creating a Community of unlimited duration, having... powers stemming from a limitation of sovereignty, or a transfer of powers from the States to the Community, the Member States have limited their sovereign rights, albeit within limited fields, and have thus created a body of law which binds both their nationals and themselves.[29]

[27] Art 8 of the Treaty reaffirmed that the market should be 'progressively established in the course of a transitional period of twelve years'. Of course, it was barely any more firmly established at the end of the twelve year period than it was at the start.

[28] According to Pavlos Eleftheriadis, it is 'the most important constitutional issue of the Community legal order'. See P Eleftheriadis, 'Aspects of European Constitutionalism', (1998) 21 *European Law Review*, 257.

[29] *Costa v ENEL* 6/64 [1964] ECR 593.

From this early decision it was clear that notions of 'unitary' constitutional sovereignty would have no sensible meaning in any Member State. The implications were laid bare once again in *Internationale Handelsgeselschaft* in 1970:

> In fact, the law stemming from the Treaty, an independent source of law, cannot because of its very nature be overridden by rules of national law, however framed, without being deprived of its character as Community law and without the legal basis of the Community itself being called into question. Therefore the validity of a Community measure or its effect within a Member State cannot be affected by allegations that it runs counter to either fundamental rights as formulated by the constitution of the State or the principles of a national constitutional structure.[30]

The principle was further refined in the 1978 *Simmenthal* case, where the Court affirmed that the principle of supremacy must 'render automatically inapplicable any conflicting provision of current national law'.[31]

Alongside the principle of supremacy, the Court of Justice also devised a principle of direct effect, designed to ensure the enforceability of Community law. Directives, the primary form of Community law, transfer responsibility for implementation to nation-states. Direct effect is meant to ensure that implementation is 'fully effective', holding Member States directly responsible for any failure to do so.[32] It has been suggested that the *Van Gend* case, in which the Court first advanced the idea of 'direct' responsibility, 'represented the first step in the judicial contribution towards the building of a more federal Europe'.[33] The Court was certainly prepared to assert that the new Community 'constitutes a new legal order of international law for the benefit of which Member States have limited their sovereign rights'.[34]

The implications of direct effect are considerable. First, Member State governments are responsible not merely for their own actions, if they appear to infringe a citizen's Community law rights, but also for the actions of other citizens. This principle, termed 'indirect effect', was developed in cases such as *Von Colson* and *Marleasing*.[35] Second,

[30] *Internationale Handelsgeselschaft* 11/70 [1970] ECR 1134.

[31] *Amministrazione della Finaze Dello Strato v Simmenthal*, 106/77 [1978] 643–44.

[32] For a discussion, see I Ward, *A Critical Introduction to European Law* (London, Butterworths, 2003), 74–80.

[33] See P Craig, 'Once Upon a Time in the West: Direct Effect and the Federalization of EEC Law', (1992) 12 *Oxford Journal of Legal Studies*, 458.

[34] *Van Gend en Loos v Nederlandse Belastingadministratie* 26/62 [1963] ECR 12.

[35] *Von Colson and Kamann v Land Nordrhein-Westfalen* 14/83 [1984] ECR 1891, *Marleasing v CIA* 106/89 [1990] ECR I-4135.

not only are governments now subject to legal action if they fail to implement Community law effectively, but so too are they subject to a full range of remedies, including, if necessary, injunctions and damages. This is so, even if, as in the UK, such remedies would not ordinarily be available. In the *Francovich* case, the Court agreed that the availability of such remedies was 'particularly essential' if Community law was to be fully effective.[36]

The legal principles of supremacy and direct effect have had a seminal impact on the evolution of the common market. As one judge of the European Court famously opined, the dynamic of legal integration was originally transmitted by the 'founding fathers' in the 'genetic code' of the Community.[37] Law, it is often suggested, is the essential Community 'method'. The problem with this conclusion, however, lies in the fact that the original Community made little attempt to approach the questions of democracy and legitimacy that define liberal democratic polities. No one thought too deeply about politics in 1958; just markets and the legal regimes necessary for their optimal efficiency. Forty years on, the 'new' Europe looks very different indeed. The European Economic Community has become a European political Union.

The idea of a political 'union', as the next stage in European integration, had been prescribed in Article 1 of the 1986 Single European Act, which talked of 'concrete progress towards European unity'. The 1992 Maastricht Treaty on European Union duly established a three 'pillar' structure; composing the Community Treaty and two further 'pillars', on Common Foreign and Security Policy, and Justice and Home Affairs. Article 1 (ex A) of the Union Treaty declared that the Union represents:

> a new stage in the process of creating an ever closer union among the peoples of Europe in which decisions are taken as closely as possible to the people.

Whereas the rhetoric of the Community Treaty had sought to entice Europeans with the allure of 'sustainable and non-inflationary growth', the Union Treaty is altogether grander in aspiration, proclaiming, in Article 6 (ex F), a politics of 'liberty, democracy, respect

[36] *Francovich and Bonifaci v Italy* 6, 9/90 [1991] ECR I-5357. For a commentary, see T Hartley, *Constitutional Problems of the European Union*, (Oxford, Hart, 1999), 59–61.

[37] F Mancini & D Keeling, 'Democracy and the European Court of Justice', (1994) 57 *Modern Law Review*, 186.

for human rights and fundamental freedoms, and the rule of law, principles which are common to the Member States'.[38] It also established a notional European citizenry in Article 17 (ex 8) of the Community Treaty.

It did not, however, address the corrosive problem of affinity, or lack of it. Politicians in Strasbourg are no more loved than those in Westminster, or Paris or Berlin. There is, as Joseph Weiler rightly affirms, a current crisis 'at all levels of European governance'.[39] Union citizenship should, as Olivia O'Leary suggests, be derived 'from the inherent dignity of the human person'.[40] At present, it is meaningless; as meaningless, indeed, as the new declaratory, but not justiciable, Union Charter of fundamental rights inaugurated at the Nice intergovernmental conference in 2000.[41]

The situation of the citizen in the 'new' Europe, and the 'new world order', is precarious. Government appears to be getting bigger and bigger, the markets ever less easily governed. Juergen Habermas confirms that the European experience is semiotic. We need to conceive of radically alternative ideas of democracy and citizenship in our 'post-metaphysical world'.[42] Ultimately,

> If Europe is to be able to act on the basis of an integrated, multilevel policy, then European citizens, who are initially characterized as such only by their common passports, will have to learn to mutually recognize one another as members of a common political existence beyond national borders.[43]

[38] Though not, of course, the Union itself. The reach of the Court of Justice is effectively limited to the operation of the Community. See M Zuern, 'Democratic Governance Beyond the Nation-State: The EU and Other International Institutions', (2000) 6 *European Journal of International Relations*, 191, 195–200.

[39] JHH Weiler, *The Constitution of Europe*, (Cambridge UP, 1999), 98, 275–76.

[40] O O'Leary, 'The Relationship Between Community Citizenship and the Protection of Fundamental Rights in Community Law', (1995) 32 *Common Market Law Review*, 541–43, 553.

[41] On citizenship, see Weiler, above n 39, 324, 336 and also E Guild, 'The Legal Framework of Citizenship of the European Union', in D Cesarini & M Fulbrook (eds), *Citizenship, Nationality and Migration in Europe*, (London, Routledge, 1996), 30 suggesting that it presently represents nothing more than 'some fancy words on a piece of paper'. For a discussion of the Charter, see Lord Goldsmith, 'A Charter of Rights, Freedoms and Principles', (2001) 38 *Common Market Law Review*, 1201–16, A Heringa, 'Towards an EU Charter of Fundamental Rights?', (2000) 7 *Maastricht Journal of European and Comparative Law*, 111–16 and I Ward, 'Tempted by Rights: The European Union and its New Charter of Fundamental Rights' (2001) 11 *Constitutional Forum*, 112–22.

[42] J Habermas, *Between Facts and Norms: Contributions to a Discourse Theory of Law and Democracy*, (Cambridge, Polity, 1996), 44–52, 430–52.

[43] J Habermas, *The Postnational Constellation*, (Cambridge, Polity, 2001), 99.

If, Habermas continues, Europe is to move beyond a state of 'barbaric nationalism', the nexus between citizenship and the right of democratic participation is critical.[44] The idea resonates with Weiler's suggestion that a European *ethos* must be defined in terms of 'tolerance' and 'plurality'.[45] With the end of 'unitary' sovereign states, citizens will be citizens of various overlapping political communities; a condition that the German jurist Ulrich Preuss describes as a 'multiplicity of associative relations'.[46] In this way, as Neil Walker maintains, the 'new' Europe is a testing ground for a new kind of 'constitutional pluralism'.[47] According to Jo Shaw this may well emerge as a 'post-national constitutionalism', one the strength of which is gauged by the vigour of its 'continuing conversation'.[48] We shall see.

An Awkward Partner

The idea of a 'post-national constitutionalism' does not, however, appeal to everyone. It has certainly met with a mixed reception in the United Kingdom. We, it is commonly said, have been the 'awkward partner' in the 'new' Europe. A visceral scepticism can be traced back to Attlee's post-war government. Deploying a suitably confused metaphor, Attlee's Foreign Secretary, Ernest Bevin, famously commented, 'I don't like it. I don't like it. When you open a Pandora's Box you'll find it full of Trojan horses'.[49] Churchill's Foreign Secretary, in turn, declared that joining the new Community was 'something which we know in our bones we cannot do'. Another of Churchill's senior ministers, Selwyn Lloyd, airily dismissed the idea of a European community as 'much ado about nothing', whilst Eden's successor at the Foreign Office, Harold Macmillan, declaimed an idea that, he opined, was put about by 'the Jews, the planners, and the old cosmopolitan element'.[50] According to

[44] Habermas, *ibid*, 76–77, 103.

[45] Weiler, above n 39, 343–47.

[46] U Preuss, 'Problems of a Concept of European Citizenship', (1995) 1 *European Law Journal* 1995, 280.

[47] N Walker, 'The Idea of Constitutional Pluralism', (2002) 65 *Modern Law Review* 2002, 317–50

[48] J Shaw, 'Process and Constitutional Discourse in the European Union', (2000) 27 *Journal of Law and Society*, 19–24.

[49] In S Greenwood, *Britain and European Cooperation since 1945*, (Oxford, Blackwell, 1992), 30.

[50] See Greenwood, *ibid*, 42–43, 64–67, 76–77, A Milward, *The European Rescue of the Nation State*, (London, Routedge, 1992), 432, and J Young, *Britain and European Union 1945–1992*, (Basingstoke, Macmillan, 1993), 29–44.

Roy Hattersley, the refusal to take a constructive part in the formation of the Community was the defining 'historical error of post-war Britain'.[51]

In large part, this historical truculence can be ascribed to the stubborn hold of Diceyan conceptions of unitary sovereignty in our constitutional and political psyche. As he ushered the 1972 European Communities Bill through a suspicious Parliament, Prime Minister Edward Heath felt moved to utter the specious assurance that 'Joining the Community does not entail a loss of national identity or an erosion of essential national sovereignty'.[52] The essential word was, of course, 'essential'. For the intervening thirty years, however, politicians and lawyers alike have clung to the illusion that Heath was somehow right; even though, as Larry Siedentop has recently argued, the very idea of 'sovereignty' makes little or no sense in the 'new' Europe.[53] Throughout the 1980s, successive Thatcher governments loudly broadcast their determination to protect national sovereignty. In a notorious speech given at Bruges in 1990, Thatcher herself waxed poetically, if a little incredibly, about the threat which the Community posed to the Magna Carta.[54] In the end the Conservative Party eventually tore itself apart trying to work out what 'essential' really meant.

The present 'new' Labour government has appeared to be rather more enthused about the 'new' Europe. On arriving in Downing Street, Prime Minister Blair declared his intention to place Britain at the 'heart' of Europe. Initially, at least, there seemed to be a superficial resonance between the European 'way' and certain precepts of the much-vaunted 'third way'. More concrete, perhaps, was the symbiosis that appeared to exist between a Human Rights Act and the aspirations of a new European 'union'. However, the extent to which we, and our present government, really embrace all the implications of the new, and significantly enlarged, Union remains moot. Hugo Young suggests that the European question, the most pressing which currently faces the UK, has been deliberately cast into a

[51] R Hattersley, *Fifty Years On: A Prejudiced History of Britain Since the War*, (London, Little Brown, 1997), 54.

[52] See Hattersley, *ibid*, 224. The statement repeated the assertion given in a 1971 White Paper, that 'There is no question of any erosion of essential national sovereignty. What is proposed is a sharing and an enlargement of individual national sovereignties in the general interest'.

[53] L Siedentop, *Democracy in Europe*, (London, Penguin, 2000), 25–28.

[54] M Thatcher, *The Downing Street Years*, (London, Harper Collins, 1993), 744–45.

'quotidian banality'.[55] So long as the question of the single currency remains unresolved, it is likely to stay there.[56]

The constitutional aspect of accession was determined by section 2.1 of the 1972 Act which stated that:

> All such rights, powers, liabilities, obligations and restrictions from time to time created or arising under the Treaties, and all such remedies and procedures from time to time provided for under the Treaties, as in accordance with the Treaties are without further enactment to be given legal effect or used in the United Kingdom shall be recognised and available in law, and be enforced, allowed and followed accordingly; and the expression 'enforceable Community right' and similar expressions shall be read as referring to one to which this subsection applies.

As we have already noted, the 1972 Act is, thus, an 'enabling' act. It is intended to prescribe the future manner of legislative enactment. It is also, of course, just the kind of statute that Dicey so mistrusted.

Precisely what section 2.1 really meant was left to the judges to decide. Relying on the idea of 'self-embracing' sovereignty, Lord Denning was able to cling to the idea that Westminster had managed to retain its sovereign authority. The 'priority' of European law, he declared in *Macarthy's v Smith*, 'is given by our law':

> It is given by the European Communities Act 1972 itself. Community law is part of our law: and, whenever there is any inconsistency, Community law has priority. It is not supplanting English law. It is part of our law which overrides any other part which is inconsistent with it.[57]

Trevor Allan termed it 'Lord Denning's dexterous revolution'.[58]

The problem is that Denning's 'revolution' was premised upon a 'dualistic' conception of constitutional law; with alternative regimes of domestic and Community law.[59] This approach was followed in a number of cases, such as *Garland* in 1983, *Pickstone* in 1989 and *Litster*

[55] H Young, *This Blessed Plot: Britain and Europe from Churchill to Blair*, (Basingstoke, Macmillan, 1998), 490. See also A Duff, 'Britain and Europe: The Different Relationship', in M Westlake (ed), *The European Union Beyond Amsterdam: New Concepts of European Integration*, (London, Routledge, 1998), 45–46.

[56] A Rawnsley, *Servants of the People: The Inside Story of New Labour*, (London, Hamish Hamilton, 2000,) 73, 76–81, 235–36.

[57] *Macarthy's v Smith* [1981] QB 200.

[58] T Allan, 'Parliamentary Sovereignty: Lord Denning's Dexterous Revolution' (1983) 3 *Oxford Journal of Legal Studies*, 22.

[59] See T Allan, 'The Limits of Parliamentary Sovereignty', (1985) *Public Law*, 25.

in 1990.[60] But it is not the kind of constitutional settlement preferred by the European Court of Justice, and the full implication of legal 'integration' was about to be laid bare in the notorious *Factortame* cases.

In 1991, the Divisional Court was asked to rule on the validity of British licensing arrangements for fishing rights and quotas; arrangements that were subject to the overarching provisions of the Community's Common Fisheries Policy. It was argued that the licensing arrangements contained in the 1988 Merchant Shipping Act were in contravention of Regulation 170/83 Article 4. In simple terms they discriminated against Spanish vessels. The Divisional Court was thoroughly bemused, and requested a preliminary ruling from the European Court of Justice. In the meantime it granted interim relief and set aside the domestic regulations. The Court of Appeal promptly reversed the interim relief decision. The House of Lords upheld the reversal, but decided that a preliminary ruling should also be sought regarding the interim relief question.

The Court of Justice decided the interim relief question first, and, following *Simmenthal*, held that interim relief must be made available if it is most appropriate to making Community law 'fully effective'.[61] In due course, it applied the same principle to the substantive question, instructing the court to disapply the 1988 regulations. In the House of Lords, Lord Bridge reflected on the implications of the interim relief decision:

> If the supremacy within the European Community of Community law over the national law of Member States was not always inherent in the EEC Treaty it was certainly well-established in the jurisprudence of the European Court of Justice long before the UK joined the Community. Thus, whatever limitations of its sovereignty Parliament accepted when it enacted the European Communities Act 1972 it was entirely voluntary. Under the terms of the Act of 1972 it has always been clear that it was the duty of a UK court, when delivering final judgment, to override any rule of national law found to be in conflict with any directly enforceable rule of Community law. Similarly, when decisions of the Court of Justice have exposed areas of United Kingdom statute law which failed to implement Council directives, Parliament has always loyally accepted the obligation to make appropriate and prompt amendments. Thus there is nothing in any way novel in according supremacy to rules of Community law in those areas to which they apply and to insist that, in the protection of rights under Community law, national

[60] *Garland v British Rail Engineering* [1983] 2 AC 751, *Pickstone v Freemans* [1989] AC 66, *Litster v Forth Dry Dock and Engineering Co* [1990] 1 AC 546.

[61] *R v Secretary of State for Transport ex p Factortame* [1991] 1 All ER 70.

> courts must not be inhibited by rules of national law from granting interim relief in appropriate cases. It is no more than a logical recognition of that supremacy.[62]

The resignation of absolute sovereignty was starkly conceded. *Factortame*, it has been suggested, drove a 'stake' through the very heart of 'unitary' sovereignty.[63] Trevor Allan suggests that it complements a wider appreciation that post-Diceyan public law will owe rather more to residual ideas of 'common law constitutionalism' than the mythologies of unitary sovereignty.[64]

And the 'European way', as Denning termed it, made further demands of domestic constitutional law. If judges are empowered with the capacity to review domestic legislation, so too must they be equipped with an alternative method of judicial reasoning. As Denning opined in the 1974 *Bulmer* case, they must now seek to 'divine the spirit of the treaty and gain inspiration from it'.[65] Accordingly, they must also interpret domestic legislation so that it is in line with Community law, even if that interpretation is clearly at variance with the original intent of Parliament. A veritable host of judges have registered their discomfort with such an interpretive responsibility, most sharing Lord Hoffmann's refusal to acknowledge that the 'partial surrender of sovereignty' effected by the 1972 Act, meant that he and his colleagues were now endowed 'with quasi-legislative powers'.[66] A similar degree of discomfort has also been expressed with certain principles of Community administrative law. As we have already seen, the principle of proportionality has met with a particularly chilly reception, summarily dismissed by the House of Lords in *Brind*, and only grudgingly taken on in the Sunday Trading cases, *Stoke* and *Peterborough*.[67] And even when a court has appeared to be rather more receptive, its enthusiasm has been blunted by sheer bewilderment.[68]

[62] *Factortame* 107–8.

[63] N MacCormick, *Questioning Sovereignty: Law, State and Nation in the European Commonwealth*, (Oxford UP, 1999), 95, 131–33. Wade reached a similar conclusion, in his 'Sovereignty—Revolution or Evolution?'(1996) 112 *Law Quarterly Review*, 568–75.

[64] T Allan, 'Parliamentary Sovereignty: Law, Politics and Revolution', (1997) 113 *Law Quarterly Review*, 443–52.

[65] *Bulmer v Bollinger*, [1974] 2 All ER 1237–38.

[66] *Stoke on Trent CC v B & Q* [1991] 4 All ER 221.

[67] See *R v Secretary of State for the Home Department ex p Brind* [1991] 1 AC 766–67, *Smith Do-It-All Ltd v Peterborough CC* [1991] 4 All ER 210 and *Stoke*, 235.

[68] *R v Chief Constable of Sussex ex p International Trader's Ferry*, [1998] 3 WLR 1260.

It is clear that there is still a distance to go before the UK and its courts can be said to have finally embraced all the challenges posed by the 'new' Europe.[69] And yet, as Lord Donaldson famously observed in the *M* case, the present situation whereby Community law appears to exist in some kind of parallel constitutional universe is 'anomalous' and 'wrong in principle'.[70] Six years later, Lord Woolf expressed the same sentiments in the fifth of the *Factortame* cases, suggesting that the time had come to 're-examine', not just the immediate implications of Denning's 'dualism', but also the wider condition of domestic constitutional law in the context of European integration.[71]

II THE END OF EMPIRE

The Setting Sun

The idea that the British should embrace the 'new' European empire, however grudgingly, carries its own array of ambiguities. The British have always liked the idea of empire; just so long as it was theirs. Dicey's *Law* was written as a paean to imperialism, to the 'outer' empire over the seas, and the 'inner' empire next door.[72] The very idea of Britain was founded on empire.[73] The Henrician Act in Restraint of Appeals referred to the realm of England as an 'empire'. The complementary Act of Supremacy vested in Henry an 'imperial crown', one that was apparently descended from Brutus, Arthur and the Roman Emperor Constantine.[74] The English reformation was an imperial venture; the first of many.

Fairyland, as David Cannadine suggests, was thus an imperial state, a vast 'imaginatively constructed artefact' dedicated to the 'cult of monarchy'.[75] In time, the Henrician empire gave way to the grand

[69] For a recent reassertion, see Lord Nolan, 'General Introduction', in Nolan & Sedley (eds) *The Making and Remaking of the British Constitution*, (London, Blackstone, 1997), 5.

[70] *M v Home Office* [1992] 4 All ER, 139.

[71] *R v Secretary of State for Transport ex p.Factortame (No 5)* [2000] 1 AC 524.

[72] D Cannadine, *Ornamentalism: How the British Saw Their Empire*, (Oxford UP, 2002), 36.

[73] M Loughlin, 'The State, the Crown and the Law', in M Sunkin & S Payne (eds), *The Nature of the Crown: A Legal and Political Analysis*, (Oxford UP, 1999), 43–48.

[74] Henry was keen that his realm should rank with that of the Pope's primary champion, the Holy Roman Emperor.

[75] Cannadine, above n 72, 3, 21.

vistas of Victorian 'evangelical imperialism'.[76] Generations of impressionable school children, force fed the names of distant imperial outposts, would be informed, time and again, that the sun never set on the Empire. They would come to know that a quarter of the world's land-surface, and approximately a quarter of its population, around 444 million in 1909, was under British rule.[77] For relaxation they could read the novels of Rider Haggard and Rudyard Kipling, and reassure themselves that the subjugation of native peoples was in everyone's best interests. After all, as John Stuart Mill had reassured their parents, England was 'incomparably the most conscientious of nations', the 'power which of all in existence best understands liberty', and the one that best appreciated the value of free markets and 'capital'.[78] And anyway, it was God's work. As 'Chinese' Gordon, the martyr of Khartoum, affirmed, to dedicate one's life to Empire 'was to know the resurrection'.[79]

Successive Victorian jubilees were given over to a celebration of empire; the marriage of Godliness and utility, the 'dignified', as Bagehot put it, and the 'efficient'. Thirty-thousand jubilee mugs and Bath buns were provided for all the children who attended the 1887 Hyde Park celebrations. A grateful Empire gave its Fairy Empress two Indian servants, whilst the Fairy Empress, reassured that she would never actually have to go there, set about learning Hindustani and cultivating a taste for curry. *The Times* celebrated a 'festival of patriotism'. A decade later, diamond jubilee mugs were once again the gift of the discerning worshipper. A quarter of million pounds was spent on street decorations in London and new-fangled light bulbs. Empire, like monarchy, as Lord Lytton wrily observed, always looks brighter with a 'bit of bunting.[80]

And yet, as the English and their various subservient peoples supped their tea and admired their decorations, the end of empire was already approaching. In his *Recessional*, written in 1897, Rudyard Kipling warned:

[76] N Ferguson, *Empire: How Britain Made the Modern World*, (London, Penguin, 2003), 125.

[77] Ferguson, *ibid*, 240.

[78] Quoted in Ferguson, *ibid*, 140–41.

[79] *Ibid*, 265.

[80] See Cannadine, above n 72, 109–10, Ferguson, above n 76, 203–4, and I Ward, *A State of Mind? The English Constitution and the Popular Imagination* (Gloucester, Sutton, 2000), 201–2.

Far-called, our naves melt away;
On dune and headland sinks the fire:
Lo, all our pomp of yesterday
Is one with Ninevah and Tyre!
Judge of the Nations, spare us yet,
Lest we forget – lest we forget![81]

For a while the economics of empire had made sense. Governing a quarter of the world and its markets cost barely 2.5% of net national product in 1898. England had created a vast quasi-federal Empire, with a series of essentially autonomous, self-governing countries whose only obligation was to service the 'mother' country.[82] But even 2.5% seemed too much, and by the time God's 'chosen people' emerged from the carnage of the Great War, they could not get rid of their Empire quickly enough.

In its place came a 'Commonwealth of Nations', and in time another 'new' world order. The plumage would, of course, continue; after all there had to be something for the dispossessed emperors to do, even if it was little more than opening athletic pageants and hosting tea parties for the motley band of petty dictators that make up the bulk of Commonwealth 'heads' of state.[83] But other than this, the English gave away their Empire, and save for Noel Coward and one or two other nostalgic racists, hardly anyone seemed to mind, or really notice.

Dating the 'end' of the empire is difficult. Niall Ferguson suggests the years immediately following 1918, when, haunted by the economic reality that Empire must anyway come to a rapid end, the idea itself passed from being the subject of unimpeachable pride to a source of music-hall ribaldry, when images of Gordon and Livingstone gave way to Colonel Blimp and the satirical asides of Woodhouse and Billy Bunter. Suddenly, the English realised what John Buchan dared to admit, that Empire was not only ridiculously expensive, but also morally contemptible, a torrid excuse for 'callous racial arrogance'.[84] Embarrassed self-deprecation seemed to be the only recourse, along with a hasty shedding of the colonies themselves.

David Cannadine suggests that the end really came with Winston Churchill's grand ceremonial funeral; 'a requiem for Britain as a great

[81] R Kipling, *Selected Poetry*, (London, Penguin, 2001), 131.
[82] See Ferguson, above n 76, 245, and J Kendle, *Federal Britain*, (London, Routledge, 1997), 12–13.
[83] Cannadine, above n 72, 158–67.
[84] Ferguson, above n 76, 317–19.

power'.[85] In many ways, Churchill summed up all the many paradoxes of empire. He lived for empire, for all its 'glitter, pomp and iced champagne'.[86] But he had also regretted the cost of it all, particularly the cost in terms of human misery:

> Yet as the mind turns from the wonderful cloudland of aspiration to the ugly scaffolding of attempt and achievement, a succession of opposite ideas arise . . . The inevitable gap between conquest and dominion becomes filled with the figures of the greedy trader, the inopportune missionary, the ambitious soldier, and the lying speculator, who disquiet minds of the conquered and excite the sordid appetites of the conquerors. And as the eye of thought rests on these sinister features, it hardly seems possible for us to believe that any fair prospect is approached by so foul a path.[87]

The title of Churchill's grand *History of the English Speaking Peoples*, meanwhile, spoke to the deeper paradoxes of English imperialism. And when the funereal pageantry had passed, he was laid to rest in a quiet Oxfordshire churchyard, his headstone reading, not Prime Minister of Britain, but Prime Minister of 'England'. When all was said and done, England was all that was left, and all that really mattered anyway. As the Victorian historian John Seeley declared, there was no such thing as a 'British' empire, just a 'vast English nation'.[88] This was certainly the empire to which Churchill and Kipling belonged, and Bagehot and Dicey too.

Of course, the end of empire was done in the best possible style; with lots of bunting, hoisted flags and dropped flags, brass bands and native dancing. And it was done properly, the constitutional mechanics facilitated by section 4 of the 1931 Statute of Westminster, which, as we have already seen, prescribed the manner of any future legislation on dominion matters. Independence, as Lord Sankey observed in *Edwards v A-G for Canada*, once given cannot be taken back.[89] Bits of empire remain, scattered rocky outcrops in the southern Atlantic and parts of the Caribbean and Pacific Oceans. And then there is the BBC World Service and Test Match Cricket. But not much else. One of the few remaining colonies of any substance, Hong Kong, was returned in to China in 1997; exactly a hundred years after Victoria's second imperial jubilee The days of empire have finally passed; the sun has set. As David Cannadine puts it:

[85] Cannadine, above n 7, 36–37, and above n 72, 196.
[86] Cannadine, above n 7, 134–35.
[87] In Ferguson, above n 76, xxv.
[88] In K Kumar, *The Making of English National Identity*, (Cambridge UP, 2003),189.
[89] *Edwards v A-G for Canada* [1930] AC 136–37.

> The captains and the kings have departed; the squadrons and the legions have come home; the plumed hats and the ceremonial swords have been put away; the Union Jack has been hauled down again and again and again; Britannia no longer rules the waves at Heaven's command; and even the royal yacht has ceased to sail the seas.[90]

So much for the 'outer' empire. The fate of the 'inner' empire, however, the empire of successive Unions, with Wales, Scotland and Ireland, is altogether less clear.

The End of Greater England

Once again, the idea of a 'united' Kingdom of Great Britain can be traced back to the Henrician reformation; even if the empire lauded in the Act in Restraint did amount to little more than a notional union of England, Wales and those bits of Ireland, around Dublin, where English troops could venture without being cut to pieces. In a sense, Henry VIII's 'empire' established the inner core of an 'inner' empire. The Tudors made much of their Welsh antecedents. Henry Tudor flew the banner of Cadwallader over Bosworth Field in 1485, whilst Shakespeare's *Richard III* dutifully eulogised the unity of English and Welsh nations, and dynastic branches conjoined by 'God's fair ordinance'.[91] The idea that Wales was part of England's dominion had already been advanced in medieval statues such as the 1284 Statute of Wales. But it was the Tudors who forced the issue.

The 'union of the crowns' between England and Scotland came rather later in 1603, when James VI of Scotland became James I of England. The union was finally set in legislative stone with the Acts of Union of 1706 and 1707. Aside from a delineated Scottish Church and Scottish legal system, pretty much everything else was removed to Westminster. The Scottish Parliament, in a final gesture, approved the Union by 110 votes to 69, thus dissolving itself, and giving England's newly reshaped inner empire a kind of legitimacy. In novels such as *Waverley* and *The Heart of Midlothian*, Sir Walter Scott sought to confirm a union of equals 'happily fulfilled'.[92] The truth was more

90 Cannadine, above n 72, xiii.

91 W Shakespeare, *Richard III*, (London, Routledge, 1981), 5.5.31.

92 W Scott, *Waverley*, (Harmondsworth, Penguin, 1972), 491. For a commentary, see I Ward, 'Scott and the Waverley Constitution: A Study in Literary Constitutionalism', (1998) 79 *English Studies*, 193–211.

prosaic. Scotland was broke. And for a sum of just under £400,000 it was 'bought and sold', as a bitter Robert Burns observed, mortgaged by a 'parcel of rogues' for 'English gold'.[93]

The Acts of Union sealed the empire of 'Greater England', as the Victorian imperialist Charles Dilke termed it, the 'virtual confederation of the English race'. [94] The interests of God's 'chosen people' were paramount. The 1707 Union, as Tom Nairn suggests was nothing more than a 'political convenience' for England; a view recently reaffirmed by Krishan Kumar, who suggests that the 'artefact' of 'Great' Britain was invented to give the English something suitably messianic to do whilst making money.[95] It is for this reason, as Tony Wright concludes, that the English have always assumed that Dilke was right, that 'Britain was just England by another name'.[96] The very idea of an Anglo-British Empire was founded in the need to justify England's presumed status as a 'chosen' nation.[97] As Linda Colley has revealed, the very idea of British-ness only emerged as that of Empire took off during the later part of the eighteenth century, and slowly encased residual ideas of England within it.[98] 'Great Britain' was invented in order to provide a sheen of constitutional respectability to the more mercenary desire to make money out of foreigners; whether they be foreigners in Africa and India, or foreigners in Scotland and Ireland.[99]

But, as with the outer empire, so too has it become apparent that the inner empire is an expensive luxury; and, in places, a thoroughly troublesome one. Britain has become a 'problem'.[100] Stripped of its imperialist pretences, the British 'isles' are seen to be fragmentary and fragmenting.[101] Talk of devolution has bounced around for a century

[93] See Davies, above n 2, 620–22, 656.

[94] In D Newsome, *The Victorian World Picture*, (London, Fontana, 1998), 132.

[95] See T Nairn, *Pariah: Misfortunes of the British Kingdom*, (London, Verso, 2002), 33, 37, and *After Britain: New Labour and the Return of Scotland*, (Cambridge, Granta, 2000), 15, and Kumar, above n 88, 187.

[96] T Wright, 'England, Whose England', in S Chen & T Wright (eds), *The English Question*, (London, Fabian Society, 2000), 12.

[97] Nairn, above n 95, 33. For the same conclusion, see M Hickman, 'A new England through Irish eyes?', in S Chen & T Wright (eds), above n 95, 101–3

[98] L Colley, *Britons: Forging the Nation 1707–1837*, (London, Vintage, 1994), particularly 1–6, 176–77, 385–97. For the same conclusion, see A Dummett, 'Citizenship and National Identity', in R Hazell (ed), *Constitutional Futures: A History of the Next Ten Years*, (Oxford UP, 1999), 215–16.

[99] Davies, above n 2, xxxviii.

[100] J Pocock, 'British History: A Plea for a New Subject', (1975) 47 *Journal of Modern History*, 601–28.

[101] Davies, above n 2, particularly, 1039–54.

or more, finding an early expression in Gladstone's desire to promote 'local patriotism', as well as Joseph Chamberlain's idea of a 'federative' United Kingdom. The governing classes, however, craved the idea of empire, even if it was ever more geographically compressed, and the idea failed to make any headway until the last part of the twentieth century.[102]

Finally, in 1978, devolutionary legislation for Scotland and Wales passed through Parliament. Only 11.9% of the Welsh electorate supported the proposal, and whilst a slim majority of Scots favoured the proposals, the number was insufficient to cross the threshold which required the support of 40% of all those eligible to vote. For the moment the idea of devolution retreated, unable to compete with the revived imperial cravings of the Thatcher years.[103] Ironically, however, these same years played a major part in nurturing a critical sense of democratic deficit in the Celtic margins. Whilst successive Conservative governments enjoyed a majority in Westminster, its share of the popular vote remained slight in both Scotland and Wales.[104]

Sensing the mood, 'new' Labour placed referenda on devolution in its 1997 manifesto. The promise was realised, and the referenda produced majority support for devolution, albeit only just in Wales, where, on a turnout of just 50.1%, a bare majority of 50.3% voted in favour. The vote in Scotland was marginally more enthusiastic. On a turnout of 60%, 74.3% voting in favour of a Scottish Parliament, with a separate vote of 63.5% in favour of tax-varying powers. In practice, then just under half of the Scottish people had bothered to turn out and support devolution, whilst only a quarter in Wales had. The only strikingly positive referendum was in Northern Ireland, where 71.1% approved the 'Good Friday Agreement' in an 81% turnout.

Variable Devolution

With this rather variable support, a very variable process of devolution was instigated. Each of Scotland, Wales and Northern Ireland would experience devolved government, but these experiences would be very

[102] M O'Neill, 'Great Britain: From Dicey to Devolution', (2000) 53 *Parliamentary Affairs*, 70–71.

[103] O'Neill, *ibid*, 73–74

[104] See R Rawlings, 'The New Model Wales', (1998) 25 *Journal of Law and Society*, 466–67.

different, with different powers devolved in different ways to different bodies. The idea of 'asymmetrical' devolution was coined by the Kilbrandon report in 1973. Another popular descriptor is 'variable geometry'. According to Michael O'Neill it can best be termed 'untidy'; a phrase also deployed by Abimbola Olowofoyeku, who adds that rider that it is also 'constitutionally unsound'.[105] The break-up of Britain, it seems, will be messy, if vaguely consensual.

The common establishment of national assemblies, with various legislative powers, First Ministers and executives, provided a sheen of uniformity, whilst also maintaining the delusive fantasies of formal Union. The pretences of Parliamentary sovereignty would be played out in Edinburgh, Cardiff and Belfast, just as they are in Westminster, whilst the latter body would maintain its constitutional authority, notional or not, over all.[106] The system of devolved government, as Tom Nairn concludes, has been 'born decrepit'.[107] As if any confirmation was required, it was felt that there remained a need for Scottish and Welsh offices at Whitehall; even if their status was ever more obviously diminished in the pantheon of ministerial responsibility [108]

In establishing a Scottish Parliament, section 1 of the 1998 Scotland Act seemed to realise Donald Dewar's desire, articulated in the White Paper a year before, to 'strengthen democratic control and make government more accountable to the people of Scotland'.[109] Primary legislative competence was transferred to the Scottish Parliament in all areas, save for those 'reserved' to Westminster. In practice, the legislative activity of the Assembly has proved to be rather limited; abolishing archaic systems of land tenure, reforming the law relating to the financial arrangements of mentally deficient adults, worrying about MSP expense accounting, and so on.[110] Undoubtedly, the most controversial area of legislative competence is the power to vary the base rate of tax by three pence in the pound; something stigmatised by oppo-

[105] See O'Neill, above n 102, 78, and A Olowofoyeku, 'Decentralising the UK: The Federal Argument', (1999) 3 *Edinburgh Law Review*, 83.

[106] For a discussion of the Westminster 'model', see M Smith, 'Reconceptualizating the British State: Theoretical and Empirical Challenges to Central Government', (1998) 76 *Public Administration*, 45–46. See also R Brazier, 'The Constitution of the United Kingdom', (1999) 58 *Cambridge Law Journal*, 100, 102–3.

[107] Nairn, above n 95, 83–85.

[108] C Munro, *Studies in Constitutional Law*, (London, Butterworths, 1999), 37–9.

[109] A Brown, 'Designing the Scottish Parliament', (2000) 53 *Parliamentary Affairs*, 547.

[110] J Bradbury & J Mitchell, 'Devolution: New Politics for Old?', (2001) 54 *Parliamentary Affairs*, 269.

nents as a 'tartan tax'. It is, of course, a relatively small sum, and in practice the effective funding of Scotland still comes from its wealthier southern neighbours; a matter of increasing resentment in England, and quiet embarrassment in Scotland.[111]

The rather limited legislative activity bears witnesses both to the need to accommodate alternative political interests in a more consensual system of government as well as the extent of 'reserved' powers. Section 29 precludes the Assembly from legislating on those matters 'reserved' in Schedule 5. The Schedule describes a series of 'general' and 'specific' reservations. The 'general' reservations relate to such matters as the 'constitution', the 'registration and funding of political parties', the 'conduct of foreign affairs', and matters of 'public service, defence and treason'. The 'specific' matters relate to eleven areas of public policy, ranging from 'home affairs' to 'transport' to 'media and culture'. The sharing of competences in such a way, devoid of firm federal determinants, can be termed 'co-operative inter-governmentalism'.[112]

Alongside 'reserved' legislative competence, and the kind of differentiated legislative procedure that is exemplified by the variable tax regime, there is a residual power for the Westminster Parliament to legislate on all matters which fall within the competence of the Scottish Assembly. Section 27.7 of the Scotland Act declares that section 28 which grants the Assembly its broad legislative competence 'does not affect the power of the UK Parliament to make laws for Scotland'.[113] In order to preclude the obvious potential for dispute, this area is governed by the Sewell 'conventions', with which the Scottish Assembly is supposed to first signal its assent to Westminster legislation on any particular matter. Amidst all the excitement surrounding Scotland's newly acquired legislative powers, the extent to which Sewell conventions are used is too easily forgotten.[114] One way or another, much of the legislation which affects Scotland continues to emanate from Westminster.

The new Scottish Parliament consists of 129 MSPs, 73 of whom are elected by constituencies on the 'first past the post' system, whilst a

[111] R Hazell & B O'Leary, 'A Rolling Programme of Devolution: Slippery Slope or Safeguard of the Union?', in Hazell (ed), above n 98, 27.

[112] O'Neill, above n 102, 79–80.

[113] For a critical discussion of this inevitably complex and controversial provision, see J McFadden, 'The Scottish Parliament: Provisions for Dispute Resolution', (1998) *Juridical Review*, 225–28.

[114] See A Page & A Batey, 'Scotland's Other Parliament: Westminster Legislation about Devolved Matters in Scotland since Devolution', (2002) *Public Law*, 501–23.

further 56 are elected under proportional representation from 'party lists' drawn up in eight regions. The system was geared to preclude absolute majorities in the Scottish Parliament, something which was also intended to promote consensus government. By happy coincidence, it also seemed to preclude the chance of an SNP majority; and also, it was fondly hoped, any chance of full Scottish independence.[115] A First Minister, vested with great seals of government and associated fripperies, heads the accompanying Scottish Executive. In practice, the Minister's primary responsibility is to provide a link between the alternative Edinburgh and Westminster parliaments; something that is likely to prove easier so long as there is a coincidence of party affiliation between alternative 'premiers', but rather more difficult if there is not.

Welsh devolution is rather different, both in theory and practice; devolution 'lite' as the more cynical have observed. Certainly, the institutional arrangements are conspicuously diluted. The 1998 Government of Wales Act concentrates more on setting up the necessary institutions for executive devolution than empowering legislative autonomy. The sixty member Welsh Assembly is established under section 1 of the 1998 Act, whilst sections 21 and 22 then describe its legislative powers. These powers are dramatically more limited than those enjoyed by the Scottish Assembly, extending only so far as the capacity to draft subordinate legislation as it is transferred on an essentially *ad hoc* basis from Westminster.

The electoral system for the Welsh Assembly is again convoluted, with 40 seats elected by 'first part the post' and 20 through the regional 'party lists'.[116] Again, this is supposed to promote consensus government, as is the system of 'concordats' intended to ease cross-party governance, and the concentration on multi-functional committee government.[117] Wales, like Scotland, now possesses a devolved Executive, consisting of nine of the sixty Assembly members, only this time headed by a First 'Secretary' as opposed to a First Minister. The terminological sleight speaks to an office that is intended to be altogether more efficient than it is dignified; part of a model that was made for effective governance as much as it was for democratic engagement.[118]

[115] Bradbury & Mitchell, 'Devolution', 258, and Brown, 'Scottish Parliament', 550–55.

[116] O'Neill, above n 102, 80.

[117] See Rawlings, above n 104, 480–85, 501–2.

[118] M Laffin &A Thomas, 'Designing the National Assembly for Wales', (2000) 53 *Parliamentary Affairs*, 557–76.

All in all the impression remains that Cardiff is the 'poor relation' to Westminster, as well as to Edinburgh and Belfast.[119]

Troubles

Traditionally, of course, the 'poor relation' in England's 'inner' Empire is Ireland, a province rather more obviously subjugated than enjoined in happy union. Whereas the conquest of Wales was proclaimed in distant medieval chronicles, and the Scottish Union eased by financial necessity, the Anglo-Irish union was, and has remained, an altogether more gruesome and bloody affair; an 'experimental laboratory' of conquest and subjugation, as Niall Ferguson, has termed it.[120] Edmund Spenser's *View of the Present State of Ireland*, composed in the 1590s, legitimated 'savage justice' in missionary terms. Oliver Cromwell likewise felt that the torching of Irish towns, and the murder of their inhabitants, was God's work, the kind of thing that a 'chosen people' was supposed to do. Notably, when Cromwell lay in state in 1658, his effigy was topped with an 'Imperial Crown', recognition of his successful suppression of the Irish.

Henry VIII had declared himself King of Ireland as early as 1541. But it was the Act of Union of 1800 that was supposed to vest English governance with some kind of supervening constitutional legitimacy. Once again the Irish Parliament obligingly voted itself out of existence; this time 'for ever'. In the end, 'for ever' meant a hundred and thirty-seven years. The overwhelming majority of the incorporated Irish, with the exception of a handful of English and Scottish settlers who seized land in the northern provinces, remained recalcitrant. A million died in the famines of 1845–46, and a further million were forced into emigration; 'Outcast weeds by a desolate sea/ Fallen leaves of humanity', as one contemporary put it.[121] By the second part of the nineteenth century, the Irish 'Question' was dominating British politics. Gladstone repeatedly tried to force Home Rule legislation, in 1886 and 1893, and repeatedly failed. Finally, in 1922, a series of statutes recognised an Irish Free State, representing all but the six northerly counties. And in 1937, the republic of Eire was established. The northern counties have remained

[119] Hazell & O'Leary, above n 111, 35–36. For a similar conclusion, see Brazier, above n 106, 108–10.

[120] Ferguson, above n 76, 64.

[121] Lady Wilde, quoted in Davies, above n 2, 761.

in a state of civil unrest, if not civil war, for most of the intervening sixty-seven years.

As late as 1886, amidst the controversy surrounding Gladstone's Home Rule proposals, Dicey could genuinely believe that any form of Irish secession would lead inexorably to the 'utter demoralisation of politics, and the ruin of the United Kingdom'.[122] The disappearance of southern Ireland from the imperial map served to remove the tidy congruence of the 'united', and unitary, kingdom, and the British 'isles'. Instead there was the recast, and inherently muddled, notion of a 'United Kingdom of Great Britain and Northern Ireland'; a piece of verbiage that testifies to a history of confusions.

For a while it was hoped that the Stormont 'settlement', which included a Parliament comprising two 'houses' together with an executive, replete with Prime Minister and Cabinet, might resolve the pending 'troubles'. A more obviously English constitutional settlement, of course, was hard to imagine. But, then, as its former Prime Minister, Lord Brookeborough, declared, Stormont was always intended to be a 'Protestant Parliament for a Protestant People'.[123] Unsurprisingly, the Catholic minority that remained in Northern Ireland were unappeased by the Stormont settlement, and amidst increasing violence, forced its abrogation and replacement by direct rule in 1972.

The idea of 'power-sharing', which raised the spectre of cross-border governance duly foundered on Unionist opposition, and for much of the next two and half decades, the vast majority of residents of Northern Ireland watched in despair as the more psychotic grasped the opportunity to shoot and bomb each other into a seeming oblivion. The 1985 Anglo-Irish Agreement, whereby the Westminster and Dublin governments agreed to coordinate security measures, represented a modest step forward; but it barely halted the slaughter. The Downing Street 'Declaration' in 1993, in which the British government for the first time disclaimed any 'selfish strategic or economic' interest in the province, was rather more significant, leading directly to the formal cessation of hostilities by the leading loyalist and republican terror organisations.

Finally, the 'Good Friday Agreement' in 1998, the product of multiparty talks between all the interested parties, cleared the way for the

[122] In R Cosgrove, *The Rule of Law: Albert Venn Dicey, Victorian Jurist*, (Chapter Hill, Univ of North Carolina Press, 1980), 137.

[123] Bradbury and Mitchell, above n 110, 266.

Northern Ireland Act and a measure of devolved governance.[124] In order to ensure that just about everyone was reasonably happy with just about everything, the 1998 Agreement guaranteed a 'triple lock', the principle behind which was to ensure that the final settlement would be negotiated rather than imposed, and would receive the support of all parties, as well as the people of Northern Ireland, and the respective British and Irish governments. The requirement that the people of Northern Ireland approve the proposed settlement was then written into the section 1 of the 1998 Act.

The 1998 Northern Ireland Act is a remarkably complex document, as one commentator has recently averred, the 'epitome of constitutional sophistication'.[125] It is commonly suggested that the various arrangements, by which power in Northern Ireland is to be radically dispersed, is 'consociational'.[126] There are four primary characteristics of the Anglo-Irish consociational model; cross-community power-sharing, the proportionality rule, segmental authority, and the mutual veto. Above all, the Good Friday Agreement and the 1998 Act sought to preclude majority dictat.[127] Rarely has so much effort been put into designing a system which guarantees a measure of power to everyone who agrees to take part, regardless of the relative strength of actual democratic mandates.

The composition and the procedure of the Northern Ireland Assembly testifies to this desire to disperse political power. The Assembly of 108 members is elected under a single transferable vote system, with all members obliged to designate themselves either 'nationalist', 'unionist' or 'other'. This latter requirement is needed in order to effect proportionate and balanced membership of all committees and executive bodies. The procedure for resolving 'key' matters such as the election of First and Deputy Ministers of the Executive, is a further testament to the overriding desire to ensure accommodation.

[124] For an overview, see E Tannam. 'Explaining the Good Friday Agreement: A Learning Process', (2001) 36 *Government and Opposition*, 493–518, and E Meehan, 'The Belfast Agreement—Its Distinctiveness and Points of Cross-Fertilization in the UK's Devolution Programme', (1999) 52 *Parliamentary Affairs*, 19–31.

[125] J Morison, 'Democracy, Governance and Governmentality: Civic Public Space and Constitutional Renewal in Northern Ireland', (2001) 21 *Oxford Journal of Legal Studies*, 287.

[126] An idea associated with the social and political theorist Arend Lijphart. See most famously, A Lijphart, *The Politics of Accommodation: Pluralism and Democracy in the Netherlands*, (Univ of California Press, 1968).

[127] See R Wilford, 'Designing the Northern Ireland Assembly', (2000) 53 *Parliamentary Affairs*, 578–80.

Such matters require both 'weighted majorities' and 'parallel consent'; meaning the approval of both Unionist and Nationalist blocs, as well as the majority of the Assembly itself. The operation of the Executive, a 'voluntary coalition' of the four main parties, Ulster Unionist, Social and Democratic Labour, Democratic Unionist and Sinn Fein, is also subject to a 'mutual veto' power, enabling any party to veto proposed legislation in any area. The Executive is thus duly charged with the particular responsibility of encouraging 'discussion' and forging a 'common position'.

The Good Friday Agreement referred to three 'strands' of government. The first 'strand' was the establishment of the Northern Ireland Assembly. The second 'strand' involves the establishment of a 'north-south' Ministerial Council to develop 'consultation, cooperation and action within the island of Ireland, including thorough implementation on an all-island and cross-border basis—on matters of mutual interest'. There are now six cross-border implementation bodies intended to ensure broad administrative cooperation between Belfast and Dublin.

The third and final 'strand' makes provision for a British-Irish Council, which can run alongside the British-Irish Intergovernmental Conference originally advanced as part of the Anglo-Irish Agreement in 1985. The stated aim of the Council is to promote 'the harmonious and mutually beneficial development of the totality of relationships among the people of these islands'. What is perhaps most intriguing about this body is the inclusion of all the 'people' of the British 'isles'. As such it includes representatives of the Scottish, Welsh and Northern Irish Councils, as well as the Channel Islands and the Isle of Man; everyone, indeed, except the English. The idea of a confederal Council of the British 'isles' has long bounced around as a possible solution to the British 'problem'.[128] It is intended that the Conference and Council should forge 'common policies' in a variety of areas, such as transport, agriculture and education.

The precise status of the Anglo-Irish Union after 1998, like that of the Anglo-Scottish, remains a matter of constitutional controversy. Republican politicians are keen to stress that English rule is effectively coming to a close. 'The British government', the Irish premier Bertie

[128] For a discussion, see E Meehan, 'Britain's Irish Question: Britain's European Question? British-Irish Relations in the Context of the European Union and the Belfast Agreement', (2000) 26 *Review of International Studies*, 83–97.

Ahern commented in 1998, 'are effectively out of the equation'.[129] In strictly constitutional terms, however, the situation is less clear. Article 75 of the Government of Ireland Act reserved ultimate statutory authority 'over all persons, matters and things', to the Westminster Parliament. There is no express repeal of Article 75 in the 1998 Act, and so its force is only diminished if it is accepted that Union legislation can be 'impliedly' repealed, and this remains a controversial issue. Moreover, section 5.6 of the 1998 Act reaffirms the 'power' of the Westminster Parliament to 'make laws for Northern Ireland'. According to Brigid Hadfield, section 5.6 'is the substantive equivalent' of section 75.[130] And beyond the realm of constitutional nicety, brute politics suggests that Westminster retains its overarching sovereignty. The suspension of the devolved institutions by the Northern Ireland Secretary of State in February 2000 provides the starkest evidence of this residual capacity.

Aside from its impact upon Anglo-British constitutional law, the Good Friday Agreement had a striking effect on the Irish Constitution, requiring the radical rewriting of Articles 2 and 3. Whereas the Preamble and the first three Articles of the Constitution had previously talked explicitly of a united Irish 'nation' and 'the national territory', and had even been interpreted in Irish case-law to imply a 'claim' to the northern province in international law, the amended Articles are notably more conciliatory. Article 2 now states that 'it is the entitlement and birthright of every person born in the island of Ireland' to 'be part of the Irish nation'. The language of entitlement is very different from that of claim; one is made by individuals, the other by nation-states. The recast Article 3 is just as striking:

> It is the firm will of the Irish nation, in harmony and friendship, to unite all the people who share the territory of the island of Ireland, in all the diversity of their identities and traditions, recognising that a united Ireland shall be brought about only by peaceful means with the consent of a majority of the people democratically expressed, in both jurisdictions in the island.

The invocation of a pluralist, rather than state-oriented, idea of political, and national, identity is one of the striking effects of the recent

[129] In B Hadfield, 'The Belfast Agreement, Sovereignty and the State of the Union', (1998) *Public Law*, 599.

[130] For a discussion of this issue, see Hadfield, *ibid*, 601–4.

attempt to settle the Irish 'troubles'.[131] And it might just be a means of settling the wider British 'problem' too.

III THE BRITISH PROBLEM

Looking for an Exit

So what then does the future hold for the increasingly fragmentary peoples of Britain? The former Welsh Secretary Ron Davies famously suggested that 'Devolution is a process. It is not an event and neither is it a journey with a fixed end-point. The devolution process is enabling us to make our own decisions and set our own priorities, that is the important point'. The view was reinforced by the President of the Welsh Assembly, Lord Elis-Thomas, who observed that 'We are not at the beginning of a new constitution for Wales. We are at the beginning of the end of the old constitution.'[132] There was no blueprint for devolution. Indeed, it is hard to think of anything that was less coherently planned.

For this reason projecting the future is not easy. The possibilities are various. One solution would be to recognise the 'logic' of devolution and to establish a formal federal Britain; a view supported by an increasing number of academic commentators. 'Long live the Federal Kingdom', Timothy Garton Ash declared in 2000.[133]

Federalism, however, has never enjoyed a great deal of intellectual, or indeed, popular currency in Britain. The ruling classes have preferred to seek solace in the lingering mythologies of the Diceyan 'unitary' state, at the apex of which can be found the related fantasies of a 'Fairy Queen' and a sovereign Parliament. All the cultural baggage that attaches to empire, from *Rule Britannia* to a British army to the 'Union' Jack also militate against federalism. The 1973 Kilbrandon Commission on the Constitution duly concluded that federalism was inappropriate for a Britain 'which had been governed in a spirit of unity

[131] For a broad discussion of these issues, see D Clarke, 'Nationalism, the Irish Constitution and Multicultural Citizenship', (2000) 51 *Northern Ireland Legal Quarterly*, 100–19.

[132] Bradbury & Mitchell, above n 110, 274–5, and M Marinetto, 'The Settlement and Process of Devolution: Territorial Politics and Governance under the Welsh Assembly', (2001) 49 *Political Studies*, 318.

[133] In Nairn, above n 95, 10. See also O'Neill, above n 102, 94, Olowofoyeku, above n 105, 83 and Brazier, above n 106, 126–27.

and co-operation for centuries'.[134] A quarter of a century on, however, the supposed 'spirit of unity' is rather less convincing.

Federalism is the obvious solution; some kind of 'semi' or 'quasi' federal compromise, descriptive of a process of continuing devolution, a possible panacea.[135] This latter possibility is, perhaps, the more likely if only because it smacks of muddling along; a strategy the English have always favoured in the governance of empire. It might be that the British-Irish Council ventured in the third 'strand' of the Good Friday Agreement will describe some kind of semi- or quasi-federal structure in due course.[136] The idea of a 'federalist culture', of 'habits of tolerance and co-operation' in lieu of formal federalism, is also popular.[137]

Regionalism offers itself as a second solution. It is attractive for a multitude of reasons, not least the fact that it could complement some kind of federal or quasi-federal settlement. It is, moreover, a solution that is actively encouraged in the 'new' Europe, at the heart of which is the idyll of a 'Europe of the regions'. The Catalan autonomous region is often presented as the obvious example of such a process. The same is true of decentralised authorities in Austria and Belgium. There is no member state of the European Union that more readily presents itself as a candidate for regional government than the increasingly disunited kingdom of Great Britain. Of course, regionalism suggests more than the immediate devolution of powers to the four 'nations'. Its logic demands a far more radical and far more vigorous decentralisation of legislative, executive and judicial power; so radical indeed that it seems, once again, to most obviously fit a properly federal model of governance. Ultimately, it seems, all roads lead back to the one obvious solution; coherent federal settlement, with properly demarcated spheres of legislative competence, and a series of interlocking regional bodies with equivalent powers.

Obvious it may be. But that does not make it likely. The shrewd money is on muddle. Indeed, devolution so far is a testament to muddle, resembling, as one commentator has suggested, a 'lottery in which winners and losers are selected by chance but in which no one has come up with the big prize'; a quite deliberate strategic 'muddle' designed to establish a 'dynamic for change by creating instability but also space

134 Royal Commission on the Constitution, 1973, Volume 1.

135 See Munro, above n 108, 46, and R Hazell, 'Reinventing the Constitution: Can the State Survive?' (1999) *Public Law*, 92.

136 See Nairn, above n 95, 4.

137 O'Neill, above n 102, 83.

for innovation'.[138] And a good each-way bet might be placed on muddle's ever-present bedfellow; cock-up. The refusal to institute a clear and definitive federal, or even quasi-federal, and regional settlement might lead to further fragmentation. The 'united' kingdom might finally fall apart by accident. Although nationalist parties in Scotland and Wales are currently struggling for support, it is not inconceivable that either or both nations might, in due course, assert independence.[139] There is a critical sense of incompleteness about the present devolution settlement. It will be taken further. But no one really knows where. As Tam Dalyell suggests, it is a 'motorway' without an obvious 'exit'.[140]

The possibility of future moves to full independence in any of the constituent nations of the 'United' Kingdom raises a number of intriguing constitutional questions. Not least is the possibility of legislation emerging from a devolved assembly that appears to be either in apparent contravention of the 1998 statutes or otherwise unwelcome at Westminster. The threat of such legislation clearly lay behind section 31 of the Scotland Act which contains a provision whereby relevant ministers must certify the lawfulness of legislation. Section 35 similarly permits the Secretary of State to intervene in order to prevent the submission of a bill for royal assent. The question of *vires* hovers ominously.

And the possibility of judicial intervention cannot be excluded. Powers of review in devolutionary matters have, with a certain irony, been placed in Westminster's ancient colonial court, the Judicial Committee of the Privy Council. The potential tensions are considerable, not least because it is unclear how the Judicial Committee is supposed to work with the ordinary courts in either England and Wales or in Scotland. The matter would become spicier still if, for example, an Edinburgh Court decided to exercise review, and came to a different conclusion from the Judicial Committee. The spirit of devolution would surely suggest that a Scottish court should enjoy jurisdiction, even if a strict interpretation of the 1998 Act suggested otherwise.[141] At present it might seem unlikely, but the future election of a strongly

[138] G.Stoker, 'Life is a Lottery: New Labour's Strategy for the Reform of Devolved Governance', (2002) 80 *Public Administration*, 417–18.

[139] For this suggestion, see Brazier, above n 106, 128, and Nairn, above n 95, 121–22.

[140] In Hazell & O'Leary, above n 111, 23.

[141] See P Craig & M Walters, 'The Courts, Devolution and Judicial Review', (1999) *Public Law*, 274–303, Rawlings, above n 104, 495–96, and also, prospectively, T Jones, 'Scottish Devolution and Demarcation Disputes', (1997) *Public Law*, 283–97.

'unionist' Conservative government at Westminster could easily raise the temperature, particularly if there was a strong nationalist majority in either the Scottish or Welsh assemblies.

As we have already seen, 'constitutional' matters are amongst those 'reserved' to Westminster, with the clear implication that any putative attempt by a devolved assembly to legislate for independence is precluded. 'Scotland', the White Paper affirmed uncompromisingly, 'will remain firmly part of the United Kingdom'.[142] Such phrases, attempting to prescribe the future, are always hostages to fortune. Within the particular context of devolution this is particularly so. The 1707 and 1800 Acts of Union, as we have seen, also tried to prescribe the future. If either the Westminster Parliament, or perhaps one of the devolved assemblies, decided to legislate for independence, then the precise nature of sovereignty would, once again, come into question. The 1998 Act might simply be repealed, or it might, following the classical doctrine of 'continuing' sovereignty, be deemed to be impliedly repealed.

Notably, each of the 1998 statutes subscribes to the classical notion of 'continuing' sovereignty. Section 35 of the Scotland Act, for example, provides that 'The Union with Scotland Act 1706 and the Union with England Act 1707 have effect subject to this Act', meaning that the 1998 Act has overridden those of 1706 and 1707, despite their presumption to bind future Parliaments. Presumably the 1998 Acts can be overridden in precisely the same way. There again, as Noreen Burrows has suggested, it is far from clear that any devolved Assembly should feel itself bound to accept the repeal of its devolved powers. According to Burrows the 1998 statutes 'transferred' rather than merely 'conferred' powers, and so any attempt to retrieve them would be constitutionally invalid, as well as politically vacuous. If this is not the case, she pointedly concludes, then 'devolution is a waste of time and effort'.[143] In this sense, the 1998 Acts should, perhaps, be viewed in the same light as the 1931 Statute of Westminster.

The prospects for Scottish and Welsh independence might, in practice, seem to be rather remote. The chances of an independent Northern Ireland, or more likely a reunited Ireland, are considerably greater. Schedule 1 paragraph 2 of the 1998 Act, moreover, contains the provision for a later referendum 'if at any time it appears likely' to the Secretary of State 'that a majority of those voting would express a wish

[142] In Brazier, above n 106, 101.

[143] N Burrows, *Devolution*, (London, Sweet & Maxwell, 2000), 56–65.

that Northern Ireland should cease to be part of the United Kingdom and form part of a united Ireland'. It represents, indeed, a binding obligation. Though, once again, it is open to debate whether, technically at least, future legislation could repeal Schedule 1 paragraph 2.[144]

The English Question

But what of England? As Brigid Hadfield has observed, the 'key element of the asymmetry' of devolution 'is a failure to address the constitutional arrangements for England'.[145] The constitutional, political, and indeed cultural, ramifications of the English 'question' are, of course, all the greater because devolution has gone off at such a half-cock. If Scotland, Wales and Northern Ireland were to become truly independent, or alternatively if they were to become part of a coherent federal settlement, then England's position would be defined, or at least rather better defined. As it is, it exists in a constitutional twilight world, a kind of quasi-country that has, as Tom Nairn comments, emerged 'helplessly unplanned'.[146] As a Charter 88 report concludes, 'The English have little reason to celebrate. The governance of England represents a gaping hole at the centre of the Government's devolution programme'.[147] The English 'question' raises issues of both constitutional integrity and cultural indeterminacy.

As it presently stands, without 'Great' Britain, England is a geopolitical and constitutional rump. Of the many constitutional incongruities, the most notorious is the famed 'West Lothian Question', originally formulated by the veteran Scottish anti-devolutionist Tam Dalyell. The 'Question' addresses the obvious anomaly that whilst English MPs at Westminster will no longer vote on matters devolved to the Scottish Assembly, Scottish MPs will be able to vote on matters relating to English governance. It was articulated by the English MP Douglas Hogg in the Parliamentary debates leading up to devolution:

[144] For a discussion, see Brazier, above n 106, 112–13.

[145] B Hadfield, 'Towards an English Constitution', (2002) 55 *Current Legal Problems*, 151. See also R Hazell et al. 'The Constitution: Coming in from the Cold', (2002) 55 *Parliamentary Affairs*, 222.

[146] Nairn, above n 95, 72.

[147] J Tomaney & M Mitchell, *Empowering the English Regions*, (London, Charter 88, 1999).

> It is absolute nonsense that Scottish members, under the devolution proposals, will be able to express a view and vote, perhaps decisively, on the domestic policies of England whereas I shall have no say about what happens in Scotland. It is little more bizarre that the Hon. Member for Linlithgow will be able to express a view on what happens in Lincolnshire, but will have no say on the domestic policies that affect his constituents. That is a constitutional affront.[148]

The Question is pressing, and as yet no-one has been able to hazard any sensible justification for the 'affront'. The sceptical argue that devolution of power to an English assembly would be the final stage in replacing the 'union' with a 'federation'. Moreover, the federation, the argument continues, would be critically unbalanced, with England very obviously dominant in terms of size and economic muscle.[149]

It is a valid issue. But it is not insurmountable, particularly if designed as part of a wider regional settlement.[150] At one level, this might simply describe a grand English region, replete with its own English Parliament. William Hague ventured this possibility in 1999, but hastily recanted when it became clear that the idea was not popular amongst Conservative constituency parties in the Home Counties. Robert Hazell has hazarded the alternative thought that the Westminster Parliament may anyway resemble more and more a *de facto* English Parliament.[151] There is no principled reason why an English parliament should be a problem; except, of course, that it would be another clear step towards some kind of federal constitutional settlement.

But regionalism can, and should, be taken rather further. The demand for a greater measure of devolved regional governance has become louder and louder, particularly in those putative regions furthest from London, such as Cornwall, the north-west, the north-east, and Yorkshire and Humberside. The idea of regional 'assemblies' is particularly popular. According to one northern MP, Austin Mitchell, the 'north' is 'ready, willing, able and waiting'.[152] The present government

148 In Olowofoyeku, above n 105, 59.

149 For an account see Hadfield, above n 145, 162–65.

150 Olowofoyeku, above n 105, 70–71, 83.

151 See R Hazell, 'Regional government in England: Three policies in search of a strategy', in S Chen & T Wright (eds), *The English Question*, (London, Fabian Society, 2000), 36.

152 P John and A Whitehead, 'The Renaissance of English Regionalism in the 1990s', (1997) 25 *Policy and Politics*, 9, 11–15, Hazell, above n , 37–38, and A Mitchell, 'Manifesto for the North', in S Chen & T Wright (eds), *The English Question*, (London, Fabian Society, 2000), 45–62.

has flirted with the idea of regionalism. Back in the 1997, Deputy Prime Minister John Prescott's White Paper 'committed' the government 'to move to directly-elected regional government in England, where there is demand for it'.[153] But then the political mood appeared to change. It is all too easy to assume that the 'demand' is not evident, particularly as no one is inclined to inquire after it too urgently. A private member's Referendum (England Parliament) Bill in 1997 failed to make any progress. The establishment of Regional Development Agencies (RDAs) feinted towards a regional instinct. But the real reason for the RDAs is efficiency rather than principle, and the desire to establish provincial 'outposts' for certain Whitehall departments. The collateral idea of Regional 'Chambers', meanwhile, was quietly shelved.[154]

More recently, the idea of regional assemblies has been ventured once again, with the promise of referenda to come in the north-east, the north-west and Yorkshire and Humberside. At the same time, however, as we shall see in the next chapter, local government 'reform' makes no meaningful gesture towards regional governance. If ever there was a case for 'joined-up' government it would be here. The election of mayors in London and a handful of other cities and towns, moreover, does more to illustrate the haphazard nature of 'devolution' in England than it does a coherent and principled approach to decentralized governance.[155]

Yet, the idea of regionalism in England makes very obvious sense, even more so within the context of a coherent federal Britain. Neil MacCormick's suggestion, that there might be a reinvested Anglo-Saxon heptarchy, with its seven historic regions, might seem rather whimsical; until we consider the paucity of credible alternatives.[156] The fear is that Westminster will just muddle on, hoping things somehow just work themselves out. At some point, something will have to be done with England. Just as it will with a Britain that has clearly reached its sell-by date; for as Nairn concludes, the Union has 'actually ceased to exist'. 'British Unionism', he affirms, 'was a short-lived pseudo-transcendence whose day is over'.[157] Neither the British 'problem' nor the English 'question' has been resolved. Indeed, the collapse of the 'inner' empire has barely begun.

[153] In Hazell & O'Leary, above n 111, 38.
[154] Hazell, above n 151, 32–35.
[155] O'Neill, above n 102, 90.
[156] MacCormick, above n 63, 195.
[157] Nairn, above n 95, 128–33, 154, and above n 95, 10–11.

The English Mind

The constitutional component of the English 'question' is irreducibly linked to the cultural. In simple terms, it is not easy to work out what England is supposed to be. As Tom Paulin observes, 'England no longer has a defining identity. It has no shape: you can't define it'.[158] Cultural identity was long ago sacrificed to the greater aspirations of 'Greater England', and in time 'Great Britain'.[159] Today, however, there is a veritable cottage-industry springing up around the English 'question'. A century ago, GK Chesterton famously alluded to the 'people of England, that have not spoken yet'. But they are certainly making up for it now. The search for an English cultural and political identity is on, and with a vengeance.[160]

A number of populist tomes have tended to the nostalgic. Roger Scruton's *England: An Elegy* is of this ilk.[161] So, too, is Simon Heffer's *Nor Shall My Sword*. The echoes of Bagehot are decidedly resonant in Heffer's assertion that the English are 'a simple and politically unsophisticated people', and, the implication follows, it would be best if they stayed that way. The prospective aspect to Heffer's vision of England is the suggestion that it might be refounded on an ethic of 'tolerance and pluralism'. It is an attractive thought, though not one that is hazarded with any great confidence.[162] The nostalgic struggles to detach itself from the melancholic. It was under this mournful spell that Lord Denning's courtrooms would periodically fall, conjuring images of 'young men mustered with their bows and arrows' on the commons of England.[163]

One of the most sophisticated of these latter-day pilgrimages into England's imagined past is Peter Ackroyd's *Albion*. According to Ackroyd the English imagination is described by an 'enchanted circle', an unending process of looking back in order to chart the future.

[158] Quoted in M Wood, *In Search of England: Journeys Into The English Past*, (London, Penguin, 2000), 92.

[159] Kumar, above n 88, ix.

[160] See Kumar, above n 88, x–xi.

[161] R Scruton, *England: An Elegy*, (London, Pimlico, 2001).

[162] S Heffer, *Nor Shall My Sword: The Reinvention of England*, (London, Weidenfeld & Nicolson, 1999), 11, 45.

[163] *New Windsor Corp v Miller* [1975] 1 Ch 386; *Myers v Milton Keynes Development Corp* [1974] 2 All ER 1098. For a discussion of Denning's 'other Eden', see D Klinck, ' "This Other Eden": Lord Denning's Pastoral Vision', (1994) 14 *Oxford Journal of Legal Studies*, 25–55.

Ackroyd places Bede and his *History of the English People* at the origins of a distinctive English identity. It was Bede who first chronicled an English people, who invested them with an 'authentic English sensibility', and so equipped them to imagine themselves. It is this tradition, Ackroyd argues, that passed down the centuries to Milton and Bunyan, Blake and Coleridge, an intensely historical and aesthetic sense of what England has been and what it could become.[164] Musing on the 'ancient Peace' of England, and her 'dewy pastures' and 'dewy trees', Tennyson cast a predictably wistful mid-Victorian tone.[165]

The same essential sentiment was caught in Rupert Brooke's *The Soldier*:

> Her sights and sounds; dreams happy as her day;
> And laughter, learnt of friends; and gentleness,
> In hearts at peace, under an English heaven.[166]

But there is something else here too; the invocation of 'gentleness'. It finds an echo in comments of the American philosopher, George Santayana, made half a century ago, that underneath the pompous and already decaying façade of the British state could be found the 'England of the countryside, and of the poets, domestic, sporting, gallant, boyish, of a sure and delicate heart'.[167] It could also be found in Tennyson's *Locksley Hall Sixty Years After*, the idea that England's freedom lay, not merely in its laws and institutions of state, but in its 'kindlier, higher, holier' sense of communal identity.[168] Raphael Samuel has more recently reached a similar conclusion, suggesting that whilst the artificial 'state' of Britain might seem to be forbidding and austere, the countervailing idea of England carries a certain poetic warmth, even 'charm'.[169]

It is this England that the conservative-minded politician has long sought to invoke. It is the England over which Stanley Baldwin rhapsodied in 1926. The:

[164] P Ackroyd, *Albion: The Origins of the English Imagination*, (London, Chatto & Windus, 2002), xix, 33–5, 49–53, 109–10.

[165] 'The Palace of Art', ll.86, 88, in A Tennyson, *Selected Poems*, (London, Penguin, 1991), 46.

[166] 'The Soldier', ll.13–15, in R Brooke, *Collected Poems*, (London, Sigwick & Jackson, 1987), 316.

[167] G Santayana, *Soliloquies in England, and Later Soliloquies*, (New York, Charles Scribner, 1922), 3.

[168] 'Locksley Hall Sixty Years After' ll.159–60, in Tennyson, above n 165, 338–39.

[169] R Samuel 'Preface' to Samuel (ed), *Patriotism: The Making and Unmaking of British National Identity*, (London, Routledge, 1989), x–xiii.

> sounds of England, the tinkle of the hammer on the anvil in the country smithy, the corncrake on a dewy morning, the sound of the scythe against the whetstone, the sight of a plough team coming over the brow of the hill, the sight that has been seen in England since England was a land, and may be seen in England long after the Empire has perished and every works in England ceased to function, for centuries the one eternal sight of England.[170]

Sixty-seven years later, John Major ventured along the same imaginary path, when he invoked an England of 'long shadows on county grounds, warm beer, invincible green suburbs, dog lovers', and 'as George Orwell said, old maids bicycling to Holy Communion through the morning mist'.[171]

But Orwell knew better. He knew that this England of 'morning mist', the England that was 'somehow bound up with solid breakfasts and gloomy Sundays, smoky towns and winding roads, green fields and red pillar-boxes', was essentially imaginary. As he concluded in his essay *The Lion and the Unicorn*, this England represents 'nothing but an enormous gush of country sentiment, a sort of accumulated vomit from a stomach stuffed with place-names'. Rather than the 'jeweled isle' of Shakespearian invocation, post-war England, he concluded, better resembles a 'family with the wrong members in control', where 'most of the power is in the hands of irresponsible uncles and bedridden aunts'.[172] Orwell knew that the nostalgic should always be balanced by the sceptical. Above all, he knew that the historical imagination can be a treacherous guide.

The search for an English identity has encouraged a complementary search for an English 'moment'; a moment when the English first identified themselves. Krishnan Kumar has recently suggested that this can be found in the later nineteenth century, when the fragile façade of empire looked about for cultural ballast and alighted upon the idea of promoting the Fairy Queen to Fairy Empress.[173] For essentially the same reasons, Linda Colley has preferred an eighteenth-century 'moment'.[174] The sixteenth-century alternative was famously preferred

[170] P Clarke, *Hope and Glory: Britain 1900–1990*, (London, Penguin, 1996), 134–35 and Paxman, above n 8, 142–43.

[171] J Major, *The Autobiography*, (London, Harper Collins, 1999), 376. It was the same John Major who startled everyone, particularly those in Scotland, Wales and Ireland, with the assertion that the 'British nation has a monarchy founded by the Kings of Wessex over eleven hundred years ago'. See Kumar, above n 88, 4.

[172] G Orwell, *Essays of George Orwell*, (London, Penguin, 1984), 116–17.

[173] Kumar, above n 88, 175–225. See also Davies, above n 98, 880–81.

[174] Colley, above n 98, particularly 1–4, 386–92.

by the likes of Maitland and Sir Geoffrey Elton, both of whom made much of the Henrician statutes of reformation as the founding texts of a political state that was English in reality and British in aspiration. Liah Greenfield has ventured the thought that the moment can really be located a century later, when these great statutes reached their political fruition in the establishment of a distinctive English 'commonwealth'.[175] We shall revisit this particular thought in rather greater depth in the next chapter.

Reaching considerably further back in history, Michael Wood has recently suggested that a distinctive English identity can be perceived in the emergent Anglo-Saxon kingships of the eighth and ninth centuries. Like Ackroyd, Wood makes much of Bede's *History*, and its determination of an identifiable '*imperium*' south of the Humber. The English were a 'chosen people' because they had an English church, and also a 'common law'.[176] As we shall again see in the next chapter, the idea of a common law set back in the mists of the dark ages might seem to be quintessentially mythic. But, as Woods emphasises, it is precisely this mythic quality that made it so compelling to subsequent generations. In the 'matter' of England, as the medieval chroniclers termed it, 'the myths create their own reality'; they 'help make us what we are' and 'they become part of history too'.[177]

It is an enticing thought; the suggestion that a distinctive, if dormant, English identity might actually be rooted in the idea of an English common law and a distinctive English constitutionalism. Norman Davies has recently made a similar assertion with regard to the constitutional nature of later medieval state building in England; a process that appeared to complement, even promote, an emergent sense of Englishness.[178] In this context, the search for an English constitution becomes all the more important; the location of England depending upon the location of its constitutional imagination. It is not, of course, a new thought. Writing at the end of the eighteenth century, Edmund Burke aligned the English constitution with an 'English mind'; a 'mind' that

[175] L Greenfield, *Nationalism: Five Roads to Modernity*, (Cambridge, Mass, Harvard UP, 1992), particularly 42–50, 420–26. For a similar suggestion, see Davies, above n 2, 456–57, 467.

[176] Wood, above n 158, 61, 95, 99–106, 286–87. See also Davies, above n 2, 198–200, 267–69. For a printed version of the fragmentary codes and of Alfred's will, see S Keynes & M Lapidge (eds), *Alfred the Great: Asser's 'Life of King Alfred' and Other Contemporary Sources*, (Harmondsworth, Penguin, 1983), 163–70, 173–78.

[177] Wood, above n 158, 69.

[178] Davies, above n 2, 367–69.

was characterised by its 'conscious dignity, a noble pride, a generous sense of glory and emulation'.[179] The 'spirit' of England could be found in the 'ancient' principles of a constitution that was an 'entailed inheritance', something which had been passed from generation to generation of Englishmen. It was also a 'prescriptive' constitution, one that inhered a 'presumption in favour' of a 'settled scheme of government against any untried project'.[180]

And the most revered of all prescriptions, of course, was that of the 'great and glorious' revolution of 1689; the revolution which conservatives such as Burke, and later Dicey, were so desperate to sequester. It was this revolution, and its Declaration, that had entrenched all the 'ancient fundamental principles of government', most prominent of which are the 'security' of 'law and liberty'.[181] And it was this England that another great Victorian conservative, Alfred Lord Tennyson, lauded as:

> A land of settled government,
> A land of just and old renown,
> Where Freedom slowly broadens down
> From precedent to precedent.[182]

All in all, the English constitution, according to Burke, was in 'harmony' with nature, 'placed in a just correspondence and symmetry with the order of the world', perfected by the 'disposition of stupendous wisdom, moulding together the great mysterious incorporation of the human race' as received through the 'principles of our forefathers' and described in the shared icons of a national community, 'our state, our hearths, our sepulchres, and our altars'. The English, Burke concluded, have a 'zeal' for order and conservation, and their constitution is the ultimate expression of this.[183] It is, finally, a deferential frame of mind, 'We fear God; we look up with awe to kings; with affection to parliaments; with duty to magistrates; with reverence to priests; and with respect to nobility'.[184] A mind that is defined by its constitution must, Burke affirmed, be a conservative mind.

[179] E Burke, *Reflections on the Revolution in France*, (London, Penguin, 1986), 92, 137.

[180] Burke, *ibid*, 106–7, 119. For a commentary, see J Pocock, 'Burke and the Ancient Constitution: A Problem in the History of Ideas', (1960) 3 *Historical Journal*, 15–43.

[181] Burke, *ibid*, 100, 117–19.

[182] 'You ask me, why, tho' ill at ease', 1842, quoted in Kumar, above n 88, 8.

[183] Burke, above n 180, 120–21, 180–87, 315.

[184] Burke, *ibid*, 182.

Perhaps so. But there again perhaps not. Burke was writing in order to promote one particular constitutional tradition, and one particular idea of England. It would be this tradition which, a century later, Dicey would sequester for the Anglo-British Union and Empire. But back at the turn of the eighteenth century, as Burke well knew, the nature of the 'English mind' was up for grabs, and the smarter money might have been on the triumph of a very different constitutional tradition and a very different idea of English-ness. For the self-styled 'friends of liberty', against whom Burke levelled his pen, the English constitution was a very different thing indeed; an instrument of radical liberty, equality and democracy. Today, after a century or more of Dicey's imperial orthodoxy, with England's various empires in steady decline, incapable of withstanding the myriad pressures of geopolitics and globalisation, the time has perhaps come to revisit this more radical alternative.

5

In Search of an English Constitution

IN AUGUST 1997 Princess Diana, the estranged wife of the heir to the throne and aspiring 'Queen of Hearts' was killed in a car driven by the drunken and drugged chauffeur of her Egyptian boyfriend. The world was momentarily unbalanced. Three quarters of a million watched the funeral: virtual mourning on an unparalleled scale. Psychiatrists are still trying to make sense of what has become known as the Diana 'effect'—if there is any sense to be had. The funereal theatre was enhanced by a glorious familial spat, as Diana's brother took the opportunity to make a series of disparaging remarks about the royal family. It was all too much. By the time they had listened to the Prime Minister of the day ham his way through a passage from Corinthians and Elton John stagger through a recast version of 'Candle in the Wind', controversially but strikingly re-titled 'Goodbye England's rose', the 'chosen people' waiting outside in the Mall were apparently hallucinating. Reports of premonitions were rife. Even Diana's eldest son, Prince William, admitted to having felt that something was 'wrong' just before he heard news of the crash.

Diana had been 'England's' rose, and England seemed to be particularly discombobulated. Crowds hung around Buckingham Palace for days on end, some reported seeing ghostly cloud formations resembling the profile of the lost Princess. Thousands queued to sign remembrance books. Little shrines to 'Saint Di' popped up around Kensington and along the Mall. People suddenly went to church again; at least for a couple of weeks. Thousands more bought ceramic images of Diana portrayed as the Virgin Mary.[1] Those who turned to the media for a voice of reason were to be disappointed. Paul Johnson, writing in the *Daily Mail*, felt himself possessed, confessing that 'In all sincerity, and at the risk of seeming blasphemous, I am reminded of the Blessed

[1] The most famous of these Diana icons, in the figure of a latter-day Virgin Mary was displayed as part of a show entitled 'Heaven' at the Liverpool Tate gallery in early 2000.

Virgin who, told of her destiny, answered with proud modesty "I am the handmaiden of the Lord".' There was, he assured his awed readers, a 'new spirit' abroad, 'moving across the country'. The 'surge of feeling', he concluded, 'has been a spontaneous collective religious act by the Nation'.[2]

But what precisely had happened to Britain? What could explain this collective loss of reason? In a notorious television interview Diana had claimed to represent a 'constituency of the rejected'. If this were true, the heroine of the 'outcasts', as David Cannadine describes her, did seem to represent an awfully big constituency.[3] Moreover, if, as the *Guardian* hazarded in one leader, Diana actually represented an anti-monarchical party, then the accompanying suggestion that her death might herald a republic did not seem to be quite so far-fetched.[4] It is certainly true that Diana had appeared to represent an alternative monarchy, if not an alternative to monarchy. Reaching back to the wave of popular excitement in 1984, when Diana married Charles, Diana Simmonds recalled that the 'presence of the Queen on her throne, with her Dutiful Son and his Beautiful Wife waiting at her side is one thing that really stops little England from facing up' to the 'ghastly reality' that pretty much everything else about 'Great' Britain is a sham.[5]

Four centuries earlier, the Elizabethan courtier Sir John Harrington admitted that the whole purpose of monarchy is to transform the mundanity of governance into a 'kind of Romanze'.[6] Just for a moment, Diana seemed capable of doing this. But then she died, and the 'chosen people' were abandoned once again. And all the dark thoughts returned.

[2] For various accounts of Diana's death and its aftermath, see A Morton, *Diana: Her True Story*, (London, Michael O'Mara, 1997), 270–82, B Campbell, *Diana, Princess of Wales: How Sexual Politics Shook the Monarchy*, (London, Women's Press, 1998), 242–45, and D Merck, *After Diana: Irreverent Elegies*, (London, Verso, 1998), 7–9, 85.

[3] See D Cannadine, *History in Our Time*, (London and New Haven, Yale UP, 1998), 78.

[4] Merck, above n 2, 5, 21–24, 29–32, Morton, above n 2, 278–80, and Campbell, above n 2, 202–3, 247–48.

[5] In T Nairn, *The Enchanted Glass: Britain and its Monarchy*, (London, Picador, 1988), 26.

[6] S Greenblatt, *Renaissance Self-Fashioning*, (Univ of Chicago Press, 1980), 168–69.

I CASTING DOWN IMAGINATIONS

Busy Doing Nothing

According to Neil MacCormick, we presently 'live in times of exciting and profound constitutional debate'.[7] Indeed, it has even been suggested that the present Prime Minister, Tony Blair, is 'the most far reaching, radical reformer of the formal edifice of the constitution since Oliver Cromwell'.[8] It is an arresting claim; though the phrase 'formal edifice' is, perhaps, critical. The 'new' Labour government that came to office in the spring of 1997 promised much. The mantra was 'modernization'; something which, as Dawn Oliver has rightly observed, does not necessarily guarantee meaningful reform.[9] Even so, it was reasonable to suppose that an age of political and constitutional reform, iconoclasm even, had dawned; an age, indeed, when the very idea of England, and an English constitution, might be recast.[10]

Even Parliament, that most revered of icons, was due for an overhaul. The House of Commons, as one former Clerk of Committees to the House observed, needed to be 'reformed and revitalised', and 'urgently' if it is 'to command the respect of the people' once more.[11] To date, however, despite some adjustment to the timings of sittings, little seems to have disturbed the cobwebs. It might be true that MPs no longer need to wear hats when raising points of order during divisions. But the abolition of the manifestly absurd is hardly an achievement that warrants loud applause. Much of Parliamentary business in the chamber still appears to be conducted by juvenile delinquents.

The need to do something about the House of Lords, the home as Lloyd George put it, of 'five hundred men, chosen accidentally from

[7] N MacCormick, *Questioning Sovereignty: Law, State and Practical Reason*, (Oxford UP, 1999), 78. The sentiment is enjoined by Nevil Johnson, in 'Taking Stock of Constitutional Reform', (2001) 36 *Government and Opposition*, 331–54.

[8] J Morison, 'The Case Against Constitutional Reform?', (1998) 25 *Journal of Law and Society*, 510.

[9] D Oliver, *Constitutional Reform in the UK*, (Oxford UP, 2003), 3–4, 353.

[10] For the suggestion that constitutional reform might aid the political and cultural redefinition of England, see A Dummett, 'Citizenship and National Identity', in R Hazell (ed) *Constitutional Futures: A History of the Next Ten Years*, (Oxford UP, 1999), 215–17.

[11] M Ryle, 'House of Commons Procedures', in R Blackburn & R Plant (eds), *Constitutional Reform: The Labour Government's Constitutional Reform Agenda*, (Harlow, Longman, 1999), 135.

amongst the unemployed', was plainer still.[12] A century and half ago, Bagehot noted its 'feeble and forlorn' condition, and suggested that its only real function was to further nurture that innate 'reverence for rank' which the 'bovine' populace craves.[13] Reform of the House was high on Lloyd George's agenda, and he played a major role in securing the passage of the 1911 Parliament Act which ended the House's power to block finance bills, as well as limiting the power to delay other forms of legislation. The Preamble to the 1911 Act declared that 'It is intended to substitute for the House of Lords as it at present exists a Second Chamber constituted on a popular instead of hereditary basis'. A handful of years short of a century later, we are still waiting.

Prior to gaining office, Tony Blair loudly declaimed that 'Perhaps the least defensible part of the British constitution is the power wielded by hereditary peers in the House of Lords'. And, he continued, 'It is in principle wrong and absurd that people should wield power on the basis of birth not merit or election'.[14] Successive Labour party manifestos proclaimed an intention to reform the second chamber, even if they did not say precisely how. Blair was, of course, right. As Robert Blackburn has observed, the 'composition and appearance' of an hereditary second chamber was wholly 'lacking' in 'democratic credibility'.[15] But the declamation was hardly original. Labour party leaders had been making the same promise since Clement Attlee.

Unfortunately, reform of the second chamber has turned into a bit of a mess. The first stage of reform saw the removal of most, but not all, of the hereditary peers. The handful that remain, ironically, are elected by their peers; giving them a degree of democratic legitimacy that will not be shared by any invited or 'selected' colleagues. The final composition of the second chamber remains uncertain, though, at present, it appears that it will be largely, even exclusively, selected. Various alternatives have been mooted. The Wakeham Commission suggested that there should be a mixture of members; some elected on a regional basis, a number of crossbenchers appointed by a Commission, a majority of party members and a smattering of bishops.[16] The House of

[12] P Clarke, *Hope and Glory: Britain 1900–1990*, (London, Penguin, 1996), 61.

[13] W Bagehot, *The English Constitution*, (Cambridge UP, 2001), 68–70, 93.

[14] Quoted in R Blackburn, 'The House of Lords' in R Blackburn & R Plant *Constitutional Reform: The Labour Government's Constitutional Reform Agenda*, (Harlow, Longman, 1999), 9–11.

[15] Blackburn, *ibid*, 27.

[16] For commentaries on Wakeham and its proposals, see variously Johnson, above n 7, 346–48, Shell, above n 16, 298, 301–7, and D Smith, 'A House for the Future: Debating

Commons appears to be quite baffled by the alternatives. It is the government, or rather the Prime Minister, who seems to favour a largely 'selected' chamber; largely selected by a Commission selected by the government. Bagehot favoured a 'selected' second chamber; precisely because it was an alternative to democracy. It will, as Robert Blackburn, observes, be a 'minimalist solution'.[17]

On his dismissal from government in 1998, the former Leader of House of Lords, Lord Richard, commented that he did not think that the Prime Minister's 'mind has been engaged' with the matter of second chamber reform 'in any concentrated way'.[18] Maybe not. But it has certainly been energetically engaged with the matter of creating new peers; a hundred and seventy being created in just the first two years of government, compared with two hundred in all eleven years of Thatcher administrations. And the smell of something rotten lingers. Lords Sainsbury, Bragg, Puttnam and Levy lead the way among peers who just happened to make large donations to the Labour Party in recent years, and then just happened to find themselves garbed in ermine.[19]

It might seem to be a fairly gentle kind of constitutional abuse; the selection of favoured supermarket owners and film makers to help populate Parliament and run the government. But is still abuse all the same; and it appears to have entered the soul of modern British politics. And it is no more suited to a modern liberal democracy than the vicissitudes of genetic selection. Money talks; every bit as much now as it did a century ago when US President McKinley's campaign manager famously remarked that 'There are two things that are important in politics. The first is money, and I can't remember the second one'. It should not, and it need not, be this way.

The idea that there should be reform to party financing and expenditure in British politics has bounced around for some time. It gained the rhetorical support of the Labour party in the run up to the 1997 election. Once in power, however, it was to be 'business' as usual. The Ecclestone 'affair', in which a prominent Labour party donor secured an audience with the Prime Minister, and by happy chance

Second Chamber Reform in the United Kingdom' (2000) 35 *Government and Opposition*, 325–44.

[17] R Blackburn, 'The House of Lords', in R Blackburn & R Plant (eds), above n 14, 39.

[18] In D Shell, 'Labour and the House of Lords: A Case Study in Constitutional Reform', (2000) 53 *Parliamentary Affairs*

[19] See J Paxman, *The Political Animal: An Anatomy*, (London, Penguin, 2002) 256.

the adjustment of government policy in his favour, was as disgraceful as it was sadly predictable. When the 'affair' seeped out, the Prime Minister, as is his wont, duly apologised profusely and admitted that there was a 'powerful case' for reform. A couple of years later, the same Prime Minister was on the phone to the Romanian premier on behalf of another businessman who wished to buy a Romanian steel company. Strangely enough, he too had just made a large donation to the party. The media expressed its disappointment; something which attracted the displeasure of the Chairman of the Labour Party who opined, with as straight a face as he could manage, that such negative reporting promoted a 'dangerous antipathy in politics'.[20]

The 2000 Political Parties, Elections and Referendums Act, inspired by the Neill Report in 1998, might have gone some way to curbing excessive election expenditure, requiring declaration of donations exceeding £5000. But it is hardly a deterrent. Indeed, given the overall limitation on election expenditure, the impact of particular substantial donations can become all the greater. Sir Paul Getty's donation of £5 million to the Conservative Party in 2001 would now represent 40% of the national campaign expenditure; a significantly higher percentage than previously.[21] The only way that such corruption can be erased from the political scene is by enforcing limits on individual donations; not simply requesting declarations. Substantial donations are made for a reason; to influence policy and to buy favour.

It is simply wrong. As Martin Linton observes:

> The most basic principle is that democracy should treat people as political equals. That does not just mean that they should all have a vote and that their votes should count the same, but that they should have the same access to information on which to make their decision. And that means, looking at it from the other side of the fence, that candidates and political parties should have the same access to voters through advertising, broadcasting and the press, the same resources to spend in elections and the same claim on public resources.[22]

[20] See M Linton, 'The Funding of Political Parties', in R Blackburn & R Plant (eds), above n 14, 50–55, M Harrop, 'An Apathetic Landslide: The British Election of 2001', (2001)*Government and Opposition*, 297–9, and J Rowbottom, 'Political Donations and the Democratic Process: Rationales for Reform', (2002) *Public Law*, 760–63.

[21] Rowbottom, *ibid*, 759, and P Webb, 'Parties and Party Systems: Modernisation, Regulation and Diversity', (2001) 54 *Parliamentary Affairs*, 312–19, and also 'Parties and Party Systems: More Continuity than Change', (2002) 55 *Parliamentary Affairs*, 372.

[22] Linton, above n 20, 48.

If we cannot get beyond a politics so obviously perverted by over-mighty parties and over-mighty governments, we might at least endeavour to constrain those who most blatantly abuse their might.

And party reform merges into the matter of electoral reform. Here, once again, rather more has been promised than delivered. The Jenkins Commission, established by 'new' Labour in 1997, castigated the 'first-past-the-post' system as a sorry apology for democracy.[23] And it seems that the present government is happy, in principle, with proportional representation here and there; though happier with it there than here. It is good enough for the Scots, Welsh and Northern Irish. It is also good enough, apparently, for European elections. It is not, however, good enough for British general elections. The present Prime Minister has announced his 'reservations' regarding electoral reform; which we can reasonably infer to be reservations about giving up the certainty of his party being one of the only two that is guaranteed a place on the merry-go-round of political power that passes for representative democracy in modern Britain.[24]

Of course, it would be foolish to underplay the political and constitutional reforms that have been made. The impact of devolution is undoubted, and the Human Rights Act might, in time, prove to be of considerable importance. Proposed reforms to the judiciary, including the establishment of a Supreme Court and greater openness regarding judicial appointments, are also to be applauded. The abolition of the office of the Lord Chancellor, an office which Bagehot termed a 'heap of anomalies', is also striking. The position of the Lord Chancellor, as a member of the House of Lords, both in a legislative and judicial capacity, and as a member of government, clearly breached the principle of the separation of powers.[25] It was, as Lord Steyn argued, 'no longer sustainable'; a view obliquely reinforced by the European Court of Human Rights in the *McGonnell* case, which suggested that the existence of such offices breached Article 6 of the European Convention.[26]

[23] See I McLean, 'The Jenkins Commission and the Implications of Electoral Reform for the UK Constitution', (1999) 34 *Government and Opposition*, 143–60, and also R Plant, 'Proportional Representation', in R Blackburn & R Plant (eds), above n 14, 72–73.

[24] P Norris, 'The Twilight of Westminster? Electoral Reform and its Consequences', (2001) 49 *Political Studies*, 896–97.

[25] See, for example, D Woodhouse, 'The Office of Lord Chancellor' (1998) *Public Law* 624–32.

[26] *McGonnell v UK* No 28488/95 (20.10.98, 8.2.00) European Commission of Human Rights. See also Steyn, 'The Weakest and Least Dangerous Department of Government' (1997) *Public Law*, 85. A clearly piqued Lord Irvine responded that the Steyn was 'not a

Overall, however, there is a sense of both bewilderment and frustration. The former is well described by Peter Hennessy, when he refers to the 'Tommy Cooper—or "just like that"' school of reform; each successive reform apparently pulled out of a hat, leaving the rest of us to gape in astonishment and wonder how it happened at all.[27] The apparent lack of overall direction, the 'inconsistency and hesitations' as Robert Hazell puts it, is unsettling.[28] Dawn Oliver similarly regrets a lack of 'coherent vision' which leaves the 'modernization' process 'in many respects incoherent and incomplete'.[29] Tom Nairn complains that the present reform 'package' appears to be little more than 'a shifting pattern of stratagems and *ad hoc* arrangements, where it is becoming harder and harder to find fixed points of reference'.[30]

The frustration is, in part, a product of the original Faustian pact which defines our relationship with our politicians. So much was promised, and we were so willing to believe.[31] As Pippa Norris suggests, we should not perhaps be so surprised that reform is so piecemeal, so hesitant; with 'constitutional reform, like Johnson's dog singing in a bar, the amazement is not due to the grace of the voice but to the fact that it is happening at all'.[32] Hennessy records being informed by one Whitehall insider that 'Most senior Ministers involved in constitutional reform either don't believe in it, aren't interested in it or don't understand it'.[33] But, if we have been conned, we should not unduly ashamed. We have been conned before, and probably will be again.

And the reason, as Hennessy implies, is not that difficult to discern. Our political 'establishment', the 'Thing' as William Cobbett termed it two centuries ago, is not enamoured by the idea of change. After all, that is why it is established. If there is to be reform, it should only, as

political scientist' and so could not know about the 'internal workings of Government'. It was not a convincing repost. For his comments see, R Stevens, *The English Judges*, (Oxford, Hart, 2002) 128.

27 P Hennessy, *The Prime Minister: The Office and its Holders since 1945*, (London, Penguin, 2001) 510.

28 R Hazell, 'Reinventing the Constitution: Can the State Survive?' (1999) *Public Law*, 102.

29 Oliver, above n 9, 3–4.

30 T Nairn, *After Britain: New Labour and the Return of Scotland*, (Cambridge, Granta, 2000) 33, 156–57, 278. For a similar conclusion, see Johnson, 'Reform', 352–54

31 A Rawnsley, *Servants of the People: The Inside Story of New Labour*, (Hamish Hamilton, 2000), 382–83.

32 Norris, 'Consequences', 896.

33 Quoted in R Hazell, above n 28, 86.

Bagehot observed, extend to removing the most patent of constitutional 'oddities', those that are obviously 'mischievous'.[34] As the great conservative idealogue, Edmund Burke, observed, 'A state without the means of some change, is without the means of its conservation'.[35] This quintessentially Whiggish mindset was beautifully encapsulated in the adage of Trollope's fictional Prime Minister, the Duke Omnium. According to Omnium, whilst Prime Ministers must appear to be busy, their ultimate responsibility to the constitution and the country is to do as little as possible, for 'The safest way in the world is to do nothing'.[36] We presently live in an age of Whig reform; another one.

Casting Down Imaginations

Thomas Hobbes would not have been particularly puzzled by the Diana 'effect'. The English, he concluded in his great treatise, *Leviathan*, seemed to relish life in the 'kingdome of darkenesse', possessed by the 'Phantasms of the braine', given to the 'worship of such images', enchanted by 'illusions' and the 'vaine and impious Conjurations' of priests and princes.[37] It was this propensity to wild and impious 'imaginations' that so troubled Hobbes's contemporary, the poet John Milton. Before there could be any reform of the constitution, Milton urged in 1649, such 'imaginations' must be 'cast down'.[38] As the radical Thomas Rainsborough had opined a couple of years earlier in the famous Putney 'debates', there must be 'root and branch' reform; for there can be no pretended hierarchies in a truly free and equal 'commonwealth'.[39] And so they were. Monarchy, Church and House of Lords; all were cast down in 1649.

But the mindset proved to be rather harder to reform. A century and a half later, Tom Paine's *Rights of Man* bemoaned a 'constitution' that

[34] Bagehot, above n 13, 182–83.

[35] E Burke, *Reflections on the Revolution in France*, (London, Penguin, 1986), 106.

[36] A Trollope, *Phineas Finn*, (London, Penguin, 1985), 574. For a general commentary on the present Whig mindset, see T Nairn, *Pariah: Misfortunes of the British Kingdom*, (London, Verso, 2002), 88–90, and Morison, above n 8, 525–26.

[37] For Hobbes's denunciation of such constitutional idolatry, see T Hobbes, *Leviathan*, (London, Penguin, 1985), 405, 435, 466, 475–79, 498–99, 568–71, 657–77, 705–13.

[38] See I Ward, 'Casting Down Imaginations: Politics and Poetry in the English Republic', (2002) 21 *Journal of Legal History*, 101–14.

[39] A Woodhouse, *Puritanism and Democracy*, (London, Dent, 1986), 61, 69, 71.

still bore the marks of a fantastic 'burlesque'. Above all, he railed against a 'form of government' that was still underpinned by a barely comprehensible reverence for 'hereditary' kings and queens, nobles and political classes. Such reverence, he urged, is 'ridiculous'. And of course it is. But it is a reverence that we still retain. Paine, too, would have been unsurprised by the events of autumn 1997. All too often, he bemoaned, the English mind 'pities the plumage, but forgets the dying bird'.[40] The English, he feared, would never bring themselves to abolish the monarchy so long as they could fret over the misfortunes of pretty princesses.[41]

All the present constitutional reforms, the tinkering with Parliament, the half-hearted attempts to deal with political corruption, even the Human Rights Act and devolution, pale into comparison with the most glaring and pressing need; to abolish Church and Crown. There is a point of principle, as the republican James Harrington observed in his *Oceana* published in 1656; for 'where there is equality of power, there can be no monarchy'.[42] But there is a point of practice too. Monarchs are not harmless old maids, trundling round the country opening flood barriers and being nice to people. They are the embodiment of executive power, its excuse and its abuse; as much a menace to liberty and democracy today as they were in 1649.[43] As Tony Benn commented, if the monarchy vanished, it would rapidly become apparent to all that we are governed by a 'medieval monarchy located at No 10 Downing Street'.[44] Small wonder that the present Prime Minister prattles on about the Queen being 'simply the best of British'; whatever that means. As Jonathan Freedland rightly observes, the monarchy continues to instill 'fresh generations' with 'a feudal history of inequality'.[45]

[40] T Paine, *Rights of Man*, (London, Penguin, 1984) 51. According to Frank Prochaska, Paine's polemic was the 'great opening salve against the modern British Crown'. See F Prochaska, *The Republic of Britain 1760–2000*, (London, Allen Lane, 2000), 4–5.

[41] The princess over whom everyone was fretting in 1790 was, of course, Marie Antoinette.

[42] J Harrington, *A Commonwealth of Oceana*, (Cambridge UP, 1992), 60.

[43] See R Brazier, 'A British Republic', (2002) 61 *Cambridge Law Journal*, 368–69, and also 'Constitutional Reform and the Crown', in M Sunkin & S Payne (eds), *The Nature of the Crown: A Legal and Political Analysis*, (Oxford UP, 1999), 350–58.

[44] In T Nairn, above n 5, 111.

[45] J Friedland, *Bring Home the Revolution: The Case for a British Republic*, (London, Fourth Estate, 1998), 191, 194.

A century ago, the radical Charles Bradlaugh observed that whilst 'monarchy is for children', republicanism is for 'grown-ups'.[46] And yet, champions can still be found entering the lists. Vernon Bogdanor, for example, suggests that monarchy can be an 'aid to reforming government'. It fixes 'constitutional landmarks and a degree of institutional continuity in a changing world', ensuring 'not conservatism' apparently, but 'legitimacy'. And most importantly, the monarchy 'alone can represent the whole nation in an emotionally satisfying way; it alone is in a position to interpret the nation to itself'.[47] Fairy Queens have survived on such mystical nonsense for centuries.[48]

One of the most common defences, famously advanced by Bagehot, is that Britain is anyway a 'disguised republic', and so the physical presence of a Queen hardly matters. It was a common recourse amongst the more troubled mid-Victorians. Henry Labouchere agreed that 'Although theoretically a Monarchy, this country is practically a Republic with a hereditary President at the head of it'.[49] Tennyson averred to the same matter in his idea of a 'crown'd Republic's crowning common-sense' in his *Idylls of the King*. More recently, Frank Prochaska has reminded us that the idea of republic speaks most immediately to the positive aspect of civic governance, rather than the negative aspect of abolishing monarchy.[50] This is true. But it is no reason to maintain a monarchy. It is simply an excuse for not doing anything about it. It is the solution that the Duke of Omnium would undoubtedly have recommended.

Bagehot, of course, was fully aware that an 'unroyal form of parliamentary government' was generally to be preferred to a royal one; provided the common man could be educated in his civil responsibilities.[51] George Bernard Shaw likewise consoled himself with the thought that once the English have educated themselves, then the 'universal hallucination' of monarchy will pass.[52] But not, it seems, just yet. As one of Shaw's fellow intellectual travellers, the early socialist Beatrice Webb observed, when it comes to contemplating monarchy the British

[46] In Prochaska, above n 40, 128.

[47] V Bogdanor, *The Monarchy and the Constitution*, (Oxford UP, 1995), 301.

[48] See D Cannadine, *History in our Time*, (London and New Haven, Yale UP, 1998), 23–24.

[49] Prochaska, above n 40, 137.

[50] Prochaska, *ibid*, xvi–vii.

[51] Bagehot, above n 13, 170.

[52] In Prochaska, above n 40, 145.

appear to be afflicted by a sudden 'softening of the brain'.[53] The affliction has yet to pass.

And the same, it appears, applies to the established Church, of which the monarch is hereditary Governor. Over half a century ago, George Orwell brilliantly evoked the image of a 'chosen people' who no longer believed in God, but who retained a peculiar fondness for a 'nice cup of tea' and a church of their 'own'.[54] Bagehot similarly attested to the desperate faith of a people who still believed that their Church, like their monarch, was gifted them 'by grace of God'.[55] For much of the previous four centuries, the idea that the monarch should be Governor of the established Church, and thus of an 'entire nation at prayer', was credible.[56] It is not now. Only 4% of us confess to being Anglican; a figure which, as Norman Davies has suggested, undercuts any claim that either England or the United Kingdom 'could reasonably claim to be a Protestant country'.[57] Indeed, given the reality of an increasingly multicultural England, the existence of a privileged Church veers from the whimsical to the offensive.[58] And yet, amidst the chatter of constitutional reform, the idea of disestablishing the Church barely earns a murmur.

The place of the Church, like that of the monarch, reflects the continuing influence of what Nairn terms, our imagined 'national spirit-essence'.[59] There is no logic or sense to either. But we cannot quite let go. Indeed, as our empires fall around us, we seem to be more and more determined to hang on to whatever glitter remains; no matter how tarnished.[60] Republicanism is deemed to be beyond the pale of respectable political debate, treated, as Nairn affirms, as some kind of 'defiant form of eccentricity'. With a civil list of £8 million a year, it has become ever more obvious that the 'Queen and her lot are on the game, and getting away with it on a gargantuan scale'. But we just do not care that much.[61] As David Cannadine concludes, 'as long as people find it

53 In Prochaska, *ibid*, 184.
54 G Orwell, *Essays of George Orwell*, (Harmondsworth, Penguin, 1984), 146–47, 283.
55 Bagehot, above n 13, 37–38.
56 Bogdanor, above n 47, 220–21.
57 N Davies, *The Isles: A History*, (Basingstoke, Macmillan, 1999) 915.
58 D Cannadine, *In Churchill's Shadow: Confronting the Past in Modern Britain*, (Oxford UP, 2002), 26.
59 Nairn, above n 5, 91–93.
60 Cannadine, above n 58, 21, 49, 75, and also *Ornamentalism: How the British Saw Their Empire*, (Oxford UP, 2002), 21.
61 Nairn, above n 5, 50–56, 61.

amusing, and want to be amused by it, they will be happy to see it undermined, but uneager to kill it off'.[62]

Sadly, there will be no serious constitutional reform until we do. As one government minister recklessly acknowledged, the monarchy is a 'scandal-ridden anachronism'.[63] But its abolition is also reckoned to be vote-loser; and nothing is worth risking an election for. Rather than being cast down, monarchy, like so much else in our constitution, is merely being refurbished. A few hangers-on, will hang-on rather less securely, just as a few more hereditary peers will retire to their country estates, and a few more party donors might have admit the extent of their political patronage. It hardly amounts to 'root and branch' reform. But it seems to be as much as the English, or more precisely its governing elite, are prepared to countenance; at least for now.[64]

II COMMONWEAL, COMMON GOOD AND COMMON LAW

Commonweal and Common Good

Aside from a desire to effect 'root and branch' institutional reform, what really drove men like Milton and Rainsborough four centuries ago was the idea of forging a better society, one that was more free, more democratic, more equal, and, indeed, more virtuous. They imagined an English commonwealth or 'common weal'. More recently, Neil MacCormick has resurrected the same idea, envisaging a reconstituted Britain, and Europe, that is composed of a series of interlocking commonwealths. According to MacCormick:

> The particular point of what we can call a 'commonwealth' is that it should comprise a group of people to whom can reasonably be imputed some consciousness that they have a 'common weal', something which really is a common good, and who are able to envisage themselves or their political representatives and governing authorities realizing this or striving after it through some form of organized political structure, embodied in some common constitutional arrangements.[65]

[62] D Cannadine, *History in Our Time*, (Yale UP, 1998) 8.

[63] R Blackburn & R Plant, 'Monarchy and the Royal Prerogative', in R Blackburn & R Plant, above n 14, 140.

[64] Nairn, above n 5, 54, 61, 388–91.

[65] N MacCormick, above n 7, 145.

Whilst the immediate context is given by the geopolitical challenges of devolution and the 'new' Europe, the historical antecedents of the idea, as MacCormick admits, are rooted in the classical ideas of commonwealth projected in the seventeenth and eighteenth centuries.[66]

The intellectual genealogy is critical. There is nothing particularly new about the idea of a distinctive English commonwealth, devoid of monarchy, established Church, hereditary peerage and so on. Indeed, prior to the pretensions of imperialism, English constitutional thought was inextricably linked to classical ideas of *res publica*. And it carried a radical charge. Passing down the generations under the guise of the 'good old cause', it would fire 'friends of liberty' with a devout belief that the 'revolution principles' of 1689 meant not just the sovereignty of the Parliament, but the rule of law and the fundamental liberty and equality of all Englishmen. Blair Worden has recently emphasised the continuing hold of 'roundhead reputations' during the eighteenth and nineteenth century, nurturing on the one hand a desire for liberty, and on the other a deep suspicion of government.[67]

The relation between constitutional reform and the idea of the 'common good' was vividly described by Milton in his essay written in defence of the idea of an English *res publica* in 1649, *The Tenure of Kings and Magistrates*. Opening with the assertion that 'No man who knows ought can be so stupid to deny that all men naturally were borne free, being the image and resemblance of God himself', Milton could affirm that power exercised by 'kings and magistrates is nothing else, but what is only derivative, transferr'd and committed to them in trust from the People, to the common good of them all'. Power, in short, 'remains fundamentally' with the 'commonwealth' of Englishmen.[68] It was this kind of rhetoric that could be found in radical republican tracts of the late 1640s, such as John Lilburne's *Agreement of the People* and John Wildman's *London Liberties*.[69]

Whilst Milton's republic would founder after barely a decade, the principles of the 'cause' would pass into radical mythology. And foremost amongst the mythologists was the civil war hero and republican martyr Algernon Sidney, whose *Discourses Concerning Government*, composed between 1681–83, bluntly asserted that the pretended 'right

[66] MacCormick, *ibid*, 167.

[67] For an overview of his thesis, see B Worden, *Roundhead Reputations: The English Civil Wars and the Passions of Posterity*, (London, Penguin, 2001), 1–19.

[68] J Milton, *Political Writings*, (Cambridge UP, 1991), 8–11.

[69] See Woodhouse, above n 39, 342–79.

of paternity as to dominion', meaning hereditary authority, 'is at an end'.[70] Sidney composed his *Discourses* as a rebuttal to Sir Robert Filmer whose *Patriarcha* had resolutely defended the idea of monarchical absolutism, and done so by suggesting that the right of the Stuart monarchs was secured by 'Adamic succession', through their descent from Old Testament kings. The notion, Sidney suggested, was absurd. Moreover, monarchy must be abolished not simply because it offends principles of equality, but because it impedes the 'publick good', the promotion of which is the 'end of all government'.[71] Magistrates, of whatever seniority, should only be selected in accordance with their ability to promote this good. The 'virtuous' magistrate is, indeed, 'distinguished from other men, by the power with which the law invests them for the publick good'.[72] Better still, of course, citizens should govern themselves; for the practice of self-government 'makes men generous and industrious' and 'fills their hearts with love' for the community within which they live.[73] This latter thought would really catch fire a century later.

Sidney's contemporary, John Locke, was equally convinced of the relation between 'common good' and good government. In his *Essay on Toleration*, written in 1667, he suggested:

> That the whole trust, power, and authority of the magistrate is vested in him for no other purpose but to be made use of for the good, preservation, and peace of men in that society over which he is set, and therefore that this alone is and ought to be the standard and measure according to which he ought to square and proportion his laws, model and frame his government.[74]

The same principle underpinned Locke's later and more famous *Treatises on Civil Government*, the first part of which was also composed as an immediate repost to Filmer. The 'proper remedy for the inconveniences of the state of nature', the second *Treatise* argued, is 'commonwealth' and civil government. Such a 'commonwealth', he famously argued, is described by a series of contracts between citizens and sovereign institutions, 'by positive engagement and express

[70] A Sidney, *Discourses Concerning Government*, (Liberty Fund, 1996), 56. For Sidney's particular 'reputation' amongst the martyrs of the 'cause', see Worden, above n 67, 122, 129–33.

[71] Sidney, *ibid*, 357.

[72] Sidney, *ibid*, 51. See also, 49, 74, 79–83.

[73] Sidney, *ibid*, 166, 199.

[74] J Locke, *Essay on Toleration*' in *Political Essays*, (Cambridge UP, 1997), 135.

promise and compact'.[75] In this way, as Sidney had also affirmed, ultimate sovereignty remains in the citizenry itself. No parliament, in a free society at least, can enjoy 'absolute' or 'arbitrary' power.[76] It was for this reason that Locke made so much of the 'separation of powers' in a balanced constitution.

The residual influence of the 'cause', as it was variously interpreted by the likes of Milton, Sidney and Locke, cannot be overestimated. The English 'mind' remained 'haunted by the Civil War' for centuries after.[77] Writing at the end of the eighteenth century, the poet Robert Southey observed that the enduring 'passions' of the civil wars had 'continued to this day'.[78] For zealots such as Horace Walpole, who kept copies of Magna Carta and Charles I's death warrant under his bed, the 'cause' was England's 'sacred' constitutional political inheritance. Bagehot was in no doubt that the 'spirit' of Cromwell remained 'potent'. Indeed, it 'founded the English constitution'.[79] The observation was not meant as a complement.

The Best Laws

Alongside its invocation of the 'common good', the classical idea of commonwealth was also founded on the principles of common law and the rule of law. The reason, as James Harrington affirmed, is simple, a 'commonwealth is government by laws and not men'.[80] Seventeenth century political and constitutional debate was riven by disputes regarding the inheritance of the 'ancient' constitution, and more particularly the precise relation of king and law. According to John Pocock, these jurisprudential debates helped to define English radicalism.[81]

Absolutists such as Sir Robert Filmer were quite convinced that there were 'kings long before there were any laws', and so, for this simple

[75] J Locke, *Two Treatises of Government*, (London, Dent, 1989) 123–24, 179, 183.

[76] Locke, *Treatises*, 184–87.

[77] Prochaska, above n 40, 2.

[78] In Worden, above n 67, 6.

[79] Cromwell's reputation amongst the Victorians was decidedly variable. Thomas Carlyle both admired and despised him. The Chartists lauded him, which goes some way to explaining Carlyle's more negative sentiments. Such ambiguity was widely shared. For a commentary see, Worden, above n 67, 215–25, 246–58, 264–67, 288–95. For Bagehot's observation, see above n 13, 177–78.

[80] Harrington, above n 42, 35.

[81] See J Pocock, 'A discourse of sovereignty', in N Phillipson & Q Skinner (eds), *Political Discourse in Early Modern Britain*, (Cambridge UP, 1993), 377–428.

reason, 'there can be no laws without a supreme power to command or make them', and so 'in a monarchy the king must of necessity be above the law'.[82] It was a view famously preferred by King James I, who asserted that he sat 'upon God his Throne in the earth'. Even by 'God himselfe', he affirmed, kings 'are called Gods'.[83] Famously, however, his Lord Chief Justice, Sir Edward Coke, thought differently. Whilst he did not challenge the royal prerogative, Coke did challenge the implication that the king might determine its jurisdiction. Such a determination, he countered, was always limited by the common law itself; a jurisprudence which, he confirmed, is the 'absolute perfection of reason'.[84]

In a series of famous cases, including *Dr Bonham's Case* and the *Cases of Prohibitions*, *of Proclamations*, and *of Commendams*, Coke thwarted James's attempts to use his prerogative as a means of subverting the authority of the ordinary courts. Eventually, Coke overreached himself, warning Parliament that it 'must look about, or the common law will be overthrown', and was visited with the full wrath of an irate monarch who berated judges who 'did both meddle with the King's prerogative, and had incroached upon all other courts of justice'.[85] But not before Coke's invocation of a 'common law constitution' had passed into republican and later Whig jurisprudential folklore.[86] Myth countered myth; that of divine right countered by that of the common law.

Eventually the 'chosen people' went to war with themselves in a bid to resolve the meaning of their constitution. For parliamentarians such as John Pym, 'the ancient and fundamental law, issuing from the first

[82] R Filmer, *Patriarcha and Other Writings*, (Cambridge UP, 1991) 7–11, 44. For commentaries on Filmer's idea of monarchy, see G Burgess, *Absolute Monarchy and the Stuart Constitution*, (London and New Haven, Yale UP, 1996), 31–32, 67–75, J Somerville, *Politics and Ideology in England 1603–1640*, (Harlow, Longman, 1986), 23–36, and J Daly, *Sir Robert Filmer and English Political Thought*, (Univ of Toronto Press, 1979), 22–24, 57–81.

[83] King James, *Political Writings*, (Cambridge UP, 1994), 64, 181.

[84] For a commentary on Coke's constitutionalism, see Burgess, above n 82, 166–69, G Knafla, *Law and Politics in Jacobean England*, (Cambridge UP, 1977), 180–84, J Pocock, *The Ancient Constitution and the Feudal Law: A Study of English Historical Thought in the Seventeenth Century*, (Cambridge UP, 1957), 43–55, and more critically J Goldsworthy, *The Sovereignty of Parliament: History and Philosophy*, (Oxford UP, 1999), 44–45.

[85] See King James, above n 83, 210–13, 225, and also M Kishlansky, *The Monarchy Transformed: Britain 1603–1714*, (Penguin, 1997), 35–38.

[86] For a recent commentary, see M Loughlin, *Sword and Scales: An Examination of the Relationship between Law and Politics*, (Oxford, Hart, 1998) 71–75.

frame and constitution of the kingdom', was well worth rebelling for.[87] And the struggle was not to be engaged solely on the battlefield. Across the libraries of England, legal scholars and antiquarians hurled authorities at each other. England was awash with hoary medieval jurisprudence. The common lawyers alighted on Bracton's assertion that an anointed English monarch is 'subject' to the 'law', as well as Sir John Fortescue's affirmation that English monarchy was 'royal and political', rather than merely 'royal'. According to Fortescue this meant that a 'king of England is not able change the laws of his kingdom at his pleasure, for he rules his people with a government not only royal but also political', and for this reason 'there is no gainsaying nor legitimate doubt but that the customs of the English are not only good but the best'.[88] And, then, rather more recently, there was the much-admired Richard Hooker, helpfully reaffirming that 'What power the King hath he hath it by law, the bounds and limits of it are known'.[89]

The need to limit the power of the king leant to the idea of balance. As Hooker's contemporary, William Lambarde, affirmed poetically, 'from such, and so well-tuned a base, mean and treble, there proceeds a most exquisite content, and delicious melody'.[90] The idea that constitutions should be balanced and 'separated' would become a mainstay of early Whig political thought. It found similarly poetic expression in Harrington's *Oceana*, published in 1656:

> Let them who will have it that power if she be confined cannot be sovereign tell us whether our rivers do not enjoy a more secure and fruitful reign within their proper banks, than if it were lawful for them, in ravishing our harvests, to spill themselves?[91]

And likewise at the root of Sidney's *Discourses* could be found the argument that the power and prerogative of the Crown was defined, and thus limited, by law. Sidney dwelt at considerable length on the Anglo-Saxons and their Witanagemot, from which he surmised the common law to be drawn, upon Bracton and Magna Carta, and all the other revered texts of the 'ancient' constitution.[92] 'Our ancestors

[87] In Goldsworthy, above n 84, 109–10.

[88] J Fortescue, *On the Laws and Governance of England*, (Cambridge UP, 1997), 6–9, 14–17, 49–52. For a commentary, see N Doe, *Fundamental Authority in Late Medieval Law*, (Cambridge UP, 1990), 1–14, 26–8, 60–83.

[89] R Hooker, *Of the Laws of Ecclesiastical Polity*, (Cambridge UP, 1989), 145–47, 217.

[90] In Goldsworthy, above n 84, 75.

[91] Harrington, above n 42, 66.

[92] Sidney, above n 70, 313, 366–68, 410–15, 470–74, 486.

were born free', Sidney asserted, 'and as the best provision they could make for us, they left us that liberty entire, with the best laws they could devise to defend it'.[93] And it is for this reason, as Coke confirmed, that kings are subject to the law; for those who 'place kings within the power of the law, and the law to be a guide to kings, equally provide for the good of king and people'.[94] No single institution, as Locke would famously affirm, should enjoy absolute power, king, council or even Parliament; for no legislature should ever assume powers that are 'absolutely arbitrary over the lives and fortunes of the people'.[95]

It has recently been suggested that much of this historiography is flawed. John Goldsworthy suggests that the 'common law constitution' is a 'myth', and that the principle of parliamentary sovereignty always enjoyed greater jurisprudential legitimacy.[96] This may be right. But truth matters little in a politics of competing mythologies. Coke's *Institutes*, as Norman Davies has recently affirmed, served as a 'bible' for all sides during the seventeenth century.[97] And as Blair Worden has confirmed, the jurisprudential precision of Coke's defence of the common law constitution mattered far less than its capacity to inspire the radical English mind. The idea that an English commonwealth was founded, not on the sovereignty of king or parliament, but on the sovereignty of its citizens would pass down the centuries, describing, as Tom Nairn has recently put it, the 'stubborn half-life' of English radicalism.[98]

Friends of Liberty

As we have already noted, memories of 1689, even 1649, retained their hold throughout the eighteenth and nineteenth century. Dicey's *Law* was dedicated to projecting one particular interpretation of the 'great and glorious revolution' and its particular constitutional 'principles'. The same was true, a century earlier, of Edmund Burke's *Reflections on the Revolution in France*. For Burke, as we have already seen, the

[93] Sidney, *ibid*, 365–66.
[94] Sidney, *ibid*, 303. See also 364.
[95] Locke, above n 75, 184–87.
[96] Goldsworthy, above n 84, particularly 6–7.
[97] Davies, above n 57, 567–67.
[98] Nairn, above n 5, 146.

constitutional settlement of 1689 defined the 'English mind'. In its broadest, most general, sense it was an assertion upon which everyone could agree. Precisely what the settlement actually meant, however, was altogether more contentious. As Roy Porter has recently affirmed, the debates surrounding the meaning of the 'Cause' were the ultimate intellectual catalyst of the radical English Enlightenment.[99]

For 'friends of liberty' such as Tom Paine and William Godwin, 'revolution principles' meant, not just classical conceptions of civic republicanism and virtue, but also real democratic empowerment. Seventeenth century ideas of the 'common weal' were recast in the altogether more modern guise of social and democratic reform. It was, as Paine affirmed, a matter of 'common sense'. In his *Discourse on the Love of Our Country*, published in 1790, another of the 'friends', Richard Price, observed:

> And now methinks I see the ardour for liberty catching and spreading, a general amendment beginning in human affairs, the dominion of kings changed for the dominion of laws, and the dominion of priests giving way to the dominion of reason and conscience.[100]

The 'gift of liberty', as John Thelwall's journal *The Tribune* kept reminding its readers, was England's true constitutional tradition.[101] The mystical poet, William Blake assured his readers that 'Jerusalem' would be 'built' one again in 'England's green & pleasant land'; and it would be built by them, the 'friends of liberty'.[102]

The democratic implications found their sharpest statement in William Godwin's *Enquiry Concerning Political Justice*. Famously, Godwin advised that all government was an infringement of liberty and democracy, at best, a necessary evil:

> Above all we should not forget, that government is an evil, an usurpation upon the private judgment and individual conscience of mankind; and that,

[99] R Porter, *Enlightenment: Britain and the Making of the Modern World*, (London, Allen Lane, 2000), 28, 193. For similar assertions, see J Black, *The Politics of Britain 1688–1800*, (Manchester UP, 1993), 10–12, and also EP Thompson, *The Making of the English Working Class*, (London, Penguin, 1991), chapter 2 discussing the residual hold of 17th century radicalism on the radical dissenting traditions of the later eighteenth century.

[100] In R Price, *Political Writings*, (Cambridge UP, 1991), 195.

[101] See, for example, G Claeys (ed), *The Politics of English Jacobinism: Writings of John Thelwall*, (Pennsylvannia State UP, 1995), 209–17. For a commentary, see Worden, above n 67, 204–14.

[102] W Blake, 'Milton', plate 1 lines 15–16, in *The Complete Poems*, (Harmondsworth, Penguin, 1977), 514.

> however we may be obliged to admit it as a necessary evil for the present, it behoves us, as the friends of reason and the human species, to admit as little of it as possible, and carefully to observe whether, in consequence of the gradual illumination of the human mind, that little may not hereafter be diminished.[103]

The equation was quite simple; the cause of liberty lies in the diminution of government and 'positive' law.[104] It is no less simple today.

Like so many of the 'friends', Godwin had little time for the kind of representative democracy that was designed to foreclose deliberative and participatory alternatives. Whereas generations of anxious Victorians would live in the state of mortal dread prescribed in turn by both Bagehot and Dicey, Godwin urged that there was nothing to fear in the sharing of political power between citizens:

> Democracy restores to man a consciousness of his value, teaches him by the removal of authority and oppression to listen only to the dictates of reason, gives him confidence to treat all other men as his fellow beings, and induces him to regard them no longer as enemies against whom to be upon his guard, but as brethren whom it becomes him to assist.[105]

The sentiment would resurface once again, a generation later, with the rise of the Chartist movement, articulated in statements such as George Harding's defence of republicanism as 'simply this, self-government; the right of every individual to govern himself, either in person or by representation'.[106] Even Bagehot was moved to admit that 'government by discussion quickens and elivens thought all through society'.[107] John Stuart Mill was positively enthused by the thought, advising in his essay *Concerning Representative Government*:

> the ideally best form of government is that in which the sovereignty, or supreme controlling power in the last resort, is vested in the entire aggregate of the community; every citizen not only having a voice in the exercise of that ultimate sovereignty, but being, at least occasionally, called on to take an actual part in the government, by the personal discharge of some public function, local or general.[108]

[103] W Godwin, *Enquiry Concerning Political Justice*, in M Philp (ed), *Political and Philosophical Writings of William Godwin*, (William Pickering, 1993), vol 3, 206.

[104] For Godwin's particular critique of positive law, see *ibid,* 390–91, 413.

[105] Godwin, *Political Justice*, 268–69.

[106] In Prochaska, *Republic*, 78.

[107] W Bagehot, *Physics and Politics*, in N.St.John Stevas, *Walter Bagehot*, (Eyre & Spottiswoode, 1959), 455.

[108] J Mill, *Concerning Representative Government*, in *On Liberty and Other Essays*, (Oxford UP, 1991), 244.

The immediate future of English radicalism, however, lay with the lures of socialism, rather than the reflective utopias of 1689 and the 'Cause'. And with it came a fatal sense of inevitability. Just as Shaw presumed that monarchy would pass once the British had come to their senses, so too prominent socialists such as Friedrich Engels, William Morris and HG Wells assumed that the true republican 'spirit' of England ensured revolution. It was simply inevitable.[109] But it was not. There would be reform; but there would be no revolution. [110] And men such as Albert Venn Dicey would make sure that that the 'spirit' of the Anglo-British constitution would be innately conservative; a bastion, indeed, against both reform and revolution.

The principles of 1689 and the 'Cause' would, instead, be taken up elsewhere; as William Blake predicted, 'driven in terror' across the oceans to America.[111] For 'founders' of the American constitution, such as Thomas Jefferson and John Adams, the influence of the 'Cause' and of men such as Harrington and Sidney was a constant source of 'fresh admiration'.[112] *The Federalist Papers* are a paean to the kind of ideas found in Sidney's *Discourses* and Locke's *Treatises*. According to Jefferson, the 'ward' system of radically decentralized political authority, adopted by the puritan settlers of New England from the models of government found in Harrington and Sidney, 'proved themselves the wisest invention ever devised by the wit of man for the perfect exercise of self-government, and for its preservation'.[113] The principle of the 'separation of powers', as Jefferson affirmed, is to complement the idea of decentralised power and democratic self-government.[114] It is in this way that real democracy liberates. As Alexis de Tocqueville noted, in comparing participatory with representative democracy, 'Without local institutions a nation may give itself a free government, but in has not got the spirit of liberty'.[115]

[109] In Prochaska, *Republic*, 110, 162.

[110] Prochaska, *Republic*, 182.

[111] Blake, 'Jerusalem', plate 38 line 69, in *Works*, 709.

[112] See L.Cappon (ed), *The Adams-Jefferson Letters*, (London, Simon & Schuster, 1971), 598, for Adams reverential comments regarding Sidney. For an overview of the intellectual debates ongoing at the time of the writing of the American constitution, see P.Craig, *Public Law and Democracy in the United Kingdom and the United States of America*, (Oxford UP, 1990), 331–34.

[113] In G Hart, *Restoration of the Republic: The Jeffersonian Ideal in 21st Century America*, (Oxford UP, 2002), 77.

[114] For a recent restatement of this basic idea, see P Birkinshaw, 'The Separation of Powers in the Changing Environment', in D Campbell & D Lewis (eds) *Promoting Participation: Law or Politics?* (London, Cavendish, 1999), 234–36.

[115] A de Tocqueville, *Democracy in America*, (Fontana, 1994), 62–63, 68.

It is to this tradition that contemporary American political philosophers such as Alisdair MacIntyre, Michael Sandel and Gary Hart have turned in order to resuscitate what they perceive to be a flagging sense of 'commonwealth' and 'common good' in modern America.[116] There is a distinctive resonance in Hart's suggestion that a revitalized republicanism must reorient American politics so that 'government is for the people because it is by the people'.[117] The Jeffersonian ideal, he alleges, can:

> yield a new political culture or a polity founded upon humanity's essentially social nature; a new destiny founded on participation in community life; the restoration of a public ethic that supersedes the private, commercial self; and the elevation of a common good and of commonwealth institutions.[118]

The context may be American; but the intellectual inheritance is English.[119] As Jonathan Friedland advises, there 'is much of real value to plunder from the US, but we are missing it'. The 'founding principles of the US' were our ideas of 'liberty and democracy, which somehow slipped out of our hands and drifted across the Atlantic'. They represent 'our buried treasure, stored and preserved an ocean away', and now, moreover, 'is the time to reclaim them for ourselves'. The 'smart money', he concludes, 'says that the politics of the next century will be dominated' by the 'libertarianism' of the levellers, the roundheads and the Chartists, the 'liberalism of Locke, the anarchism of Shelley and a thousand dreamers in between'.[120] It is an inspiring thought. As Andrew Marr concludes, if there is a 'spirit of liberty' to be rekindled in contemporary England, it is to be found in the classical republican idea of self-government.[121]

[116] For MacIntryre's ideas see A MacIntyre, *After Virtue: A Study in Moral Virtue*, (Duckworth, 1985). See also Sandel, *Democracy's Discontent: America in Search of a Public Philosophy*, (Cambridge, Mass, Harvard UP, 1996) and C Taylor, *Sources of the Self: The Making of Modern Identity*, (Cambridge UP, 1989).

[117] Hart, above n 113, 10.

[118] *ibid*, 23.

[119] J Pocock, *The Machiavellian Moment: Florentine Political Thought and the Atlantic Republican Tradition*, (Princeton UP, 1975), particularly 506–7, and Craig, above n 112, 318–28.

[120] Friedland, above n 45, 14, 230–32.

[121] A Marr, *Ruling Britannia: The Failure and Future of British Democracy*, (London, Michael Joseph, 1995), 57, and also 344–46.

III A NEW CONSTITUTIONALISM AND A NEW IMAGINING

A New Constitutionalism

England needs a new constitution, a new politics, a new public philosophy. Our present system of government is rotten, our apology for democracy feeble, our received visions of unitary constitutionalism no longer credible in the 'new world order' in which we live.

The idea that a revitalized, and distinctively English, constitutionalism might be founded in a revived idea of the 'common law constitution' has gathered pace during the final decade of the last century. As we saw in chapter three, it has been carried along on the coat-tails, first of the 'renaissance' in judicial review, and then more recently the arrival of the 1998 Human Rights Act. Like so much of the present constitutional 'project', the impact of the 1998 statute waits to be seen. But for Sir Stephen Sedley, there is a very obvious historical resonance, with 'the legacy of the seventeenth century settlement by which we continue to live and be governed'. It is a legacy, he continues, that describes:

> not simply a culture of possessive individualism, though possessive individualism forms a strong strand of it. It is equally, and perhaps more importantly, a culture of republicanism—of a society which aims not merely to be composed of free individuals but to be itself free'.[122]

This ascription is not new. It was famously made by Charles McIlwain during the first part of the last century.[123] But its revival is striking. The 'genie of constitutionalism', as Dawn Oliver puts it, 'is out of the bottle'. The future, she argues, will witness the re-emergence of a more 'law-based, law-dominated' idea of the constitution.[124]

And no one has been more vigorous in promoting this revival than Trevor Allan.[125] Allan places the principle of the rule of law, rather than parliamentary sovereignty, at the apex of a recast and revitalized

[122] S Sedley, *Freedom, Law and Justice*, (London, Sweet & Maxwell, 1999), 5–6.

[123] See, for example, C McIlwain, *Constitutionalism: Ancient and Modern*, (Ithaca and NY, Cornell UP, 1947).

[124] Oliver, above n 9, 389.

[125] For this assertion, and a general commentary and critique, see T Poole, 'Dogmatic Liberalism?: TRS.Allan and the Common Law Constitution', (2002) 65 *Modern Law Review*, 463–75.

constitution that is dedicated to promoting the 'common good'.[126] It is a sentiment, intriguingly, which can be found lurking behind Lord Irvine's invocation of the 'beacon of the rule of law' as a defining instrument in English constitutionalism.[127] But then Dicey, as we have already noted, was prepared to concede this much, and there is a significant step to be made from rhetorical reverence for the rule of law, and a willingness to enforce it at the centre of a revised constitutional philosophy.

It is a step, however, that Allan is prepared to make. In his *Law, Liberty and Justice*, he repeatedly affirms that the rule of law exists as a counterbalance to the potential whimsies of legislative omnipotence. Thus:

> At its core is the conviction that law provides the means of protecting each citizen from the arbitrary will of others—including the most powerful. By being constrained to govern by means of general laws, the political rulers of society cannot single out particular persons for special treatment. The law is to constitute a bulwark between governors and governed, shielding the individual from hostile discrimination on the part of those with political power.[128]

Ultimately, and this is the crucial assertion, it 'is the rule of law that is truly absolute, constituting the basis of the legal order within which legislative sovereignty must be located and defined'.[129]

Once again, there may be a rhetorical echo of Dicey. But in terms of sentiment there is an ocean of difference; one that becomes more apparent still when Allan confirms that the 'formal conception' of the rule of law must then lead to a more nuanced idea of fairness and equality, of 'individual right and human dignity', and, perhaps most importantly, of the 'moral responsibility and independence of the ordinary citizen'. It is here that Allan's constitutional theory embraces the ethical implications of a truly liberal public philosophy. Like it or not, as Harold Laski affirmed, 'institutions with genuine power become ethical ideas'.[130] The constitution of a state cannot be sensibly divorced

[126] See, for example, T Allan, 'The Rule of Law as the Rule of Reason: Consent and Constitutionalism', (1999) 115 *Law Quarterly Review*, 237–39.

[127] Lord Irvine, 'The Spirit of Magna Carta Continues to Resonate in Modern Law', (2003) 119 *Law Quarterly Review*, particularly, 227–38.

[128] T Allan, *Law, Liberty and Justice: The Legal Foundations of British Constitutionalism*, (Oxford UP, 1993), 22.

[129] T Allan, *Constitutional Justice: Liberal Theory and the Rule of Law*, (Oxford UP, 2001) 201.

[130] In H Laski, *The Foundations of Sovereignty and Other Essays*, in P Hirst (ed), *The Pluralist Theory of the State*, (London, Routledge, 1993), 180, 192.

form the constitution of humanity. As the American legal philosopher Ronald Dworkin argues, a liberal constitution is defined by its moral capacity.[131] For Allan, accordingly, the primacy of the rule of law leads to a process of 'moral reasoning', one that is 'sensitive to settled principles regarding individual rights and expectations'; one that is, in effect, set within the context of the community in which a judge judges, and which reflects the values of that community.[132]

Allan's more recent *Constitutional Justice* is composed in the same tenor, presenting the rule of law as the central principle of a 'common law' constitution. Here, once again, the rule of law expresses 'a vision of law as the embodiment of a defensible conception of the common good'.[133] Accordingly:

> Government must be held to a broadly consistent account of the common good it purports to espouse; it cannot discriminate unfairly between citizens by selective application of general principles it claims to honour. The equal dignity of citizens, with its implications for fair treatment and respect for individual autonomy, is the basic premise of liberal constitutionalism, and accordingly the ultimate meaning of the rule of law.[134]

And again, the invocation of the rule of law carries an undeniably ethical imperative:

> The citizen of a constitutional democracy is to be honoured as an equal, autonomous, moral agent, who takes responsibility for his own actions, including his conduct in response to governmental rules and requirements. Legal obligation is therefore interpreted as a species of moral obligation; the nature and limits of the state's entitlement to obedience are questions of moral judgment that are always directly relevant to the identification and interpretation of the content of law.[135]

The echoes of Sidney and Locke and Godwin are resonant. A liberal constitution is a moral instrument because it embodies the political morality of the community, and the community is composed of citizens who are moral beings. There is, as Allan suggests, an 'intrinsic dependence' between the common law and the 'moral judgment and vision of all who participate in legal analysis and constitutional debate'; which

[131] For a strong statement of this capacity, see R Dworkin, *Freedom's Law: The Moral Reading of the American Constitution*, (Oxford, 1996).

[132] Allan, above n 128, 39, 43, 88, 125.

[133] Allan, above n 129, 123

[134] Allan, *ibid*, 2.

[135] Allan, *ibid*, 6.

should, in a genuine democracy, be all of us. For, 'in the last analysis', the 'standards of justice' are determined by the 'moral judgment of both private citizen and public official'.[136] It is for this reason that parliamentary sovereignty must 'necessarily' be 'limited' by the principle of the rule of law.[137]

It is impossible to conceive of a 'common good' as anything but a moral imperative, and so the instruments deployed to secure it must be too. This does not mean that the constitution must reach into 'abstract political philosophy'. Rather, it accepts a political morality built on 'those principles accepted as constitutionally fundamental, within a particular regime or polity, and the underlying values of human dignity and freedom that these principles characteristically assume'.[138] The ethical implications are spelled out once more:

> The law should encourage the exercise of individual responsibility, in preference to requiring conformity to collective judgments about controversial questions of value, because that approach is most consistent with the ideal of personal moral judgment that underlies the rule of law itself.[139]

In doing so, of course, the law will encourage citizens to 'question the legitimacy, and hence legality, of rules'. This is not, as Dicey would suggest, the seedcorn of anarchy. It is, rather, the 'ultimate guarantee of justice'.[140] Democracy, at least the democracy of participation and debate, is indelibly antagonistic.[141] Ultimately, Allan concludes, the idea of a 'common law' constitution, founded on principles of equality and the rule of law 'makes sense only in the context of a broadly republican conception of politics'. It is intrinsically related to the classical republican conception of 'public reason', of a political process of 'deliberate democracy' that is dedicated to nurturing the individual 'moral' and 'political judgment' of each citizen.[142] The argument is compelling.

[136] Allan, *ibid*, 249, 283.
[137] Allan, *ibid*, 220–21.
[138] Allan, *ibid*, 22.
[139] Allan, *ibid*, 312–13.
[140] Allan, *ibid*, 312.
[141] See C Mouffe, *The Democratic Paradox*, (London, Verso, 2000), particularly chapters 4–5.
[142] Allan, above n 129, 283–90, 301, 311–12.

A New Politics

And it leads inexorably to a new politics, to the thought that a remodelled English commonwealth, and a remodelled English constitution can actually promote a revitalised idea of democracy. It is here that the internal processes of decay and the external dynamics of the 'new world order' come together. As we noted in the previous chapter, the age of the nation-state, an institution that was created in order to preserve vested political interests, appears to have passed, and so too has the jurisprudence that was fabricated to clothe the Anglo-British state with some measure of constitutional legitimacy.

It is within this evolutionary context that MacCormick resurrects the idea of a European *res publica* or commonwealth:

> In this sense, both member states and the Union are commonwealths, one more intensive and localized, more strongly rooted in a sense of tradition and of personal identity and loyalty, the other more extensive and broadly inclusive. Here in Europe we have something which is a constituted order, which does have however imperfectly a legal constitution, whose members have certain vital interests in peace and prosperity that they can best pursue as common interests through policies oriented towards this common good. Commonwealth seems a natural term here to use.[143]

Massimo La Torre has similarly suggested that the future shape of Europe will resemble a 'mixed commonwealth' of constituent commonwealths, whilst Ulrich Beck likewise recommends a Europe of 'local communities' and 'cosmopolitan nations'.[144] There is a further echo in Juergen Habermas's appeal for a European 'constitutional patriotism' secured by the radical implementation of the principle of subsidiarity.[145] As it was enshrined in Articles 1 and 5 of the Union Treaty, subsidiarity is meant to effect the devolution and balancing of power between different 'competences' in Union governance, with decisions being 'taken as closely as possible to the people'. Such an approach to governance chimes with the much-vaunted ideal of a

[143] MacCormick, above n 7, 145, and also 167.

[144] U Beck, 'Democratization of Democracy—Third Way Policy Needs to Redefine Work', (2000) 5 *The European Legacy*, 177–81, and M La Torre, 'Legal Pluralism as an Evolutionary Achievement of European Community Law', in F Snyder (ed), *The Europeanisation of Law: The Legal Effects of European Integration*, (Oxford, Hart, 2000), 138.

[145] For a broad discussion of these issues, see J Habermas, *The Postnational Constellation: Political Essays*, (Cambridge, Polity, 2001), 74–76, 109.

'Europe of the regions'; and, as we noted in the last chapter, the present composition, or decomposition, of the 'united' Kingdom renders it peculiarly suited to a regionally driven form of political and constitutional reformation.[146]

There is, of course, an obvious irony here. The very idea of a 'chosen people' was, as we have seen, nurtured by a previous reformation; that which detached 'Jerusalem' from Rome. But the idea that the 'new' Europe is simply restoring the boundaries, and the politics, of the 'old' has not been lost on commentators such as the French philosopher Jacques Derrida, whose essay *On Cosmopolitanism* suggests that an incipient Union public philosophy can be founded on Aristotelian conceptions of the 'common good', on a 'politics of friendship'.[147] It is a thought that finds an echo in Larry Siedentop's observation that the very idea of Europe is founded on the classical conception of *humanitas*, a philosophy of 'universal' autonomy, difference and tolerance. The idea of the *res publica* or 'commonwealth', Siedentop alleges, provides not merely a moral or political philosophy, but the 'original constitution of Europe'.[148] The European tradition, in short, is a republican tradition, a tradition of civic empowerment and participation, of real democracy, real engagement, and real political liberty.

The historical resonances are striking. Writing in 1679, the Hanoverian philosopher Gottfried Wilhelm Leibniz suggested that the 'universal jurisprudence' that defines the European *res publica* is founded on a 'universal benevolence', a 'habit of loving' that equips the 'wise man' to pursue the 'greatest good'.[149] Three centuries later, Pierre Bourdieu can likewise recommend the very idea of Europe as being definitively 'humanist' in precisely these terms.[150] Perhaps the most compelling affirmation can be found in Vaclav Havel's suggestion that the 'salvation of this human world lies nowhere else than in the human heart, in the human power to reflect, in human modesty, and in human responsibility'. The promotion of the very 'idea of humanity', he adds,

[146] MacCormick, above n 65, 193–94.

[147] J Derrida, *On Cosmopolitanism and Forgiveness*, (London, Routledge, 2001), 11. For an exploration of this principle, see his earlier *Politics of Friendship*, (London, Routledge, 1997).

[148] L Siedentop, *Democracy in Europe*, (London, Penguin, 2000), 190–95, 200–1.

[149] See G Leibniz, *Portrait of a Prince* in *Political Writings*, (Cambridge UP, 1988), 98–99. For a commentary, see I Ward, 'Beyond Constitutionalism: The Search for a European Political Imagination', (2001) 7 *European Law Journal*, 32–40.

[150] P Bourdieu, *Acts of Resistance: Against the Tyranny of the Market*, (New Press, 1998), 40–41.

and of the politics that such a philosophy demands, of 'civic coexistence, solidarity, and participation', is Europe's destiny.[151] And England's too, perhaps.[152]

And alongside the challenge of Europe, as we also noted in the last chapter, comes the challenge of devolution. The Constitutional Convention, which mapped out the course of Scottish devolution, made much of the need to establish a 'civic forum' and promote a 'civic society'. Its concluding report expressed the 'powerful hope that the coming of a Scottish Parliament will usher in a way of politics that is radically different from the rituals of Westminster; more participative, more creative, less confrontational'. It should, the report added, promote 'a culture of openness which will enable the people to see how decisions are being taken in their name and why'.[153] There was a particular hope that a 'new politics' would also light a 'bonfire of the quangos', the apparently bottomless number of unaccountable executive bodies set up in London to administer affairs, both in England and in Scotland, Wales and Northern Ireland.[154]

Above all, however, particularly in Northern Ireland, it was hoped that talk of a 'new politics' would promote a spirit of reconciliation, even compassion. Of course, the spectacle of the Holy Cross primary school children running the gauntlet of screaming religious bigots is a salutary reminder that good intentions can only do so much. But progress is founded on hope, and, as John Morison has observed, the advance of voluntary self-help and 'healing' groups is one of the most striking aspects of post-devolution government in the province.[155]

[151] V Havel, *The Art of the Impossible: Politics as Morality in Practice*, (Fromm International, 1998), 18–19, 147–48.

[152] For this suggestion, see K Kumar, *The Making of English National Identity*, (Cambridge UP, 2003) 269–73 and also Davies, *Isles*, 1054.

[153] J Mitchell, 'New Parliament, New Politics in Scotland', (2000) 53 *Parliamentary Affairs*, 605, 611–12, and A Brown, 'Designing the Scottish Parliament', (2000) 53 *Parliamentary Affairs*, 542.

[154] See L McAllister, 'The New Politics in Wales: Rhetoric or Reality?', (2000) 53 *Parliamentary Affairs*, 595, M Marinetto, 'The Settlement and Process of Devolution: Territorial Governance under the Welsh Assembly', (2001) 49 *Political Studies*, 310, and R Rawlings, 'The New Model Wales', (1998) 25 *Journal of Law and Society*, 467–68.

[155] J Morison, 'Democracy, Governance and Governmentality: Civic Public Space and Constitutional Practice in Northern Ireland', (2001) 21 *Oxford Journal of Legal Studies*, 299–308. See also, B Rolston, 'Assembling the Jigsaw: truth, justice and transition in the North of Ireland', (2002) 44 *Race and Class*, 87–105, J Ruane & J Todd, 'The Politics of Transition?: Explaining Political Crises in the Implementation of the Belfast Good Friday Agreement', (2001) 49 *Political Studies*, 923–40, and also J Bradbury & J Mitchell, 'Devolution and Territorial Politics: Stability, Uncertainty and Crisis', 55 *Parliamentary Affairs* 2002, 311–12.

Laura McAllister has similarly applauded the work of the Welsh Civic Forum in engaging voluntary and non-political organisations.[156]

According to Morison, the truly radical potential here lies in 'hearing voices from outside traditional politics'. The Patten report into policing in Northern Ireland talked of the need for a 'real partnership between the police and the community', one that is conspicuously and radically 'de-centralised', whilst the European Union has financed a Special Support Programme for Peace and Reconciliation which is intended to nurture this 'new politics' of inter-community consensus and reconciliation. Such developments, Morison argues, recognise the reality of devolved politics as a multi-level and multi-form entity, a politics in which power is both devolved to various levels and distributed across various sectors.[157] It adds some substance to Vernon Bogdanor's prospective suggestion that the dispersal of power that should accompany devolution can 'humanise the state'.[158]

Closer to the People?

The situation in England, of course, appears to be slightly different. But appearances can deceive, and if the need for reconciliation is less apparent, the need for a revitalized democracy is just as great. At the simplest level, this need addresses the problem of local government; at present a microcosm of the wider problems reflecting public apathy towards government in general. Local election turnouts in 1998 and 1999 were 29% and 32% respectively.[159]

Another of the promises of 'new' Labour was to 'bring government back to the people'. In opposition, Tony Blair boldly announced that the 'era of big, centralized government is over', and that, if elected, he would ensure that decision-making was moved 'closer to the people'.[160] Likewise, Peter Mandelson could be found hazarding the thought that 'the era of pure representative democracy is slowly

[156] McAllister, above n 154, 602–3.

[157] Morison, above n 155, 293, 295, 306. For a discussion of the aid packages, see A Byrne & C Irvin, 'Economic aid and policy making: building the peace dividend in Northern Ireland', (2001) 29 *Policy and Politics*, 413–29.

[158] V Bogdanor, *Devolution in the United Kingdom* (Oxford UP, 1999), 6.

[159] See D Wilson, 'Local Government: Balancing Diversity and Uniformity', (2001) 54 *Parliamentary Affairs*, 299, and J Brooks, 'Labour's Modernization of Local Government', (2000) 78 *Public Administration*, 606.

[160] In Rawnsley, above n 31, 236–37.

coming to an end'.[161] There was, as ever, no shortage of rhetoric. The 1998 White Paper on local government reform duly announced the need to effect a 'fundamental shift in culture', to encourage 'in-touch' councils and councillors.[162] The resultant Local Government Act 2000 contained three elements of reform, 'community planning', new executive structures and 'best value'. The Local Government Association defines 'community planning' in terms of:

> A multi-organisational, community-based process, initiated by the council, for creating a shared vision of community identified priorities leading to a programme of actions which demonstrate the commitment and support of the organisations and groups involved.[163]

It is suggested that this notion recasts the idea of hierarchical local government in terms of a proliferation of horizontal 'governance' organisations and relationships.[164] But the diminution of hierarchy does not itself ensure greater participation or openness. It just means different pretenders to government; at present 'stakeholders' and 'quangocrats'.[165] Each year around 10,000 unknowns are appointed to the four thousand quangos that pervade local government in England.

The executive structures and 'best value' aspects of the 2000 Act are little more encouraging. The institution of Cabinet style government in local town halls is not necessarily to be welcomed, whilst the obsession with 'best value' speaks to a mindset that is far more driven by efficiency than by democracy or accountability.[166] The determination to 'weave and knit together the contributions of the various local stakeholders' originally recommended by the Green Paper on local government, is not the same as a determination to enhance local democracy, whilst the mass of 'best value' inspectorates that stalk local schools, hospitals and so forth, reinforce the sense that Whitehall is not about to resign its overarching executive commission.[167] As David Chandler

[161] Quoted in J Morison, above n 8, 514.

[162] See D Chandler, 'Active citizens and the therapeutic state: the role of democratic participation in local government reform', (2000) 29 *Policy and Politics*, 4.

[163] In V Jenkins, 'Learning from the Past: Achieving Sustainable Development in the Reform of Local Government', (2000) *Public Law*, 138.

[164] *ibid*, 139.

[165] Friedland, above n 45, 90–91.

[166] D Wilson, above n 159, 291, and also 'Exploring the Limits of Public Participation in Local Government', (1999) 52 *Parliamentary Affairs*, 248–49.

[167] See Morison, above n 155, 294, D Cooper, 'Local Government Legal Consciousness in the Shadow of Juridification', (1995) 22 *Journal of Law and Society*, 506–26, Wilson, above n 159, 295–99, 302–6 and above n 159, 248–49.

concludes, local government reform seems to be 'symbolic', proffering a 'therapeutic politics' that intends to 'give individuals a feeling of greater inclusion', rather than actually including them in the real decision-making process.[168]

Much has been made of the 'core executive' model of devolved governance across the 'united' Kingdom, with its radical distribution of power to various 'stakeholders'. It has been argued that such a model better reflects the reality of a world in which there is now a conspicuous 'absence of firm boundaries to central government'.[169] Whilst the 'core executive' model might indeed open up the possibility for greater localised governance, once again it does little to render it more accountable.[170] This latter issue nurtures the more cynical view that the reality of the new politics is as much about enhanced executive capacity as it is greater democratic participation.[171] Even if the geography might have changed, the governmental mindset in Westminster and Whitehall has not.[172] Indeed, not only does it deny the logic of devolution in England, but so too does it actively militate against devolution abroad. The Scottish Executive has been accused of revealing an 'astonishing capacity for regurgitating work done in London'.[173] It is an accusation that is ever more apposite for the reality of devolved governance in Wales.[174]

The myth of the stakeholder was much to the fore in the putative 'new' Labour philosophy of the 'third way'. According to one of its leading exponents, Antony Giddens, the 'third way' should promote 'experiments with democracy', whilst also anticipating a new form of 'life politics' that can oscillate around a 'common morality of citizenship', something which he redefines in terms of 'stakeholder' citizenship.[175]

[168] Chandler, above n 162, 10–11. See also Brooks, above n 159, 597–98.

[169] See M Smith, 'Reconceptualizing the British state: theoretical and empirical challenges to central government', (1998) 76 *Public Administration*, 47.

[170] As Ron Davies admitted, the acceptance of such a model was the price paid for the support of the Labour Party in London. See M Laffin & A Thomas, 'Designing the National Assembly for Wales', (2000) 53 *Parliamentary Affairs*, 566.

[171] See Bradbury & Mitchell, above n 155, 299–316. For a similar conclusion, in the particular context of Welsh devolution, see McAllister, above n 154, 591–92. But for a more optimistic slant, see Brown, above n 153, 556.

[172] Nairn, above n 30, 10.

[173] See Bradbury & Mitchell, above n 171, 301, and Mitchell, above n 153, 614, 618.

[174] See J Bradbury & J Mitchell, 'Devolution: New Politics for Old?' (2001) 54 *Parliamentary Affairs*, 258–54, 269–72, and Marinetto, 'Settlement', 315–16.

[175] A Giddens, *The Third Way: The Renewal of Social Democracy*, (Cambridge, Polity, 1998), 44, 65–66, 72–76, 102–8.

The stakeholder also props up Will Hutton's suggestion that a 'third way' politics should concentrate on reclaiming 'public spaces' and encouraging popular democratic 'participation'.[176] It is, of course, the kind of rhetoric that has fired American ideas of democratic participation since Jefferson. Only Jefferson believed that democracy was for everyone; not just those who could claim a 'stake'.

And there is one final, and rather obvious, failing. Local government 'reform' does not map onto any coherent idea of regional governance. Muttered promises for referenda in the north-east, Yorkshire and Humberside, and elsewhere, continue to be heard; but nothing seems to happen, and certainly nothing connected does. Indeed, the very refusal to focus reform on democracy, and instead to assume that a good council is an efficient, rather than a democratic or open, one, reinforces this failure.[177] As we noted before, the causes of democracy, regionalism and constitutional reform run together; or at least they should. As John Morison duly affirms:

> The role of radical participatory democracy is to move beyond simply fiddling with parliament and other aspects of representative democracy and to reclaim a public space where truly equal, free, and participatory discourse can take place.[178]

It is a thought that should arrest our attention. There remains no better way of restoring public trust and public interest than by passing the responsibility for government to the public itself.[179]

A New Imagining

In his study of the English imagination, Peter Ackroyd suggests that the English originally viewed government as an 'art' rather than as a science. From Bede to Milton to Blake, the English shared an intensely poetic, as well as historical, sense of themselves; an awareness that their past, and therefore their present, was innately mythic.[180] And

[176] W Hutton, *The State We're In*, (London, Jonathan Cape, 1995), 285–86, 290.

[177] For a broad, and critical, summary, see L Pratchett, 'Local Government: From Modernisation to Consolidation', (2002) 55 *Parliamentary Affairs*, 331–46.

[178] Morison, above n 8, 532.

[179] See P Dunleavy et al, 'Constitutional Reform, New Labour in Power and Public Trust in Government', (2001) 54 *Parliamentary Affairs*, 414–15.

[180] P Ackroyd, *Albion: The Origins of the English Imagination*, (London, Chatto & Windus, 2002), 128–29, 213–14, 255–59, 390–93.

being aesthetic, this view of government was necessarily humanist, even romantic; a concern with diversity and change, with the thought that 'a human being may be transfigured by god-like powers of the imagination'. It was this innately liberating sense of identity that was crushed between the Scylla and Charybdis of Empire and utility. Whereas England had identified itself in terms of poetry and mythology, the newly invented Great Britain of the late eighteenth and nineteenth centuries preferred to worship the idols of positivism, science and utility. It is only now, as Ackroyd concludes, that this particular delusion is passing.[181]

The 'friends of liberty' were, of course, thoroughly immersed in the struggle between reason and romance, sense and sensibility; what Samuel Taylor Coleridge famously termed the 'rage of metaphysics'. Tom Paine's essay on *Common Sense* vied with Mary Wollstonecraft's 'cult of sensibility', that 'most exquisite feeling of which the human soul is susceptible', the sheer 'impulses of the heart', of love for humanity itself. As her *Vindication of the Rights of Women* affirmed, no matter how much positivists might seek to assert a science of law and government, the necessary indeterminacy of a political life lived with others always 'twists the cords of love that in various convolutions entangle the heart'.[182] According to Wollstonecraft's husband, William Godwin, the politics of the good society is far more about 'moral feeling' that it is moral law.[183] Even the most committed of utilitarians was prepared to concede the political implications of sensibility. As Adam Smith admitted in his *Theory of Moral Sentiments*, in the final analysis 'Humanity does not desire to be great, but to be beloved'.[184]

The most compelling statements in the defence of sensibility were, of course, to be found in verse; in poems such as William Wordsworth's *Lines Composed Above Tintern Abbey*, with its appeal to a 'warmer love', to a politics, not of grand ideologies, but the of 'little nameless, unremembered, acts/ Of kindness and love'.[185] Perhaps its most compelling advocate was Percy Bysshe Shelley, who famously alleged that

[181] *ibid*, 433–37.

[182] M Wollstonecraft, *Mary*, (London, Penguin, 1992), 43, and *A Vindication of the Rights of Women*, (London, Dent, 1986), 154.

[183] See J Morrow, 'Republicanism and Public Virtue: William Godwin's *History of the Commonwealth of England*', (1991) 34 *Historical Journal* 1991, 650, and I Ward, *Justice, Humanity and the New World Order*, (Aldershot, Ashgate, 2003), 55–59.

[184] A Smith, *The Theory of Moral Sentiments*, (Oxford UP, 1976), 76, 166.

[185] W Wordsworth, *Lines Composed Above Tintern Abbey*, ll.33–35, in *Complete Poetical Works*, (Oxford UP, 1936), 164.

poets were the true 'unacknowledged legislators of the world'. Politicians might understand government, but poets understand humanity.[186] In his epic poem on the French revolution, *The Revolt of Islam*, Shelley lauded a politics of democratic participation that can 'found sympathy/ In human hearts', ensuring that 'those/ Who grow together cannot choose but love'.[187] And again, in *Prometheus Unbound*, he projected an England in which 'thrones were kingless, and men walked/ One with the other even as spirits do/ None fawned, none trampled'.[188] Ultimately it would be a politics of 'Familiar acts' rendered beautiful through love', a democracy of equality and liberty, of

> Man, one harmonious soul of many a soul,
> Whose nature is its own divine control,
> Where all things flow to all, as rivers to the sea.[189]

The mid-Victorian mind was fascinated by the 'rage of metaphysics', thrilled and horrified in equal measure. Both Bagehot and Dicey composed essays on Wordsworth. Typically, Dicey's *The Statesmanship of Wordsworth* shied away from the 'ethical' poet, preferring to revisit Wordsworth's later, rather dreary, *Sonnets on National Independence*. Writing in the context of the Great War, an ageing Dicey lauded Wordsworth's 'defence' of England and its constitution against the feared invasion of Napoleon. Wordsworth, according to Dicey, was an imperialist; something that made him a true Englishman.[190] Bagehot ventured a little further into the metaphysics, appraising the 'scriptures of the intellectual life' that could be found in Wordsworth's earlier work.[191] But neither was prepared to dig deep.

Rather more prepared was John Stuart Mill, who, as a young man, composed a complementary pair of essays on Bentham and Coleridge.[192] Mill's essay on *Bentham* applauded a 'great subversive',

[186] P Shelley, *A Philosophical View of Reform*, in P Foot (ed) *Shelley's Revolutionary Year*, (Redwords, 1990), 29–84.

[187] P Shelley, *The Revolt of Islam*, ll.2686–87, 3541–42, in *Complete Poetical Works* (Oxford UP, 1971), 103, 124.

[188] P Shelley, *Prometheus Unbound*, 3.4.131–34, in *ibid*, 252.

[189] *Ibid*, 4.4.400.3, 263.

[190] See A Dicey, *The Statesmanship of Wordsworth* (Oxford UP, 1917), 2–3, 5–6, 132, and also R Cosgrove, *The Rule of Law: Albert Venn Dicey, Victorian Jurist*, (Chapel Hill, NC, Univ of North Carolina Press, 1980, 268.

[191] In N St John Stevas (ed), *Walter Bagehot*, (London, Eyre & Spottiswoode, 1959), 26–27, 36–37.

[192] Dicey, interestingly, was a huge admirer of Mill. See A Dicey, *Lectures on the Relation between Law and Public Opinion in England during the Nineteenth Century*, (London, Macmillan, 1914), 426, and Cosgrove, above n 190, 12–13.

someone who was willing to 'speak disrespectfully' of the constitution, and to urge its reform. Bentham had swept away much of the 'mysticism from the philosophy of law' and for this Mill had nothing but praise. But Bentham suffered from a critical 'incompleteness' of the mind, a 'deficiency of the Imagination' that rendered him 'altogether cut off' from the 'most natural and strongest feelings of human nature'. He did not realise that a constitution is more than a set of rules or laws, but is, rather, a living organism representative of an evolving political morality.[193] Coleridge, on the other hand, was possessed of all the 'complexities of the human intellect and feelings'. His metaphysics might have been that of an 'arrant driveller', but Coleridge was redeemed by his appreciation that political communities are cultural artefacts, expressions of a 'strong and active principle of cohesion', of a dynamic narrative of change that could, and must, accommodate the demands of political reform.[194]

If England was to be truly reformed, Mill suggested, it must embrace the demands of both Bentham and Coleridge. It must have modern institutions of government, and it must nurture a sense of moral 'feelings' amongst its citizenry, a sense of commonalty and 'commonwealth'. The moral theory of utility, as he urged in his essay *Utilitarianism*, aspires to the happiness of 'individuals within the limits imposed by the collective interests of mankind'. Society, for Mill, was a 'natural condition' outside of which humanity cannot survive, and it is only in a society founded securely on principles of 'liberty', 'justice' and 'morality' that Englishmen and women can lead happy and fulfilled lives. Justice, Mill concluded, is an 'intensity' of moral 'sentiment', not a metaphysical abstraction and most certainly not a function of mere rules.[195]

The contemporary American philosopher Martha Nussbaum has deployed Mill as an exemplar of 'intelligent' liberalism; a liberalism that understands that a 'good society' is founded, not on laws or constitutions, or at least not only, but on the 'ability to think what it might be like to be in the shoes of a person different from oneself, to be an intelligent reader of that person's story, and to understand the emotions and wishes and desires that someone so placed might have'. There is, Nussbaum confirms, far 'more genuine love and friendship in the life of questioning and self-government than in submission to

193 In J Mill, *Utilitarianism and Other Essays*, (London, Penguin, 1987), 132–75.

194 *Ibid*, 173–23.

195 *Ibid*, 286–91, 304–5, 334.

authority'.[196] The rhetoric echoes Richard Rorty's assertion that a genuinely 'liberal society is one whose ideal can be fulfilled by persuasion rather than by force, by reform rather than revolution', by an understanding of 'cruelty' and 'kindness' rather than 'rights'. The politics of democracy, for Rorty, is a 'romance of endless diversity'.[197]

There is much here to ponder, not least because it chimes so obviously with the kind of rhetoric deployed originally by Leibniz and then more recently by Havel and Siedentop in the European context. The deeper sense of community that the idea of commonwealth promotes requires a concomitantly deeper sense of political morality. Law alone cannot promote the love of humanity which a flourishing and diverse society needs.[198] It was this insight that impelled Milton to compose his essay *Areopagitica*, with its justly famous defence of toleration and human dignity. And it is this insight which can accommodate the reality of our ever more diverse, multicultural England—an England which, as Milton's great disciple, William Blake, acknowledged, is defined by its 'amalgamating' peoples.[199]

It can be no coincidence that those jurists who embrace the idea of a 'common weal' and a 'moral' constitution seem most comfortable with the notion of a sentimental jurisprudence. According to Sir Stephen Sedley, for example, the 'rhetoric of law should not obscure the fact that justice' is 'in large part a matter of personal perception'; something, he continues, that has to do with 'a common sense of equity, an ethic of kindness, a morality of feeling, which does not and cannot be expected to stop at a desire for legal justice, even though that is necessarily where the law itself must stop'.[200] Likewise, for Sir John Laws, it is vital to remember that a cohesive constitutional morality must be about more than laws, that it must articulate the idea of community,

[196] M Nussbaum, *Cultivating Humanity: A Classical Defence of Reform in Liberal Education*, (Cambridge, Mass, Harvard UP, 1997), 10–11, 84.

[197] R Rorty, *Contingency, Irony, and Solidarity*, (Cambridge UP, 1989), 60–61, *Achieving Our Country: Leftist Thought in Twentieth Century America*, (Cambridge, Mass, Harvard UP, 1998), 24–25, and *Philosophy and Social Hope*, (London, Penguin, 1999), 24, 93–100, 212, 263, 270–77.

[198] See A Dummett, 'Citizenship', in R Hazell (ed), *Constitutional Futures*, (Oxford UP, 1999) 220–21.

[199] Blake, 'Jerusalem', plate 92 line 1, *Works*, 835, For a commentary on the need to advance a public philosophy that can better accommodate diversity in a changing Britain, and England, see G Younge, 'On race and Englishness', in S Chen & T Wright (eds), *The English Question*, (London, Fabian Society, 2000) 111–16, and B Parekh, 'Being British', (2002) 37 *Government and Opposition*, 301–15.

[200] Sedley, above n 122, 45, 55.

and its particular 'morality of aspiration', for the 'observance of duty is meaningless, and the flowering of human achievement impossible, except in the crucible of a life shared with others'.[201]

It is a compelling thought. There can be no sense of justice without a sensibility for compassion and kindness. If an English public philosophy can be recast in this image, and a constitution too, then we really will have something to applaud.

[201] J Laws, 'The Constitution: Morals and Rights', (1996) *Public Law*, 627, 635.

Index